FROM ADAM'S PEAK TO ELEPHANTA

FROM ADAM'S PEAK TO ELEPHANTA

SKETCHES OF CEYLON AND INDIA

EDWARD CARPENTER

GYAN

Published by

Gyan Publishing House
5, Ansari Road
Daryaganj, New Delhi-110002
Phone: 011-47034999, 9811692060
E-mail: books@gyanbooks.com

Distribution Network
gyanbooks.com
India, USA, Canada, UK, Australia, France

ISBN : 978-81-212-3411-5 (PB)
First Published, London, 1882

2nd Impression 2020

Printed at: Gyan Press, Delhi.

From Adam's Peak to Elephanta
Author: Edward Carpenter

FROM ADAM'S PEAK TO ELEPHANTA

SKETCHES IN CEYLON AND INDIA

BY

EDWARD CARPENTER

NEW EDITION, REVISED

LONDON

SWAN SONNENSCHEIN & CO. LIMITED

NEW YORK: E. P. DUTTON & CO.

1910

SEASHORE, NEAR COLOMBO

(Outrigged canoe in foreground)

PREFACE

If asked to write a book about his own country and people a man might well give up the task as hopeless—yet to do the same about a distant land in which he has only spent a few months is a thing which the average traveler quite cheerfully undertakes. I suppose this may be looked upon as another illustration of the great fact that the less one knows of a matter the easier it is to write or talk about it. But there is, it is sometimes said, a certain merit of their own in first mpressions; and I trust that this may appear in the present case. Certainly, though there are many things that are missed in a first glance, there are some things that stand out clearer then than later.

In the following pages I have tried to keep as far as possible to the relation of things actually seen and heard, and not to be betrayed into doubtful generalisations. It is so easy in the case of a land like India, which is as large as Europe (without Russia) and at least as multifarious in its peoples, languages, creeds, customs, and manners, to make the serious mistake of supposing that what is true of one locality necessarily applies to the whole vast demesne, that I must specially warn the reader not only against falling into this error himself, but against the possibility of my having fallen into it in places.

As far as actual experience of life in Ceylon and India is concerned I have perhaps been fortunate; not only in being introduced (through the kindness of local friends) into circles of traditional teaching which are often closed against the English, and in so getting to know something of the esoteric religious lore of South India; but also in obtaining some interesting glimpses behind the scenes of the Hindu ceremonial. I have too had the good luck to find friends and familiar acquaintances among all classes of native society, down almost to the lowest; and I must say that the sectional view I have thus obtained of the mass-people in this part of the world has made me feel with renewed assurance the essential oneness of humanity everywhere, notwithstanding the very marked local and superficial differences that undoubtedly exist.

The spectacle of the social changes now taking place in India is one that is full of interest to anyone who has studied and taken part in the Socialistic movement at home; and the interest of it is likely to increase. For though the movement in India is not the same as that at home, it forms a curious counterpart to the latter; and being backed by economic changes which will probably persist for years to come is not likely to die out very soon.

For the rest the book must rely on the description of scenes of nature and of ordinary human life, whose unexpected vividness forced me to portray them—though to begin with I had no intention of doing so. The illustrations are many of them taken from the excellent photographs of Messrs Scowen of Colombo, Messrs Bourn of Bombay, and Messrs Frith of Reigate.

E. C.

Nov. 1892.

PREFACE TO SECOND EDITION

IN the matter of the second edition of this book I have not much to say. A few slight corrections have been made in the text; and an Appendix has been added, dealing with the present financial condition of India. It is thought that the portraits, now first inserted, of the Gñáni to whom the visit was made, and of another Tamil Sage and Teacher, Paramaguru Swámi, will be found interesting.

E. C.

1903

CONTENTS

CEYLON

CHAPTER I

COLOMBO

CHAPTER II

KANDY AND PEASANT LIFE

CHAPTER III

KURUNÉGALA

CHAPTER VI

ANURADHAPURA: A RUINED CITY OF THE JUNGLE

CHAPTER VII

A NIGHT-FESTIVAL IN A HINDU TEMPLE

A VISIT TO A GÑÁNI

CHAPTER VIII

A VISIT TO A GÑÁNI

INDIA

CHAPTER XII

THE SOUTH INDIAN TEMPLES

CHAPTER XIII

MADRAS AND CALCUTTA

CHAPTER XIV

Benares

CHAPTER XV

The Anglo-Indian and the Native

CHAPTER XVI

Delhi and Agra

CHAPTER XVII

BOMBAY

THE OLD ORDER AND THE NEW INFLUENCES

CHAPTER XVIII

THE OLD ORDER: CASTE AND COMMUNISM

CHAPTER XIX

THE NEW INFLUENCES: WESTERN SCIENCE AND COMMERCIALISM

LIST OF ILLUSTRATIONS

CEYLON

From Adam's Peak to Elephanta

CHAPTER I

COLOMBO

IMAGINE a blue-green ribbon of water some 60 yards wide, then rough sandy dunes 10 or 20 feet high, and then beyond, the desert, burning yellow in the sun—here and there partly covered with scrub, but for the most part seeming quite bare; sometimes flat and stony, sometimes tossed and broken, sometimes in great drifts and wreaths of sand, just like snowdrifts, delicately ribbed by the wind—the whole stretching away for miles, scores of miles, not a moving form visible, till it is bounded on the horizon by a ridge of hills of the most ethereal pink under an intense blue sky. Such is the view to the east of us now, as we pass through the Suez Canal (19th October 1890). To the west the land looks browner and grayer; some reeds mark a water-course, and about 10 miles off appears a frowning dark range of bare hills about 2000 feet high, an outlying spur of the hills (Jebel Attákah) that bound the Gulf of Suez.

In such a landscape one of the signal stations, with its neat tiled cottage and flagstaff, and a few date palms and perhaps a tiny bit of garden, is quite an attraction to the eye. These stations are placed at intervals of about 6 miles all along the canal. They serve to regulate the traffic, which is now enormous, and continuous night and day. The great ships nearly fill the waterway, so that one has to be drawn aside and moored in order to let another pass; and though they are not allowed to go faster than 4 miles an hour they create a considerable wave in their rear, which keeps washing down the banks. Tufts of a reedy grass have been planted in places to hold the sand together; but the silt is very great, and huge steam-dredges are constantly at work to remove it. Here and there on the bank is a native hut of dry reeds—three sides and a flat top—just a shelter from the sun; or an Arab tent, with camels tethered by the leg around it. At Kantarah the caravan track from Jerusalem—one of the great highways of the old world—crosses the canal; there are a few wood and mud huts, and it is curious to see the string of laden camels and the Arabs in their unbleached cotton burnouses coming down—just as they might be coming down from the time of Father Abraham—and crossing the path of this huge modern steamship, with its electric lights and myriad modern appliances, the *Kaiser Wilhelm* now going half-way round the globe.

The desert does not seem quite devoid of animal life; at anyrate along the canal side you may see tracks in the sand of rabbits and hares, occasional wagtail-like birds by the water, a few crows hovering above, or a sea-gull, not to mention camels and a donkey or two, or a goat. Near Port Said they say the lagoons are sometimes white with flocks of pelicans and flamingoes, but we passed there in the night. It was fine to see the electric light, placed in the bows, throwing a clear beam and illuminating the banks for fully half-a-mile ahead, as we slowly steamed along. The driven sand looked like snow in the bluish light. The crescent moon and Venus were in the sky, and the red signal lights behind us of Port Said.

The canal is 90 miles long, and a large part of it follows the bed of a very ancient canal which is supposed to have connected the two seas. It appears that there is a very slight movement of the water through it from south to north.

We are now nearing Suez, and the heat is so great that it reverberates from the banks as from a furnace; of course the deck is under an awning. The remains of a little village built of clay appears, but the huts have broken down, split by the fierce sun-rays, and some light frame-houses, roofed and walled with shingles, have taken their place.

Gulf of Suez.—The town of Suez is a tumble-down little place, narrow lanes and alleys; two-storeyed stone houses mostly, some with carved wooden fronts, and on the upper floors lattice-work, behind which I suppose the women abide. Some nice-looking faces in the streets, but a good many ruffians; not so bad though as Port Said, where the people simply exist to shark upon the ships. In both places an insane medley of Arabs, fellahs, half-castes and Europeans, touts, guides, donkey-boys, etc., and every shade of dress and absurd hybrid costume, from extreme Oriental to correct English; ludicrous scenes of passengers going on shore, ladies clinging round the necks of swarthy boatmen; donkey-boys shouting the names of their donkeys—

"Mr Bradlaugh, sir, very fine donkey," "Mrs Langtry," "Bishop of London," etc.; fearful altercations about claimed *baksheesh*; parties beguiled into outlying quarters of the town and badly blackmailed; refusals of boatmen to take you back to the ship while the very gong of departure is sounding; and so forth. Suez, however, has a little caravan and coasting trade of its own, besides the railway which now runs thence to Cairo, and has antique claims to a respectability which its sister city at the other end of the canal cannot share.

Now that we are out in the gulf, the sea is deep blue, and very beautiful, the rocks and mountains along the shore very wild and bare, and in many parts of a strong red colour. This arm of the Red Sea is about 150 miles long, and I think not more than 20 miles wide at any point; in some places it is much less. We pass jutting capes and islands quite close on the west of us—great rocky ravine-cut masses absolutely bare of vegetation. On the east—apparently about 10 miles distant, but very clear—stands an outlying range of Sinai—Jebel Sirbal by name—looks about 5000 or 6000 feet high, very wild and craggy, many of the peaks cloven at the summit and gaping as if with the heat; farther back some higher points are visible, one of which is probably Jebel Musa. A most extraordinary land; at some places one can discern—especially with the aid of a glass—large tracts or plains of loose sand, miles in extent, and perfectly level, except where they wash up in great drifts against the bases of the mountains. Across these plains tall dark columns can be distinguished slowly travelling—the dreaded sand-clouds borne on eddies of the wind.

Indian Ocean, Oct. 25th.—Much cooler now. In the Red Sea, with thermometer at 90° in the cabins, heat was of course the absorbing topic. Everybody mopping; punkahs in full swing. I believe the *water* there frequently reaches 90° F., and sometimes 95°; but here it is quite cool, probably not much over 60°, and that alone makes a great difference. It is a queer climate in the Red Sea: there seems to be always a haze, due to dust blown from the shores; at the same time the air is very damp, owing to the enormous evaporation, clothes hung up get quite wet, and there are heavy dews. When the wind is aft the oppression from the heat is sometimes so great that ships have to be turned back and steamed against the breeze; but even so casualties and deaths are not uncommon. Owing to the haze, and the breadth of the Red Sea which is as much as 200 miles in parts, little is seen of the shores. A few rocky islands are passed, and a good many awkward reefs which the passengers know nothing of. The Straits of Bab-el-Mandeb are curious. The passage between the Island of Perim and the Arabian mainland is quite narrow, only a mile or two wide; tossed wild-looking hills on the mainland, 3000 or 4000 feet high, with French fortifications. The island itself lower and more rounded, with English fort and lighthouse; but looking very black and bare, though owing to the moisture there is some kind of stunted heathery stuff growing on it. There are a few English here, and a native town of waggon-like tents clustered round the fort; some little fishing and sailing boats along the shores. Turning eastwards along the south coast of Arabia the same awful land meets the eye as in the Gulf of Suez. A continual cloud of dust flies along it, through which one discerns sandy plains, and high parched summits beyond. There must, however, be water in some parts of this region, as it is back from here in this angle of Arabia that Mocha lies and the coffee is grown.

Colombo.—I fear that the Red Sea combined with mutual boredom had a bad effect on the passengers' tempers, for terrible dissensions broke out; and after six days of the Indian Ocean, during which the only diversions were flying-fish outside and scandal-mongering inside the ship, it was a relief to land on the palm-fringed coast of Ceylon. The slender catamarans—or more properly outrigged canoes—manned by dusky forms, which come to take you ashore, are indeed so narrow that it is impossible to sit inside them! They are made of a "dug-out" tree-trunk (see frontispiece), with parallel bulwarks fastened on only 10 inches or a foot apart; across the bulwarks a short board is placed, and on *that* you can sit. Two arms projecting on one side carry a float or light fish-shaped piece of wood, which rests on the water 8 feet or so from the canoe, and prevents the vessel from capsizing, which it would otherwise infallibly do. Impelled by oars, or by a sail, the boat bounds over the water at a good speed; and the mode of travelling is very pleasant. There is no necessity however to embark in these frail craft, for respectable civilised boats, and even steam-launches, abound; we are indeed in an important and busy port.

A great granite mole, built five years ago, has

converted an open roadstead into a safe and capacious harbour, and there is now probably no place in the East better supplied with mails and passenger boats than Colombo. It is the calling place for the great lines of steamers *en route* for Australia, for China and Japan, and for Calcutta and Burmah, not to mention smaller coasting boats from the mainland of India, and so forth. The city itself has only the slightest resemblance to a European town. There is a fort, certainly, and a Government House, and barracks with a regiment of infantry (part of whom however are generally up country); there are two or three streets of two or even three-storeyed houses, with shops, banks, mercantile offices, etc.; a few hotels and big goods stores, a lighthouse, and a large engineering works, employing some hundreds of Cinghalese and Tamil operatives; and then you have done with the English quarter. The land is flat, and round about the part just described stretch open grass-covered spaces, and tree-fringed roads, with the tiny booths or huts of the darkies on both sides of them. Here and there are knots and congeries of little streets and native markets with multifarious life going on in them. Here is a street of better built cottages or little villas belonging to Eurasians—the somewhat mixed descendants of old Dutch and Portuguese settlers—small one or seldom two-storeyed houses of stuccoed brick, with a verandah in front and a little open court within, clustering round an old Dutch church of the 17th century. Here is the residential quarter of the official English and of the more aspiring among the natives—the old Cinnamon Gardens, now laid out in large villa-bungalows and private grounds. Here again is a Roman Catholic church and convent, or the grotesque façade of a Hindu temple; and everywhere trees and flowering shrubs and, as one approaches the outskirts of the town, the plentiful broad leaves of coco palms and bananas overshadowing the roads. Nor in any description of Colombo should the fresh-water lake be forgotten, which, ramifying and winding in most intricate fashion through the town, and in one place coming within a hundred yards of the sea, surprises one continually with enchanting glimpses. I don't know any more delightful view of its kind—all the more delightful because so unexpected—than that which greets the eye on entering the Fort Railway Station at Colombo. You pass through the booking-office and find yourself on a platform, which except for the line of rails between might be a terrace on the lake itself; a large expanse of water with wooded shores and islands, interspersed with villas, cottages and cabins, lies before you; white-sailed boats are going to and fro; groups of dark figures, waist-deep in water, are washing clothes; children are playing and swimming in the water; and when, as I saw it once, the evening sun is shining through the transparent green fringe of banana palms which occupies the immediate foreground, and the calm lake beyond reflects like a mirror the gorgeous hues of sky and cloud, the scene is one which for effects of color can hardly be surpassed.

Up and down these streets and roads, and by the side of this lake, and along the seashore and through the quays and docks, goes, as may be imagined, a most motley crowd. The Cinghalese and the Tamils are of course the most numerous, but besides these there are Mohammedans—usually called Moor-men here—and some Malays. The English in Ceylon may be divided into three classes: the official English, the planters, and the small trading English (including employees on railway and other works). Then there are the Anglicised native gentry, Cinghalese or Tamil, some of whom occupy official positions, and who largely adopt European dress and habits; the non-Anglicised ditto, who keep to their own ways and costume, and are not much seen in public; the Dutch Eurasians, many of whom become doctors or solicitors (proctors); and the Portuguese, who are frequently traders in a small way.

Specimens of all these, in their different degrees of costume and absence of costume, may be seen in Colombo, as indeed in almost any place in Ceylon which can be dignified with the name of a town.

Here for instance is a great big Moor-man with high fez of plaited grass, baggy white pants and turned-up shoes; a figured vest on his body, and red shawl thrown over one shoulder. [He is probably a well-to-do shopkeeper; not an agreeable face, but I find the Mohammedans have a good reputation for upright dealing and fidelity to their word.]

Here a ruddy-brown Cinghalese man, with hairy chest, and nothing on but a red loin-cloth, carrying by a string an earthenware pot, probably of palm-beer. [A peasant. The Cinghalese are generally of this colour, whereas the Tamils tend towards black, though shading off in the higher castes to an olive tint.]

Another Cinghalese, dressed all in white, white

cotton jacket and white cloth hanging to below the knees, with elegant semicircular tortoise-shell comb on his head; a morbidly sensitive face with its indrawn nose and pouting lips. [Possibly a private servant, or small official of one of the courts, or *Arachchi.* The comb is a great mark of the low-country Cinghalese. They draw the hair backwards over the head and put the comb on horizontally, like an incomplete crown, with its two ends sticking up above the forehead—very like horns from a front view! The hair is then fastened in a knot behind, or sometimes left hanging down the back. This is a somewhat feeble face, but as a rule onc may say that the Cinghalese are very intelligent. They make excellent carpenters and mechanics. Are generally sensitive and proud.]

Cinghalese Man

Here come two Englishmen in tweed suits and tennis-shoes—their umbrellas held carefully by the middle—apparently of the planter community, young, but rather weedy looking, with an unsteady, swimmy look about the eyes which I fear is not uncommon among the planters; I have seen it already well-developed in a mere boy of eighteen.

Here a dozen or so of *chetties* (a Tamil commercial caste), with bare shaven and half-shaven heads, brown skins, and white muslins thrown gracefully round their full and sleek limbs; the sacred spot marked on their foreheads, red betel in their mouths, and avarice in their faces.

A Jaffna Tamil

There a Tamil coolie or wage-worker, nearly naked except for a handkerchief tied round his head, with glossy black skin and slight yet graceful figure.

Here a pretty little girl of nine or so, with blue beads round her neck, and the usual white cotton jacket and coloured petticoat or çilai of the Cinghalese women, walking with a younger brother.

Here three young Eurasian girls in light European costume and straw hats, hair loose or in pigtails down their backs, very pretty. [They are off for a walk along the Galle Face promenade by the sea, as the heat of the day is now past.]

Here also an English lady, young and carefully dressed, but looking a little bored, driving in her pony-trap to do some shopping, with a black boy standing behind and holding a sunshade over her.

One of the features of Colombo are the jinrickshaws, or light two-wheeled gigs drawn by men, which abound in the streets. These Tamil fellows, in the lightest of costumes, their backs streaming under the vertical sun, bare-legged and often bareheaded, will trot with you in a miraculous way from one end of Colombo to the other, and for the smallest fee. Tommy Atkins delights to sit thus lordly behind the toiling "nigger." At eventide you may see him and his Eurasian girl—he in one jinrickshaw and she in another—driving out to the Galle Face Hotel, or some such distant resort along the shore of the many-sounding ocean. The Tamils are mostly slight and graceful in figure, and of an active build. Down at the docks they work by hundreds, with nothing on beyond a narrow band between the thighs, loading and unloading barges and ships—a study of the human figure. Some of them of course are thick and muscular, but mostly they excel in a kind of unconscious grace and fleetness of form as of the bronze Mercury of Herculaneum, of which they often remind me. Their physiognomy corresponds with their bodily activity; the most characteristic type that I have noticed among them has level brows, and eyes deep-set (and sometimes a little close together), straight nose, and well-formed chin. They are a more enterprising, pushing, and industrious people than the Cinghalese, eager and thin, skins often very dark, with a concentrated, sometimes demonish, look between the eyes—will-power evidently present—but often handsome. Altogether a singular mixture of enterprise with demoniac qualities; for occultism is rife among them, from the jugglery of the lower castes to the esoteric philosophy and speculativeness of the higher. The horse-keepers and stable-boys

A Jinrickshaw
(Tamil coolie, Eurasian girl)

in Ceylon are almost all Tamils (of a low caste), and are a charming race, dusky, active, affectionate demons, fond of their horses, and with unlimited capacity of running, even over newly macadamised roads. The tea coolies are also Tamils, and the road-workers, and generally all wage-laborers; while the Cinghalese, who have been longer located in the island, keep to their own little peasant holdings and are not at all inclined to come under the thumb of a master, preferring often indeed to suffer a chronic starvation instead.

The Tamil women are, like their lords, generally of a slighter build than the Cinghalese of the same sex, some indeed are quite diminutive. Among both races some very graceful and good-looking girls are to be seen, up to the age of sixteen or so, fairly bright even in manner; especially among the Cinghalese are they distinguished for their fine eyes; but at a later age, and as wives, they lose their good looks and tend to become rather heavy and brutish.

The contrast between the Cinghalese and the Tamils is sufficiently marked throughout, and though they live on the island on amicable terms there is as a rule no love lost between them. The Cinghalese came to Ceylon, apparently from the mainland of India, somewhere in the sixth century B.C., and after pushing the aborigines up into the woods and mountains (where some of them may yet be found), occupied the whole island. It was not long however before the Tamils followed, also from India; and since then, and through a long series of conflicts, the latter have maintained their position, and now form the larger part of the population in the north of the island, while the Cinghalese are most numerous in the south. Great numbers of Tamil peasants — men, women, and children—still come over from the mainland every year, and go up-country to work in the tea-gardens, where there is a great demand for coolie labour.

In character the Cinghalese are more like the Italians, easy-going, reasonably idle, sensitive, shrewd, and just a bit romantic. Their large eyes and tortoise-shell combs and long hair give them a very womanly aspect; and many of the boys and youths have very girlish features and expressions. They have nearly always grace and dignity of manner, the better types decidedly handsome, with their well-formed large heads, short beards, and long black hair, composed and gentle, remindful of some pictures of Christ. In inferior types you have thick-featured, morbidly sensitive, and at the same time dull-looking persons. As a rule their frames are bigger and more fleshy than those of the Tamils, and their features less cleanly cut. Captain R, Knox, in his "Nineteen Years' Captivity in the Kingdom of Conde Uda" (1681), says of them: "In carriage and behaviour they are very grave and stately, like unto Portuguese; in understanding, quick and apprehensive; in design, subtle and crafty; in discourse, courteous, but full of flatteries; naturally inclined to temperance both in meat and drink, but not to chastity; near and pro-

Tamil Girl

vident in their families, commending good husbandry."

The Cinghalese are nearly all Buddhists, while the Tamils are Hindus. Buddhism was introduced into Ceylon about the fourth century B.C., and has flourished here ever since; and Buddhist rock-temples are to be found all over the island. The Tamils have a quite extensive literature of considerable antiquity, mostly philosophical or philosophico-poetical; and their language is very rich in vocabulary as well as in its grammatical forms and inflexions—though very terse, with scanty terms for expressions of courtesy (like "thank you," or "good-morning"), and a little harsh in sound, *k*'s and *r*'s flying through the teeth at a great rate. Cinghalese is much more liquid and pleasant in sound, and has many more Aryan words in it. In fact, it is supposed to be an offshoot of Sanskrit, whereas Tamil seems to have no relation to Sanskrit, except that it has borrowed a good many words. The curious thing is that, so little related as races, the Tamils should have taken their philosophy, as they have done, from the Sanskrit Vedas and Upanishads, and really expressed the ideas if anything more compactly and systematically than the Sanskrit books do. Though poor in literature, I believe, yet the Cinghalese have one of the best books of chronicles which exist in any language—the Mahawanso—giving a very reliable history of the race (of course with florid adornment of stupendous miracles, which can easily be stripped off) from their landing in Ceylon down to modern times. The Mahawanso was begun by Mahanamo, a priest, who about

460 A.D. compiled the early portion comprising the period from B.C. 543 to A.D. 301, after which it was continued by successive authors right down to British times—*i.e.* A.D. 1758!

There are two newspapers in Colombo printed in the Cinghalese language, one of which is called *The Buddhist World*; there is also a paper printed in Tamil; and there are three English newspapers. In "places of entertainment" Colombo (and the same is true of the towns in India) is very wanting. There is no theatre or concert-hall. It can be readily understood that though the population is large (120,000) it is so diverse that a sufficiently large public cannot be found to support such places. The native races have each their own festivals, which provide for them all they require in that way. The British are only few—5000 in all Ceylon, including military, out of a population of over three millions; and even if the Eurasian population—who of course go in for Western manners and ideals—were added, their combined numbers would be only scanty. An occasional circus or menagerie, or a visit from a stray theatrical company on its way to Australia, is all that takes place in that line.

For the rest there is a Salvation Army, with thriving barracks, a Theosophist Society, a branch of the Royal Asiatic Society, and various other little clubs representing different sections. Society is of course very much broken up into sections. Even the British, few as they are, are sadly divided by cliques and jealousies; the line between the official English and the "second class" English is terribly severe (as indeed all over India); and between these again and the Eurasians. Even where Cinghalese or Tamil or Eurasian families of old standing attain important official positions, an insuperable stiffness still marks the intercourse between them and the British. "Ah!" said a planter to a young friend of mine who had just shaken hands rather cordially with a native gentleman, "Ah! my boy, you won't do that when you've been here three years!" Thus a perfect social amalgamation and the sweetness of brethren dwelling together in unity are things still rather far distant in this otherwise lovely isle.

Talking about the beauty of the island, I was very much struck, even on my first landing, with its "spicy gales." The air is heavy with an aromatic fragrance which, though it forced itself on my attention for three or four weeks before I got fairly accustomed to it, I have never been able to trace to any particular plant or shrub. It is perhaps not unlike the odour of the cinnamon leaf when bruised, but I don't think it comes from that source. I am never tired of looking at the coconut palms; they grow literally by the million all along this coast to the north and south of Colombo. To the south the sea-shore road is overshadowed by them. I have been some miles along the road, and the belt of land, a hundred yards or so wide, between it and the sea, is thick with their stems right down to the water's edge, over which they lean lovingly, for they are fond of the salt spray. On the other side of the road too they grow, and underneath them are little villas and farmsteads and tiny native cabins, with poultry and donkeys and humped cows and black pigs and brown children, in lively confusion; while groups of peasant men and women in bright-colored wraps travel slowly along, and the little bullock gigs, drawn by active little Brahmin bulls with jingling bells, trot past at a pace which would do credit to an English pony—a scene which they say continues much the same the whole way to Galle (80 miles). These palms do not grow wild in Ceylon; they are all planted and cared for, whether in huge estates, or in the rood of ground which surrounds a Cinghalese cabin. The Cinghalese have a pretty saying that they cannot grow afar from the sound of the human voice. They have also a saying to the effect that a man only sees a *straight* coco-palm once in a life-time. Many of the other kinds of palms grow remarkably straight, but this kind certainly does not. In a grove of them you see hundreds of the grey smooth stems shooting upwards in every fantastic curve imaginable, with an extraordinary sense of life and power, reminding one of the way in which a volley of rockets goes up into the air. Then at the height of 50 or 60 feet they break into that splendid crown of green plumes which sparkles glossy in the sun, and waves and whispers to the lightest breeze.

Along this palm-fringed and mostly low and sandy shore the waves break—with not much change of level in their tides—loudly roaring in the S.W. monsoon, or with sullen swell when the wind is in the N.E., but seldom altogether calm. A grateful breeze tempers the 90° of the thermometer. A clumsy-hulled, lateen-sailed fishing boat is anchored in the shelter of a sandy spit; two or three native men and boys are fishing with rod and line, standing ankle-deep at the water's edge. The dashing blue waves look tempting for a bathe, but the shore is comparatively deserted; not a soul is to be seen in the water, infested as it is by the all-dreaded shark. Only 300 or 400 yards out, can be discerned the figure of a man—also fishing with a line—apparently standing up to his middle in water, but really sitting on a kind of primitive raft or boat, consisting of three or four logs of wood, slightly shaped, with upturned ends, and loosely tied together—the true catamaran (*kattu maram*, tied tree). The water of course washes up and around him, but that is pleasant on a hot day. He is safe from sharks; there is a slender possibility of his catching something for dinner; and there he sits, a relic of pre-Adamite times, while the train from Kalutara rushes by with a shriek to Colombo.

CHAPTER II

KANDY AND PEASANT LIFE

ERNST HAECKEL in his book about Ceylon says that the Cinghalese, though a long-civilised race, are as primitive as savages in their dress, cabins, etc.; and this remark strikes me as very true. As soon as you get off the railways and main roads you find them living in their little huts under their coco-palms in the most primitive fashion, and probably much as they did when they first came to Ceylon, 2000 or 3000 years ago.

On the 4th of this month (December), my friend "Ajax" landed at Colombo from England. He is on his way to Assam, in the tea-planting line, and is staying a week in the island to break the journey. He is a thorough Socialist in feeling, and a jolly fellow, always bright and good-natured, and with a great turn for music. We came up here to Kandy, and shortly after our arrival went to call on a Cinghalese peasant whose acquaintance I had lately made—Kalua by name—and found him in his little cabin, about a mile out of the town, among the hills, where he lives with his brother Kirrah. Leaving Kandy by footpaths and alongside hedgerows overrun by a wild sunflower, and by that extraordinary creeper, with a verbena-like blossom, the *lantana*, which though said to have been introduced only about fifty years ago now runs in masses over the whole island, we came at last to a lovely little glen, with rice-lands laid out in terraces at the bottom, and tangles of scrub and jungle up the sides, among which were clumps of coco-nut and banana, indicating the presence of habitations. Under one of these groves, in a tiny little mud and thatch cabin, we found Kalua; in fact, he saw us coming, and with a shout ran down to meet us. We were soon seated in the shade and talking such broken English and Tamil as we could respectively command. The brothers were very friendly, and brought us coco-nut milk and *chágeri* beer (made by cutting the great flower-bud off the *chágeri* palm, and letting the sap from the wounded stem flow into a jar, where it soon ferments; it has a musty flavor, and I cannot say that I care for it). Then their father, hearing of our arrival, came from half-a-mile off to have a look at us—a regular jolly old savage, with broad face

Kaiua

and broad belly—but unfortunately, as we could not speak Cinghalese, there was no means of communicating with him, except by signs. This little valley seems to be chiefly occupied by the brothers and their kindred, forming a little tribe, so to speak. Kalua and his father both own good strips of rice-land, and are perhaps rather better off than most Cinghalese peasants, though that is not saying much. Married sisters and their children, and other relatives, also occupy portions of the glen; but Kalua and Kirrah are not married yet. It seems to be a point of honor with the Cinghalese (and indeed with most of the East Indian races) not to marry till their sisters are wedded. Like the Irish, the brothers work to provide a dowry for their sisters; and generally family feeling and helpfulness are very strong among them. To strike a father or a mother is, all over Ceylon (and India), a crime of almost unheard-of atrocity. Kalua gives a good deal of his earnings to his parents, and buys additions to the family rice-lands—which as far as I can make out are held to a considerable extent as common property.

There was a native king and kingdom of Kandy till about eighty years ago (1814), when the British overthrew it; and it is curious that the old Kandian law—which was recognised for some time by the British—contains very evident traces of the old group-marriage which is found among so many races in their pre-civilisation period. There were two kinds of marriage treated of in the Kandian law—the Deega marriage, in which the wife went (as with us) to the house of her husband, and became more or less his property; and the Beena marriage, in which he came to live with her among her own people, but was liable to expulsion at any time! The latter form is generally supposed to be the more primitive, and belongs to the time when heredity is traced through the woman, and when also polygamous and polyandrous practices prevail. And this is confirmed by a paragraph of the Kandian law, or custom, which forbade inter-marriage between the children of two brothers, or between the children of two sisters, but allowed it between the children of a brother and a sister—the meaning of course being that two brothers might have the same wife, or two sisters the same husband, but that a brother and sister—having necessarily distinct wives and husbands—would produce children who could not be more nearly related to each other than cousins. It is also confirmed by the fact that a kind of customary group-marriage still lingers among the Cinghalese—*e.g.* if a man is married, his brothers not uncommonly have access to the wife—though owing to its being discountenanced by Western habits and law, this practice is gradually dying out.

Kalua has seen rather more of the world than some of his people, and has had opportunities of making a little money now and then. It appears that at the age of twelve or thirteen he took to "devil-dancing"—probably his father set him to it. He danced in the temple and got money; but now-a-days does not like the priests or believe in the temples. This devil-dancing appears to be a relic of aboriginal Kandian demon-worship: the evil spirits had to be appeased, or in cases of illness or misfortune driven away by shrieks and frantic gestures. It is a truly diabolical performance. The dancers (there are generally two of them) dress themselves up in fantastic array, and then execute the most extraordinary series of leaps, bounds, demivolts, and somersaults, in rhythmical climaxes, accompanied by clapping of hands, shrieks, and tom-tomming, for about twenty minutes without stopping, by the end of which time the excitement of themselves and spectators is intense, and the patient—if there is one—is pretty sure to be either killed or cured! When the Buddhists came to the island they incorporated these older performances into their institutions. Some two or three years ago, however, Hagenbeck, of circus celebrity, being in Ceylon, engaged a troupe of Kandians—of whom Kalua was one—to give a native performance for the benefit of the Europeans; and since that time the old peasant life has palled upon our friend, and it is evident that he lives in dreams of civilisation and the West. Kalua is remarkably well-made, and active and powerful. He is about twenty-eight, with the soft giraffe-like eyes of the Cinghalese, and the gentle, somewhat diffident manner which they affect; his black hair is generally coiled in a knot behind his head, and, with an ornamental belt sustaining his colored skirt, and a shawl thrown over his shoulder, he looks quite handsome. Kirrah is thinner and weaker, both mentally and physically, with a clinging affectionateness of character which is touching. Then there are two nephews, Pinha and Punjha, whom I have seen once or twice—bright, nice-looking boys, anxious to pick up phrases and words of English, and ideas about the wonderful

Western world, which is beginning to dawn on their horizon—though, alas! it will soon destroy their naked beauty and *naïveté*. To see Punjha go straight up the stem of a coco-nut tree fifty feet high is a caution! He just puts a noose of rope round his two feet to enable him to grasp the stem better with his soles, clasps his hands round the trunk, brings his knees up to his ears, and shoots up like a frog swimming!

The coco-nut palm is everything to the Cinghalese: they use the kernel of the nut for food, either as a curry along with their rice, or as a flavoring to cakes made of rice and sugar; the shell serves for drinking cups and primeval spoons; the husky fibre of course makes string, rope, and matting; the oil pressed from the nut, in creaking antique mills worked by oxen, is quite an article of commerce, and is used for anointing their hair and bodies, as well as for their little brass lamps and other purposes; the woody stems come in for the framework of cabins, and the great leaves either form an excellent thatch, or when plaited make natural screens, which in that climate often serve for the cabin-walls in place of anything more substantial. When Ajax told Kirrah that there were no coco-palms in England, the latter's surprise was unfeigned as he exclaimed, "How do you live, then?"

The other great staple of Cinghalese life is rice. Kalua's family rice-fields lay below us in larger patches along the bottom of the glen, and terraced in narrow strips a little way up the hill at the head of it. The rice-lands are, for irrigation's sake, always laid out in level patches, each surrounded by a low mud bank, one or two feet high; sometimes, where there is water at hand, they are terraced quite a good way up the hillsides, something like the vineyards in Italy. During and after the rains the water is led onto the various levels successively, which are thus well flooded. While in flood they are ploughed—with a rude plough drawn by humped cattle, or by buffaloes—and sown as the water subsides. The crop soon springs up, a brilliant green about as high as barley, but with an ear more re-

Ploughing in the Rice-Fields, with Buffaloes

sembling oats, and in seven or eight weeks is ready to be harvested. Boiled rice, with some curried vegetable or coco-nut, just to give it a flavor, is the staple food all over Ceylon among the natives—two meals a day, sometimes in poorer agricultural districts only one; a scanty fare, as their thin limbs too often testify. They use no bread, but a few cakes made of rice-flour and ghee and the sugar of the *chágeri* palm.

The brothers' cabin is primitive enough—just a

little thatched place, perhaps twelve feet by eight, divided into two—a large wicker jar or basket containing store of rice, one or two boxes, a few earthenware pots for cooking in, fire lighted on the ground, no chair or table, and little sign of civilisation except a photograph or two stuck on the wall and a low cane-seated couch for sleeping on. The latter, however, is quite a luxury, as the Cinghalese men as often as not sleep on the earth floor.

We stayed a little while chatting, while every now and then the great husked coco-nuts (of which you have to be careful) fell with a heavy thud from the trees; and then Kalua came on with us to Kandy, and we went to see the great Buddhist temple there, the Dalada Maligawa, which contains the precious tooth-relic of Buddha.

Architecturally nothing, the temple is interesting for the antique appearance of its gardens, shrines, priests' cottages, library, fishponds, etc.; sacred fish and turtles coming to be fed by the pious; rude frescoes of the infernal torments of the wicked, not unlike our mediæval designs on similar subjects; the sacred shrine itself with ivory and silver doors; the dirty, yellow-stoled priests arriving with huge keys to open it, but first washing their feet in the forecourt; the tom-toms and horns blowing; flowers scattered about; and then the interior chamber of the shrine, where behind strong bars of iron reposes a golden and bell-shaped cover, crusted with jewels —the outermost of *six* successive covers, within the last of which is the tooth itself (reported by Emerson Tennent to be about two inches long, and probably the fang of a crocodile!); then the little golden and crystal images of Buddha in various little shrines to themselves; and, most interesting of all, the library with its old MS. books written on strips of talipot palm leaf beautifully done in Cinghalese, Pali, San-

Buddhist Priest
(Librarian at the Temple at Kandy, with palm-leaf MS. book in lap)

skrit, etc., illuminated with elegant designs, and bound by silk cords in covers of fretted silver. The old librarian priest was a charming specimen of a Buddhist priest—gentle, intelligent, and apparently with a vein of religious feeling in his character—and spoke with interest about the various texts and manuscripts. It is a pity that so much cannot be said of the Buddhist priests generally, who are as a rule—in Ceylon at any rate—an ignorant, dirty, betel-chewing and uninviting-looking lot.

At the botanical gardens at Peradeniya—three or four miles out of Kandy—we saw a specimen of the talipot palm in full flower. This beautiful palm—unlike the coco-palm—grows perfectly erect and straight; it flowers only once, and then dies. Haeckel says that it lives from fifty to eighty years, and that the blossom is sometimes thirty or forty feet long. The specimen that we saw in blossom was about forty-five feet high in the stem; and then from its handsome crown of huge leaves sprang a flower, or rather a branched spike of numerous white flowers, which I estimated at fifteen feet high (but which I afterwards saw described in the newspapers as twenty feet high). Baker says that the flower bud is often as much as four feet long, and that it opens with a smart report, when this beautiful white plume unfolds and lifts itself in the sun. The natives use the great leaf of the talipot—which is circular and sometimes eight or nine feet in diameter—as an umbrella. They fold it together along its natural corrugations, and then open it to ward off sun or rain.

Kandy is very beautiful. It stands nearly 2000 feet high, by the side of an artificial lake which the old kings of Kandy made, and embosomed in hills covered by lovely woods full of tropical plants and flowers and commanding beautiful views from their slopes and summits. There is a small native town containing the usual mixed population of

General View of Kandy
(Native street on left, Buddhist temple on right, English church in centre)

Cinghalese, Tamils, and Moor-men; there are one or two English hotels, a church, library and reading-room; a few residents' houses, and a scattered population of English tea-planters on the hills for some miles round, who make Kandy their *rendez-vous.*

Ajax gets on well with the native youths and boys here; he has an easy, friendly way with them, and they get hold of his hand and walk alongside. Of course they are delighted to find any *Mahate* * who will treat them a little friendly; but I fear the few English about are much shocked at our conduct. When I first came to Ceylon my Tamil friend A. chaffed me about my way of calling him and the rest of the population, whether Tamil or Mohammedan or Cinghalese, all indiscriminately *natives*, "as if we were so many *oysters.*" I told this to Ajax, and of course there was nothing for it after that but to call them all oysters!

We find the few British whom we have come across in our travels very much set against the "oysters." There is something queer about the British and their insularity; but I suppose it is more their misfortune than their fault. Certainly they will allow that the oysters are not without merit—indeed, if one keeps them to it they will often speak quite warmly of the tenderness and affectionateness of servants who have nursed them through long illnesses, etc.—but the idea of associating with them on terms of equality and friendship is somehow unspeakable and not to be entertained. It seems almost *de rigueur* to say something disparaging about the oyster, when that topic turns

* Short for *Mahatmaya.*

up—as a way of showing one's own breeding, I suppose; after that has been done, however, it is allowable to grant that there are exceptions, and even to point out some kindly traits, pearls as it were, which are occasionally found in the poor bivalve. It strikes me however that the English are the chief losers by this insular habit. They look awfully bored and miserable as a rule in these up-country parts, which must almost necessarily be the case where there are only five or six residents in a station, or within accessible distances of each other, and confined entirely to each other's society.

One day Ajax and I went up to Nuwara Ellia. The railway carriage was full of tea-planters (including one or two wives and sisters), and there were a few at the hotel. It was curious to see some English faces of the cold-mutton-commercial type, and in quite orthodox English attire, in this out-of-the-way region. The good people looked sadly bored, and it seemed a point of honor with them to act throughout as if the colored folk didn't exist or were invisible—also as if they were deaf, to judge by the shouting. In the evening however (at the hotel) we felt touched at the way in which they cheered up when Ajax and I played a few familiar tunes on the piano. They came round, saying it reminded them of home, and entreated us to go on; so we played for about two hours, Ajax improvising as usual in the most charming way.

Nuwara Ellia is 6000 feet above the sea—a little village with an hotel or two—a favorite resort from the sultry airs of Colombo and the lowlands. Here the Britisher finds fires in the sitting-rooms and thick mists outside, and dons his greatcoat and feels quite at home. But we, having only just come from the land of fogs, did not appreciate these joys, and thought the place a little bleak and bare.

CHAPTER III

KURUNÉGALA

On my way here, on the coach, I fell in with Monerasingha, a Cinghalese of some education and ability, a proctor or solicitor. He is a cheerful little man, an immense talker, and very keen on politics. He was very amusing about the English; says they are very agreeable at first, "but after three months' stay in the island a complete change comes over them—won't speak to us or look at us—*but I can give it them back.*" His idea seems to be that representative institutions are wanted to restore to the people that interest in public life which has been taken from them by the destruction of their communal institutions under British rule. He seems to be a great hater of caste, and thinks the English have done much good in that matter. "I am loyal enough, because I know we are much better off than we should be under Russia. The English are stupid and incapable of understanding us, and don't go among us to get understanding; but they mean well, according to their lights."

This place (called Kornegalle by the English) is a little town of 2000 or 3000 inhabitants, fifty miles from Colombo and eleven miles (by coach) from Polgahawella, the nearest railway station. It lies just at the foot of the mountain region of Ceylon, and takes its name, Kurunégala or

Elephant-rock, from a huge Gibraltar-like rock, 600 feet high, at the base of which it nestles—and whose rounded dark granite structure, wrinkled with weather and largely bare of trees or any herbage, certainly bears a remarkable resemblance, both in form and color, to a couchant elephant. Ascending its steep sides, on which the sun strikes with fierce heat during the midday, one obtains from the summit a fine view—westward over low plains, eastward over mountain ranges rising higher and higher towards the centre of the island. The prevailing impression of the landscape here, as elsewhere in Ceylon, is its uniform green. There is no change of summer or winter. (Though this is the coolest time of year the daily temperature ranges from 85° to 90° in the shade.) The trees do not cast their leaves at any stated time, though individual trees will sleep at intervals, resting so. In every direction the same color meets the eye—tracts of green scrub, green expanses of forest, green rice-fields, and the massed green of bananas and coco-palms. A little monotonous this in the general landscape, though it is plentifully compensated on a near view by the detailed color of insect and flower life. One curious feature is that though the country is well populated, hardly a trace of habitation is to be seen from any high point such as this. Even Kurunégala, which lies at our feet, is only distinguishable by its court-house and prison and one or two other emblems of civilisation; the native cabins, and even in many cases the European houses—which are of one storey only—are entirely hidden by trees. Those clumps however of coco-palms which you see standing like oases in the general woods, or breaking the levels of the rice-fields, with occasional traces of blue smoke curling up through them, are sure indications of little native hamlets clustered

Native Hut
(Among banana and coco-palms)

beneath—often far far from any road, and accessible only by natural footpaths worn by naked feet.

From the top of the rock one gets a good view of the tank which supplies irrigation water for the town and neighborhood. It is about three-quarters of a mile long and half-a-mile broad, and forms a pretty little lake, over which kites hover and kingfishers skim, and in which the people daily bathe. These tanks and irrigation channels are matters of the utmost importance, to which I think Government can hardly give too much attention. Their importance was well understood in past times, as indeed the remains and ruins of immense works of this kind, over a thousand years old, in various parts of the island fully testify. A little is being done towards their renewal and restoration, but the tendency to-day is to neglect the interests of the rice-growing peasant in favour of the tea-planting Englishman. Tea, which is an export and a luxury, and which enriches the few, is thought to be so much more important than an article which is grown for home consumption and for the needs of the many. It is of course only an instance of the general commercial policy of all modern Governments; but one cannot the less for that think it a mistake, and an attempt to make the pyramid of social prosperity stand upon its apex. There is something curious—and indeed is it not self-contradictory?—in the fact that every country of the civilised world studies above all things the increase of its *exports*—is engaged, not in producing things primarily for it own use, but in trying to get other people to buy what it produces!—as if we all stood round and tried to shuffle off our bad wares on the others, in the hope that they by some accident might return us good stuff in exchange. Somehow the system does not seem as if it would work; it looks too like the case of that island where the inhabitants all earned a precarious living by taking in each other's washing. What, one may ask, is really the cause of the enormous growth of this practice of neglecting production for use in favour of production for export and for the market? Is it not simply money and the merchant interest? Production at home by the population and for its own use is and always must be, one would think, by far the most important for the population and for its own comfort and welfare, though a margin may of course be allowed for the acquirement by exchange of some few articles which cannot be grown at home. But production such as this does not necessarily mean either money or mercantile transaction. Conceivably it may very well take place without either these or the gains which flow from their use—without profits or interest or dividends or anything of the kind. But this would never do! The money and commercial interest, which is now by far the most powerful interest in all modern states, is not such a fool as to favour a system of national economy which would be its own ruin. No; it must encourage *trade* in every way, at all costs. Trade, commerce, exchange, exports and imports—these are the things which bring dividends and interest, which fill the pockets of the parasites at the expense of the people; and so the nations stand round, obedient, and carry on the futile game till further orders.

As a matter of fact, in these hot countries, like Ceylon and India, almost unlimited results of productiveness can be got by perfected irrigation, and as long as the peasantry in these lands are (as they are) practically starving, and the irrigation works practically neglected, the responsibility for such a state of affairs must lie with the rulers; and naturally no mere shuffling of commercial cards, or encouragement of an export trade which brings fortunes into the hands of a few tea-planters and merchants, can be expected to make things better.

It is sad to see the thin and famished mortals who come in here from the country districts round to beg. Many of them, especially the younger ones, have their limbs badly ulcerated. One day, going through the hospital, the doctor—a Eurasian—took me through a ward full of such cases. He said that they mostly soon got better with the better hospital diet; "but," he added, "when they get back to their old conditions they are soon as bad as ever." In fact, the mass of the population in a place like Colombo looks far sleeker and better off than in these country districts; but that only affords another instance of how the modern policy encourages the shifty and crafty onhanger of commercial life at the cost of the sturdy agriculturist—and I need not say that the case is the same at home as abroad.

It is quite a pretty sight to see the bathing in the tanks. It takes place in the early morning, and indeed during most of the day. Cleanliness is a religious observance, and engrained in the habits of the people. Of course there are exceptions, but save among the lowest castes this is the rule. An orthodox Hindu is expected not only to wash himself, but his own cloth, at least once a day. The climate makes bathing a pleasure, and the people linger over it. Men and boys, women and children, together or in groups not far distant from each other, revel and splash in the cool liquid; their colored wraps are rinsed and spread to dry on the banks, their brass pots glance in the sun as they dip the water with them and pour it over their own heads, their long black hair streams down their backs. Then, leaving the water, they pluck a twig from a certain tree, and, squatting on their hams, with the frayed twig end rub their teeth and talk over the scandal of the day. This tooth-cleaning gossiping business lasts till they are dry, and often a good deal longer, and is, I fancy, one of the most enjoyable parts of the day to the mild darkie. In unsophisticated places there is no distinction of classes in this process, and rich and poor join in the public bathing alike—in fact, there is very little difference in their dress and habits anyhow, as far as regards wealth and poverty—but of course where Western ideas are penetrating, the well-to-do natives adopt our habits and conduct their bathing discreetly at home.

The people never (except it be children) go into the water *quite* naked, and the women always retain one of their wraps wound round the body. These wraps are very long, and the skill with which they manage to wash first one end and then the other, winding and unwinding, and remaining decorously covered all the time, is quite admirable. I am struck by the gravity and decorum of the people generally—in outer behavior or gesture—though their language (among the lower castes) is by no means always select! But there is none, or very little, of that banter between the sexes which is common among the Western populations, and even among the boys and youths you see next to no frolicking or bear-fighting. I suppose it is part of the passivity and want of animal spirits which characterise the Hindu; and of course the sentiment of the relation between the sexes is different in some degree from what it is with us. On sexual matters generally, as far as I can make out, the tendency, even among the higher castes, is to be

Native Street, and Shops

outspoken, and there is little of that prudery which among us is only after all a modern growth.

The town here is a queer mixture of primitive life with modern institutions. There are two or three little streets of booths, which constitute the "bazaar." Walking down these—where behind baskets of wares the interiors of the dwellings are often visible, and the processes of life are naïvely exposed to the eye—one may judge for one's self how little man wants here below. Here is a fruit and vegetable shop, with huge bunches of plantains or bananas, a hundred in a bunch, and selling at five or six a penny; of a morning you may see the peasant coming in along the road carrying *two* such bunches—a good load—slung one at each end of a long pole, or *pingo*, over his shoulder—a similar figure to that which is so frequent on the Egyptian monuments of 3,000 years ago; pineapples, from 1*d.* up to 4*d.* each for the very finest; the bread-fruit, and its queer relation the enormous jack-fruit, weighing often as much as 12 to 14 lbs., with its pulpy and not very palatable interior, used so much by the people, growing high up over their cabins on the handsome jack-tree, and threatening you with instant dissolution if it descend upon your head; the egg-plant, murunga, beans, potatoes, and other vegetables; and plentiful ready-prepared packets of areca nut and betel leaf for chewing. Then there is a shop where they sell spices, peppers, chilis, and all such condiments for curries, not to mention baskets of dried fish (also for currying), which stink horribly and constitute one of the chief drawbacks of the bazaars; and an earthenware shop,—and I must not forget the opium shop. Besides these there are only two others—and they represent Manchester and Birmingham respectively—one where they sell shoddy and much-sized cotton goods, and the other which displays tin-ware, soap, matches, paraffin lamps, dinner knives, and all sorts of damnable cutlery. I have seen these knives and scissors, or such as these (made only to deceive), being manufactured in the dens of Sheffield by boys and girls slaving in dust and dirt, breathing out their lives in foul air under the gaslights, hounded on by mean taskmasters and by the fear of imminent starvation. Dear children! if you could only come out here yourselves, instead of sending the abominable work of your hands—come out here to enjoy this sunshine, and the society of these brothers and sisters whose skins are dark by nature rather than by art!

The opium-seller is a friend of mine. I often go and sit in his shop—on his one chair. He teaches me Tamil—for he is a Tamil—and tells me long stories, slowly, word by word. He is a thin, soft-eyed, intelligent man, about thirty, has read a fair amount of English—of a friendly *riant* child-nature—not without a reasonable eye to the main chance, like some of his Northern cousins. There are a few jars of opium in its various forms—for smoking, drinking, and chewing; a pair of scales to weigh it with; a brass coco-nut oil lamp with two or three wicks hanging overhead; and a partition for the bed at the back,—and that is all. The shop-front is of course entirely open to the thronged street, except at night, when it is closed with shutter-boards.

At the corner of the street stands a policeman, of course, else we should not know we were being civilised. But, O Lord, what a policeman! How a London street arab would chuckle all over at the sight of him! Imagine the mild and somewhat timid native dressed in a blue woollen serge suit (very hot for this climate), with a belt round his waist, some kind of turban on his head, a staff in his hand, and *boots* on his feet! A real live "oyster" in boots! It is too absurd. How miserable he looks; and as to running after a criminal—the thing is not to be thought of. But no doubt the boots vindicate the majesty of the British Government.

While we are gazing at this apparition, a gang of prisoners marches by—twenty lean creatures, with slouched straw hats on their heads, striped cotton jackets and pants, and bare arms and lower legs, each carrying a mattock—for they are going to work on the roads—and the whole gang followed and guarded (certainly Ceylon is a most idyllic land) by a Cinghalese youth of about twenty-one, dressed in white skirts down to his feet, with a tortoise-shell comb on his head, and holding a parasol to shade himself from the sun! Why do not the twenty men with mattocks turn and slay the boy with the parasol, and so depart in peace? I asked this question many times, and always got the same answer. "Because," they said, "the prisoners do not particularly want to run away. They are very well off in prison,—better off, as a rule, than they are outside. Imprisonment by an alien Government, under alien laws and standards, is naturally no disgrace, at anyrate to the mass of the people, and so once in prison they make themselves as happy as they can."

I visited the gaol one day, and thought they succeeded very well in that respect. The authorities, I am glad to say, do all they can to make them comfortable. They have each a large dish of rice and curry, with meat if they wish, twice a day, and a meal of coffee and bread in the morning besides; which is certainly better fare than they would get as peasants. They do their little apology for work in public places during the day—with a chance of a chat with friends—and sleep in gangs together in the prison sheds at night, each with his mat, pillow, and night suit; so possibly on the whole they are not ill-content.

My friend A., with whom I am staying here, is a Tamil, and an official of high standing. He became thoroughly Anglicised while studying in England, and like many of the Hindus who come to London or Cambridge or Oxford, did for the time quite outwesternise us in the tendency towards materialism and the belief in science, "comforts," representative institutions, and "progress" generally. Now however he seems to be undergoing a reaction in favor of caste and the religious traditions of his own people, and I am inclined to think that other westernising Hindus will experience the same reaction.

He lives in an ordinary one-storeyed stone house, or bungalow, such as the English inhabit here. These houses naturally cover a good deal of ground. The roof, which is made of heavy tiles or thatch, is pitched high in the middle, giving space for lofty sitting-rooms; the sleeping chambers flank these at a lower slope, and outside runs the verandah, almost round the house, the roof terminating beyond it at six or seven feet from the ground. This arrangement makes the interiors very dark and cool, as the windows open on the verandah, and the sun cannot penetrate to them; but I am not sure that I like the sensation of being confined under this immense carapace of tiles, with no possible outlook to the sky, in a sort of cavernous twilight all the while. The verandah forms an easy means of access from one part to another, and in this house there are no passages in the interior, but the rooms all open into one another; and plentiful windows — some mere Venetian shutters, without glass — ensure a free circulation of air.

Mosquitoes are a little trying. I don't think they are more venomous than the English gnat, but they are far 'cuter. The mosquito is the 'cutest little animal for its size that exists. I am certain from repeated observations, that it *watches one's eyes.* If you look at it, it flies away. It settles on the under side of your hand (say when reading a book), or on your ankles when sitting at table—on any part in fact which is remote from observation; there is nothing that it loves better than for you to sit in a cane-bottomed chair. But it never attacks your face—and that is a curious thing—*except when you are asleep.* How it knows I cannot tell, but I have often noticed that it is so. If you close your eyes and pretend to be asleep, it will not come; but as sure as you begin to drowse off you hear the ping of its little wing as it swoops past your ear to your cheek.

At night however the mosquito curtains keep one in safety, and I cannot say that I am much troubled during the day, except on occasions, and in certain places, as in the woods when there is no breeze. A. is a vegetarian, and I fancy diet has a good deal to do with freedom from irritation by insects and by heat. The thermometer reaches 90° in the shade almost every day here; to sit and run at the same time is a gymnastic feat which one

D

can easily perform, and at night it is hot enough to sleep without any covering on the bed; but I enjoy the climate thoroughly, and never felt in better health. No doubt these things often affect one more after a time than at first; but there seems almost always a pleasant breeze here at this time of year, and I do not notice that languor which generally accompanies sultry weather.

A. has most lovely vegetable curries; plenty of boiled rice, with four or five little dishes of different sorts of curried vegetables. This, with fruit, forms our breakfast—at ten; and dinner at six or seven is much the same, with perhaps an added soup or side-dish. His wife sometimes joins us at dinner, which I take as an honor, as even with those Hindu women who are emancipated there is often a little reserve about eating with the foreigner. She has a very composed and gentle manner, and speaks English prettily and correctly, though slowly and with a little hesitation; approves of a good deal of the English freedom for women, but says she cannot quite reconcile herself to women walking about the streets alone, and other things she hears they do in England. However, she would like to come to England herself and see.

The children are very bright and charming. Mahéswari (three years old) is the sweetest little dot, with big black eyes and a very decided opinion about things. She comes into the room and lifts up one arm and turns up her face and prophesies something in solemn tones in Tamil, which turns out to be, "Father is very naughty to sit down to dinner before mother comes." Then she talks

Cinghalese to her nurse and English to me, which is pretty good for a beginner in life. Mahadéva and Jayanta, the two boys (seven and nine respectively), are in the bubbling-over stage, and are alternately fast friends and fighting with each other two or three times a day, much like English boys. They are dressed more after the English fashion, though they are privileged to have bare knees and feet—at anyrate in the house; and Jayanta has a pony which he rides out every day.

A. sets apart a little room in this house as a "chapel." It is quite bare, with just a five-wicked lamp on a small table in one corner, and flowers, fruit, etc., on the ground in front. I was present the other day when the Brahmin priest was performing a little service there. He recited Sanskrit formulas, burned camphor, and gave us cowdung ashes and sandalwood paste to put on our foreheads, consecrated milk to drink, and a flower each. The cowdung ashes are a symbol. For as cowdung, when burnt, becomes clean and even purifying in quality, so must the body itself be consumed and purified in the flame of Siva's presence. A. says they use a gesture identifying the light (of Siva) within the body with the light of the flame, and also with that of the sun; and always terminate their worship by going out into the open and saluting the sun. The Brahmin priest, a man about forty, and the boy of fifteen who often accompanies him, are pleasant-faced folk, not apparently at all highly educated, wearing but little in the way of clothes, and not specially distinguishable from other people, except by the sacred thread worn over the shoulder, and a certain alertness of expression which is often noticeable in the Brahmin—though the trouble is that it is generally alertness for gain.

The priests generally here, whether Buddhist or Hindu (and Buddhism is of course the prevailing religion in Ceylon), occupy much the same relation to the people which the priests occupy in the country districts of France or Ireland—that is, whatever spiritual power they claim, they do not arrogate to themselves any worldly supremacy, and are always poor and often quite unlettered. In fact, I suppose it is only in the commercially religious—*i.e.* Protestant—countries that the absurd anomaly exists of a priesthood which pretends to the service of the Jesus who had not where to lay his head, and which at the same time openly claims to belong to "society" and the well-to-do classes, and would resent any imputation to the contrary. There are indeed many points of resemblance between the religions here—especially Hinduism—and Roman Catholicism: the elaborate ceremonials and services, with processions, incense, lights, ringing of bells, etc.; the many mendicant orders, the use of beads and rosaries, and begging bowls, the monasteries with their abbots, and so forth.

There is one advantage in a hot damp climate like this; namely, that things—books, furniture, clothes, etc.—soon get destroyed and done with, so that there is little temptation to cumber up your house with possessions. Some English of course try to furnish and keep their rooms as if they were *still* living in Bayswater, but they are plentifully plagued for their folly. The floors here are of some cement or concrete material, which prevents the white ants surging up through them, as they infallibly would through boards, and which is nice and cool to the feet; carpets, cupboards, and all collections of unremoved things are discountenanced.

Veddahs
(Aborigines of Ceylon)

A chest of drawers or a bookcase stands out a foot or two from the wall, so that the servants can sweep behind it every day. Little frogs, lizards, scorpions, and other fry, which come hopping and creeping in during or after heavy rain can then be gently admonished to depart, and spiders do not find it easy to establish a footing. The greatest harbor for vermin is the big roof, which is full of rats. In pursuit of these come the rat-snakes, fellows five or six feet long, but not venomous, and wild cats; and the noises at night from them, the shuffling of the snakes, and the squeals of the poor little rats, etc., I confess are trying.

We have three or four male servants about the house and garden, and there are two *ayahs*, who look after the children and the women's apartments. I believe many of these Indian and Cinghalese races love to be servants (under a tolerably good master); their feminine sensitive natures, often lacking in enterprise, rather seek the shelter of dependence. And certainly they make, in many instances and when well treated, wonderfully good servants, their tact and affectionateness riveting the bond. I know of a case in which an English civilian met with an accident when 200 miles away from his station, and his "bearer," when he heard the news, in default of other means of communication, *walked* the whole distance, and arrived in time to see him before he died. At the same time it is a mistake to suppose they will do anything out of a sense of duty. The word duty doesn't occupy an important place in the Oriental vocabulary, any more than it does among the Celtic peoples of Europe. This is a fruitful source of misunderstanding between the races. The Britisher pays his Indian servant regularly, and in return expects him to *do his duty*, and to submit to kicks when he doesn't. He, the Britisher, regards this as a fair contract. But the native doesn't understand it in the least. He would rather receive his pay less regularly, and be treated as "a man and a brother." Haeckel's account of the affection of his Rodiya servant-lad for him, and of the boy's despair when Haeckel had to leave him, is quite touching; but it is corroborated by a thousand similar stories. But if there is no attachment, what is the meaning of duty? The native in keeping with his weaker, more dependent nature, is cunning and lazy—his vices lie in that direction rather than in the Western direction of brutal energy. If his attachment is not called out, he can make his master miserable in his own way. And he does so; hence endless strife and recrimination.

The Arachchi here, a kind of official servant of A.'s, is a most gentle creature, with remarkable tact, but almost too sensitive; one is afraid of wounding him by not accepting all his numerous attentions. He glides in and out of the room—as they all do—noiselessly, with bare feet; and one never knows whether one is alone or not. The horse-keeper and I are good friends, though our dialogues are limited for want of vocabulary! He is a regular dusky demon, with his look of affectionate bedevilment and way of dissolving in a grin whenever he sees one. A. says that he thinks the pariahs, or outcasts—and the horse-keepers are pariahs—are some of the most genuine and good-hearted among the people; and I see that the author of *Life in an Indian Village* says something of the same kind. "As a class, hardworking, honest, and truthful," he calls them;

and after describing their devotion to the interests of the families to whom they are often hereditarily attached, adds, "Such are the illiterate pariahs, a unique class, whose pure lives and noble traits of character are in every way worthy of admiration."

It is curious, but I am constantly being struck by the resemblance between the lowest castes here and the slum-dwellers in our great cities—resem blance in physiognomy, as well as in many unconscious traits of character, often very noble, with the brutish basis well-marked, the unformed mouth, and the somewhat heavy brows, just as in Meunier's fine statue of the ironworker ("puddleur"), but with thicker lips.

CHAPTER IV

ADAM'S PEAK AND THE BLACK RIVER

JANUARY 1st, 1891.—Sitting by an impromptu wood-fire in a little hut on the summit of Adam's Peak—nearly midnight—a half-naked Caliban out of the woods squatting beside me, and Kalua and the guide sleeping on the floor. But I find it too cold to sleep, and there is *no* furniture in the hut.

Altogether an eventful New Year's day. Last night I spent at Kandy with Kalua and his brother in their little cabin. They were both very friendly, and I kept being reminded of Herman Melville and his Marquesas Island experiences—so beautiful the scene, the moon rising about ten, woods and valleys all around—the primitive little hut, Kirrah cooking over a fire on the ground, etc. We were up by moon and starlight at 5 A.M., and by walking, driving, and the railway, reached Muskeliya at the foot of the peak by 2.30 P.M. There we got a guide—a very decent young Tamil—and reached here by 7.30 or 8 P.M. Our path lay at first through tea-gardens, and then, leaving them, it went in nearly a direct line straight up the mountain side—perhaps 3000 feet—through dense woods, in step-like formation, over tree roots and up the rocks, worn and hacked into shape through successive centuries by innumerable pilgrims, but still only wide enough for one. Night came upon us on the way, and the last hour or two we had to light torches to see our route. Elephant tracks were plentiful all round us through the woods, even close to the summit. It is certainly extraordinary on what steep places and rock sides these animals will safely travel; but we were not fortunate enough to see any of them.

This is a long night trying to sleep. It is the wretchedest hut, without a door, and unceiled to the four winds! Caliban makes the fire for me as I write. He has nothing on but a cotton wrap and a thin jersey, but does not seem to feel the cold much; and the guide is even more thinly clad, and is asleep, while I am shivering, bundled in cloth coats. There is something curious about the way in which the English in this country feel the cold—when it is cold—more than the natives; though one might expect the contrary. I have often noticed it. I fancy we make a great mistake in these hot lands in not exposing our skins more to the sun and air, and so strengthening and hardening them. In the great heat, and when constantly covered with garments, the skin perspires terribly, and becomes sodden and enervated, and more sensitive than it ought to be—hence great danger of chills. I have taken several sun-baths in the woods here at different times, and found advantage from doing so.

[Since writing the above, I have discovered the existence of a little society in India—of English folk—who encourage nudity, and the abandonment as far as possible of clothes, on three distinct grounds—physical, moral, and æsthetic—of Health, Decency, and Beauty. I wish the society every success. Passing over the moral and æsthetic considerations—which are both of course of the utmost importance in this connection—there is still the consideration of physical health and enjoyment, which must appeal to everybody. In a place like India, where the mass of the people go with very little covering, the spectacle of their ease and enjoyment must double the discomforts of the unfortunate European who thinks it necessary to be dressed up to the eyes on every occasion when he appears in public. It is indeed surprising that men can endure, as they do, to wear cloth coats and waistcoats and starched collars and cuffs, and all the paraphernalia of propriety, in a severity of heat which really makes only the very lightest covering tolerable; nor can one be surprised at the exhaustion of the system which ensues, from the cause already mentioned. In fact, the direct stimulation and strengthening of the skin by sun and air, though most important in our home climate, may be even more indispensable in a place like India, where the relaxing influences are so terribly strong. Certainly, when one considers this cause of English enervation in India, and the other due to the greatly mistaken *diet* of our people there, the fearful quantities of flesh consumed, and of strong liquors—both things which are injurious enough at home, but which are ruinous in a hot country—the wonder is not that the English fail to breed and colonise in India, but that they even last out their few years of individual service there.]

There is a lovely view of cloudland from the summit now the moon has risen. All the lower lands and mountains are wrapped in mist, and you look down upon a great white rolling sea, silent, remote from the world, with only the moon and stars above, and the sound of the Buddhist priests chanting away in a low tone round the fire in their own little cabin or *pansela*.

This is a most remarkable mountain. For at least 2000 years, and probably for long enough before that, priests of some kind or another have kept watch over the sacred footmark on the summit; for thousands of years the sound of their chanting has been heard at night between the driven white plain of clouds below and the silent moon and stars above; and by day pilgrims have toiled up the steep sides to strew flowers, and to perform some kind of worship to their gods, on this high natural altar. The peak is 7400 feet high, and though not quite the highest point on the island, is by far the most conspicuous. It stands like a great outpost on the south-west edge of the mountain region of Ceylon, and can be seen from far out to sea—a sugar-loaf with very precipitous sides. When the Buddhists first came to Ceylon, about the 4th century B.C., they claimed the footmark as that of Buddha. Later on some Gnostic Christian sects attributed it to the primal man; the Mohammedans, following this idea, when they got possession of the mountain, gave it the name of Adam's Peak; the Portuguese consecrated it to S. Eusebius; and now the Buddhists are again in possession—though I believe the Mohammedans are allowed a kind of concurrent right. But whatever has been the nominal dedication of this ancient "high place," a continuous stream of pilgrims—mainly of course the country folk of the island—has flowed to it undisturbed through the centuries; and even now they say that in the month of May the mountain side is covered by hundreds and even thousands of folk, who camp out during the night, and do *poojah* on the summit by day. Kalua says that his father—the jolly old savage—once ascended "Samantakuta," and, like the rest of the Cinghalese, thinks a great deal of the religious merit of this performance.

Ratnapura, Jan. 3rd.—Sunrise yesterday on the peak was fine, though "sunrises" are not always a success. The great veil of clouds gradually dissolved, and a long level "rose of dawn" appeared in the eastern sky—Venus brilliant above it, the Southern Cross visible, and one or two other crosses which lie near it, and the half moon overhead; a dark, peaked and castellated rampart of lower mountains stretched around us, and far on the horizon were masses of cumulus cloud rising out of the lowland mists, and catching the early light; while the lower lands themselves remained partly hidden by irregular pools and rivers of white fog, which looked like water in the first twilight. A great fan-like crown of rays preceded the sun, very splendid, of pearly colors, with great beams reaching nearly to the zenith. We could not see the sea, owing to mists along the horizon, nor was any habitation visible, but only the great jungle-covered hills and far plains shrouded in the green of coco-nut groves.

The shadow of the peak itself, cast on the mists at sunrise, is a very conspicuous and often-noted phenomenon. Owing to the sun's breadth, the effect is produced of an *umbra* and *penumbra*; and the *umbra* looks very dark and pointed—more pointed even than the peak itself. I was surprised to see how distant it looked—a shadow-mountain among the far crags. It gradually fell and disappeared as the sun rose.

There is another phenomenon which I have somewhere seen described as peculiar to Adam's Peak; though this must be a pious fraud, or one of those cases of people only being able to see familiar things when they are in unfamiliar surroundings, since it is a phenomenon which can be witnessed any day at home. It is that if when there is dew or rain upon the grass, and the sun is not too high in the heavens, you look at the shadow of your head on the grass, you will see it surrounded by a white light, or "glory." It arises, I imagine, from the direct reflection of the sunlight on the inner surfaces of the little globules of water which lie in or near the line joining the sun and the head, and is enhanced no doubt by the fact that the light so reflected shows all the clearer from having to pass through a column of shadow to the eye. Anyhow, whatever the cause, it is quite a flattering appearance, all the more so because if you have a companion you do not see the "glory" round his head, but only round your own! I once nearly turned the strong brain of a Positivist by pointing out to him this aureole round his head, and making as if I could see it. He, of course, being unable to see a similar light round mine, had no alternative but to conclude that he was specially overshadowed by the Holy Ghost!

The *sripada*—"sacred foot"—is better than I expected: a natural depression in the rock, an inch or so deep, five feet long,* of an oblong

* Captain Knox, above quoted, speaks of it as "about two feet long"; but he does not appear to have actually seen it

shape, and distantly resembling a foot; but they have "improved" it in parts by mortaring bits of tile along the doubtful edges! There are no toes marked, though in "copies" of it that I have seen in some Buddhist shrines the toes are carefully indicated. The mark is curiously situated at the very summit of the rock—which is only a few feet square, only large enough, in fact, to give space for the foot and for a little pavilion, open to the winds, which has been erected over it; and on the natural platform just below—which (so steep is the mountain) is itself encircled by a wall to prevent accidents—are some curious bits of furniture: four old bronze standard lamps, of lotus-flower design, one at each corner of the platform, a bell, a little shrine, and the priests' hut before mentioned. Looking into the latter after dawn, I beheld nothing resembling furniture, but a pan in the middle with logs burning, and three lean figures squatted round it, their mortal possessions tied in handkerchiefs and hanging from the roof.

The priests were horribly on the greed for money, and made it really unpleasant to stay on the top; but I delayed a little in order to watch Caliban doing *poojah* at the little shrine I have mentioned. He brought a hot ember from the fire, sprinkled frankincense on it, burned camphor and something that looked like saltpetre, also poured some kind of scented water on the ember, causing fragrance. Very ancient gnarled rhododendron trees, twenty or thirty feet high, rooting in clefts and hollows, were in flower (carmine red) all round the top of the rock. No snow ever falls here, they say; but there are sometimes hoar frosts, which the natives mistake for snow. I don't suppose the temperature that night was below 50° Fahr., but it felt cold, very cold, after the heat of the lowlands.

The sun rose soon after six, and at 7.30 we started downwards, on the great pilgrim-track towards Ratnapura. The final cone, for about 1500 feet, is certainly a steep bit of rock. I have seen it from several points of view, but the summit angle was always under 90°. Steps are cut nearly all down this part, and chains hang alongside in all places of possible difficulty—chains upon chains, things with links six inches long, all shapes and curiously wrought, centuries and centuries old—the pious gifts of successive generations of pilgrims. Here and there are long inscriptions, in Cinghalese characters, on the rock-faces; and everywhere innumerable signs of labor of successive travellers in hewing and shaping the path all the way—not to mention resting-sheds and cabins built in convenient spots lower down. These however are largely fallen to decay; and indeed the whole place gives one the impression that the *sripada* has come somewhat into disrepute in these modern times, and is only supported by the poorer and more ignorant among the people.

Ratnapura is only 150 feet or so above the sea; and for twenty-four miles the path to it from the summit—well-marked but single file—goes down over rocks and through vast woods, without coming to anything like a road. Nearly the whole, however, of this great descent of 7000 feet is done in the first twelve miles to Palábaddala—a tiny hamlet at the very foot of the mountains—and I don't know that I ever felt a descent so fatiguing as this one, partly no doubt owing to the experiences of the day and night before, and partly no doubt to the enervation produced by the climate and want of exercise; but the path itself is a caution, and the ascent of it must indeed be a pilgrimage, with its huge steps and strides from rock to rock and from tree-root to tree-root, and going, as it does, almost straight up and down the mountain side, without the long zigzags and detours by which in such cases the brunt is usually avoided. All the same, it was very interesting; the upper jungle of rhododendrons, myrtles, and other evergreen foliage forming a splendid cover for elephants, and clothing the surrounding peaks and crags for miles in grey-green wrinkles and folds, with here and there open grassy spaces and glades and tumbling watercourses; then the vegetation of the lower woods, huge trees 150 or even 200 feet high, with creepers, orchids, and tree-ferns, the occasional rush of monkeys along the branches; butterflies and birds; thick undergrowth in parts, of daturas, pointsettias, crotons, and other fragrant and bright-colored shrubs; down at last into coco-nut plantations and to the lovely Kalu-ganga, or Black river, which we forded twice; and ultimately along its banks, shadowed by bamboos and many flowering trees.

Although, curiously enough, the fig is not grown as a fruit in Ceylon, yet the *ficus* is one of the most important families of trees here, and many of the forest trees belong to it. There is one very handsome variety, whose massive grey stem rises unbroken to a great height before it branches, and which in order to support itself throws out great lateral wings or buttresses, reaching to a height of twelve or twenty feet from the ground, and spreading far out from the base of the trunk, —each buttress perhaps three or four inches thick, and perfectly shaped, with plane and parallel sides like a sawn plank, so as to give the utmost strength with least expenditure of material. This variety has small ovate evergreen leaves. Then there are two or three varieties, of which the banyan (*ficus Indica*) is one, which are parasitic in their habit. The banyan begins existence by its seed being dropped in the fork of another tree—not unfrequently a palm—from which point its rootlets make their way down the stem to the ground. With rapid growth it then encircles the victim tree, and throwing out great lateral branches sends down from these a rain of fresh rootlets, which, after swinging in air for a few weeks, reach the ground and soon become sturdy pillars. I have thus seen a banyan encircling with its central trunk the stem of a palm, and clasping it so close that a knife could not be pushed between the two, while the palm, which had grown in height since this accident happened to it, was still soaring upwards, and feebly endeavoring to live. There is a very fine banyan tree at Kalutara, which spans the great high-road from Colombo to Galle, all the traffic passing beneath it and between its trunks.

Some of the figs fasten parasitically on other trees, though without throwing out the pillar-like roots which distinguish the banyan; and it is not uncommon to see one of these with roots like a cataract of snakes winding round the trunk of an acacia, or even round some non-parasitic fig, the two trees appearing to be wrestling and writhing together in a fierce embrace, while they throw out their separate branches to sun and air, as though to gain strength for the fray. The parasite generally however ends by throttling its adversary.

There is also the bo-tree, or *ficus religiosa,* whose leaf is of a thinner texture. One of the commonest plants in open spots all over Ceylon is the sensitive plant. Its delicately pinnate leaves form a bushy growth six inches to a foot in depth over the ground; but a shower of rain, or nightfall, or the trampling of animals through it causes it to collapse into a mere brown patch—almost as if a fire had passed over. In a few minutes, however, after the disturbance has ceased it regains it luxuriance. There are also some acacia trees which droop their leaves at nightfall, and at the advent of rain.

There are two sorts of monkeys common in these forests—a small brown monkey, which may be seen swinging itself from tree to tree, not unfrequently with a babe in its arms; and the larger *wanderoo* monkey, which skips and runs on all-fours along the ground, and of which it is said that its devotion to its mate is life-long. Very common all over Ceylon is a little grey-brown squirrel, with three yellow longitudinal stripes on its back; almost every tree seems to be inhabited by a pair, which take refuge there at the approach of a stranger, and utter a sharp little whistle like the note of an angry bird. They are very tame, however, and will often in inhabited places run about the streets, or even make their appearance in the houses in search of food.

The Hindus take no pleasure in killing animals—even the boys do not, as a rule, molest wild creatures—and the consequence is that birds and the smaller four-footed beasts are comparatively bold. Not that the animals are made pets of, but they are simply left alone—in keeping with the Hindu gentleness and quiescence of disposition. Even the deadly cobra—partly, no doubt, from religious associations—is allowed to go its way unharmed; and the people have generally a good word for it, saying it will not attack anyone unless it be first injured.

On the whole, the trouble about reptiles in this country seems to me to be much exaggerated. There are some places in the forests where small leeches—particularly in the wet seasons—are a great pest. Occasionally a snake is to be seen, but I have been rather disappointed at their rarity; or a millipede nine inches long. The larger scorpion is a venomous-looking creature, with its blue-black lobster-like body and claws, and slender sting-surmounted tail, five inches long in all; but it is not so venomous as generally supposed, and most of these creatures, like the larger animals—the chetah, the elk, the bear, the elephant, etc.—keep out of the way of man as well as they can. Of course, native woodmen and others tramping bare-legged through the tangles occasionally tread on a snake and get bitten; but the tale of deaths through such casualties, though it may seem numerically large, taken say throughout Ceylon and India, is in proportion to the population but a slight matter—about 1 in 15,000 per annum.

There are many handsome butterflies here, especially of the swallow-tail sort—some of enormous size—and a number of queer insects. I saw a large green mantis, perhaps six inches long—a most wicked-looking creature. I confess it reminded me of a highly respectable British property-owner. It sits up like a beautiful green leaf, with its two fore-claws (themselves flattened out and green, to look like lesser leaves) held up as if it were praying—*perfectly* motionless—except that all the time it rolls its stalked eyes slowly around, till it sees a poor little insect approach, when it stealthily moves a claw, and pounces.

The birds are not so numerous as I expected. There are some bright-colored kinds and a few parrots, but the woods seem quiet on the whole. The barbet, a green bird not quite so big as a pigeon, goes on with its monotonous bell-like call—like a cuckoo that has lost its second note—on and on, the whole day long; the lizards cluck and kiss, full of omens to the natives, who call them "the crocodile's little brothers"—and say "if you kill a little lizard the crocodile will come and kill you"; the grasshoppers give three clicks and a wheeze; the small grey squirrels chirrup; the frogs croak; and the whole air is full of continuous though subdued sound.

At Palábaddala, the tiny little hamlet at the foot of the mountains, I was dead-beat with the long jolting downhill, and if it had not been for the faithful Kalua, who held my hand in the steeper parts, I should fairly have fallen once or twice. Here we stopped two hours at a little cabin. Good people and friendly—a father and mother and two lads—the same anxious, tender mother-face that is the same all over the world. They brought out a kind of couch for me to lie on, but would not at first believe that I would eat *their* food. However, after a little persuasion, they made some tea (for the people are beginning to use tea quite freely) and some curry and rice—quite palatable. I began to eat of course with my fingers, native fashion; but as soon as I did so, they saw that something was wrong, and raised a cry of *Karandi!* (spoon); and a boy was sent off, despite my protests, to the cabin of a rich neighbor half-a-mile off, and ultimately returned in triumph with a rather battered German-silver teaspoon!

I felt doubtful about doing another twelve miles to Ratnapura; however thought best to try, and off we went. But the rest had done little good, and I could not go more than two miles an hour. At 4 P.M., after walking about four miles, we came out into flat land—a good path, little villages with clumps of palm and banana, lovely open meadows, and tame buffaloes grazing. Thence along the side of the Kaluganga, most lovely of rivers, through thickets of bamboo and tangles of shrubs, and past more hamlets and grazing grounds (though feeling so *done*, I thoroughly enjoyed every step of the way), till at last at a little kind of shop (*kadai*) we halted, about 6 P.M. Got more tea, and a few bananas, which was all I cared to eat; and then went in and lay down on a trestle and mat for an hour, after which we decided to stay the night. Kalua stretched himself near me; the men of the place lay down on the floor—the women somewhere inside; the plank shutters were built in, and lights put out. I slept fairly well, and woke finally at the sound of voices and with dawn peeping in through the holes in the roof. Had a lovely wash in a little stream, and an early breakfast of tea, bananas, and hot cakes made of rice, coco-nut, and sugar—and then walked four miles into this place (Ratnapura), where at last we came to a road and signs of civilisation.

The rest-house here is comfortable; have had another bath, and a good solid breakfast, and made arrangements for a boat to start with us this evening down the river to Kalutara (60 miles).

Sunday, Jan. 4th.—After walking round the town yesterday, and getting fruit and provisions for our voyage, we embarked about 6 P.M., and are now floating lazily down the Kaluganga. The water is rather low, and the speed not good; but the river is very beautiful, with bamboos, areca-palms, and other trees, leaning over in profusion.

Ratnapura (the city of jewels) is only a small town—hardly so big as Kurunégala—just about one long street of little booths and cabins, a post-office, court-house and cutcherry, and the usual two or three bungalows of the English agent and officials standing back in park-like grounds in a kind of feudal reserve. The town derives its name from the trade in precious stones which has been carried on here for long enough—rubies, sapphires, and others being found over a great part of the mountain district. In perhaps half the little shops of Ratnapura men and boys may be seen squatted on the floor grinding and polishing jewels. With one hand they use a bow to turn their wheels, and with the other they hold the stone in position. The jewels are also set and offered for sale—often at what seem very low prices. But the purchaser must beware; for the blessings of modern commerce are with us even here, and many of these precious stones are bits of stained glass supplied wholesale from Birmingham.

This boat, which is of a type common on the river, consists of two canoes or "dug-outs," each twenty feet long, and set five or six feet apart from each other, with a flooring laid across them, and a little thatched cabin constructed amidships. The cabin is for cooking and sleeping—a fire and cooking pots at one end, and mats laid at the other. At the front end of the boat sit the two rowers, and the steersman stands behind. We have a skipper and four crew (an old man, Djayánis; a middle-aged man, Signápu; and two lads, Duánis and Thoránis). The name of the skipper is Pedri. About two miles below Ratnapura we drew to the shore and stopped below a temple; and Pedri and the old man went up to offer money for a favorable voyage! They washed a few coppers in the river, wrapped them in a bo-tree leaf, which had also been washed, sprinkled water on their foreheads, and then went up. They soon came back, and then we started.

Hardly any signs of habitation along the river. Now and then rude steps down to the shore, and a dark figure pouring water on its own head. The river varying, a hundred yards, more or less, wide. At about seven it got too dark and we halted against a sandbank, waiting for the moon to rise, and had dinner—rice, curried eggs, and beans, and a pineapple—very good. Then got out and sat on the sand, while the boys lighted a fire. Very fine, the gloom on the tall fringed banks, gleams from the fire, voices of children far back among the woods, playing in some village. After a time we went back on board again, and sat round teaching each other to count, and laughing at our mistakes—*ekkai, dekkai, tonai, hattarai*—one, two, three, four. The Cinghalese language (unlike the Tamil) is full of Aryan roots—*minya*, man; *gáni*,

Rice-Boats on the Kaluganga
(A clump of bamboos on the right)

woman; and so on. The small boy Thoránis (12 years) learnt his "one two three" in no time; he is pretty sharp; he does the cooking, and prepares our meals, taking an oar between times. The man Pedri seemed good to the lads, and they all enjoyed themselves till they got sleepy and lay in a row and snored.

Started again at moonrise, about midnight; after

which I went to sleep till six or so, then went ashore and had a bath—water quite warm. Then off again; a few slight rapids, but nothing much. We go aground every now and then; but these boats are so tough—the canoes themselves being hollowed trees—that a bump even on a rock does not seem to matter much. The lads quite enjoy the struggle getting over a sandbank, and Duánis jumps down from his perch and plunges through the water with evident pleasure. The old man Djayánis steers—a shrewd-faced calm thin fellow, almost like a North American Indian, but no beak. See a monkey or a kite occasionally; no crocodiles in this part of the river, above the rapids; some large and handsome kingfishers, and the fruit-crow, whose plumage is something like that of a pheasant.

Kalua enjoys the voyage. It suits his lazy sociable temperament, and he chats away to Pedri and the crew no end. His savage strength and *insouciance* are splendid. All over Adam's Peak he walked barefoot, with no more sign of fatigue than if it had been a walk round a garden,—would lie down and sleep anywhere, or not sleep, eat or not eat, endure cold or heat with apparent indifference; yet though so complete a savage physically, it is interesting to see what an attraction for him civilisation, or the little he has seen of it, exerts. He is always asking me about Europe, and evidently dreaming about its wealth and splendor. All the modern facilities and inventions are sort of wonderful toys to this child of nature; and though I think he is attached to me, and is no doubt of an affectionate disposition, still it is partly that I am mixed up in his mind with all these things. I tried one day to find out from K. his ideas of god or devil, or supreme power of any kind; but in vain. His mind wandered to things more tangible. Many of the Cinghalese, however, have rather a turn for speculations of this kind; and at one hotel where I was staying the chamber-servant entertained me with quite a discourse on Buddha, and ended by ridiculing the Christian idea that a man can get rid of the results of sin by merely praying to God or believing in Jesus.

We have now passed the *nárraka-gála* (bad rock) rapid, which is about half-way down the river, and is the only rapid which has looked awkward, the river narrowing to five or six yards between rocks, and plunging over at a decided slope. We went through with a great bump, but no damage! The sun and smells on board are getting rather trying; this dried-fish smell unfortunately haunts one wherever there are native cabins. But we shall not be long now before reaching my landing-place, a little above Kalutara.

There are a good many boats like ours on the river, some laden with rice going down, others poling upwards—sometimes whole families on the move. Quantities of ragged white lilies fringing the shore.

Jan. 6th.—Kalua and I left our friends and their boat in the afternoon, and spent Sunday night at P's bungalow. P. is manager of a tea plantation—a bit of a Robinson Crusoe, living all by himself—native servants of course—with two dogs, a cat, and a jackdaw (and at one time a hare!) sharing his meals. Some of these planter-fellows must find the life a little dreary I fancy, living isolated on their plantations at a considerable distance from European neighbours, with very small choice of society at the best, and prevented, no doubt, by their position from associating too closely with the only folk who are near them—their own employees. The more kindly-hearted among them however do a good deal for their workers in the way of physicking and nursing them when ill or disabled, advising them when in difficulties, etc.; and in these cases the natives, with their instinct of dependence, soon learn to lean like children on their employer, and the latter finds himself, after a few years, the father (so to speak) of a large family. There are 200 Tamil coolies permanently employed on this plantation, and a hundred or two besides, mostly girls and women, who come in to work when wanted from neighboring Cinghalese villages.

But the system, like the commercial system wherever it is found to-day, is pretty bad and odious in itself, and is no doubt in many cases a cover for shameful abuses. The Tamil coolies —men, women, and children—come over in gangs from the mainland of India. An agent is sent out to tout for them, and to conduct them by sea and land to their destination. On their arrival on the tea-estate each one finds himself so many rupees in debt for the expenses of transit! An average wage is *6d.* a day, but to keep them up to the mark in productiveness their work is "set" for them to complete a certain task in a certain time, and if they do not come up to their task they get only half-pay; so that if a man is slow, or lazy, or ill, he may expect about *3d.* per diem! Under these circumstances the debt, as may be imagined, goes on increasing instead of diminishing; the estate is far up country, away from town or village, and the tea company acts as agent and sells rice and the other necessaries of life to its own coolies.

Group of Tamil Coolies, or Wage-Workers

Poor things, they cannot buy elsewhere. "Oh, but they like to be in debt," said a young planter to me, "and think they are not doing the best for themselves unless they owe as much as the company will allow." He was very young, that planter, and perhaps did not realise what he was saying; but what a suggestion of despair! Certainly there may have been some truth in the remark; for when all hope of ever being out of debt is gone, the very next best thing is to be in debt as much as ever you can. At the end of the week the coolie does not see any wage; his rice, etc., has forestalled all that, and more; only his debt is ticked down a little deeper. If he runs away he is hunted down, and gets three months in gaol. He is a slave, and must remain so to the end of his days. That is not very long, however; for poor food and thin clothing, and the mists and the cool airs of the mountains soon bring on lung diseases, of which the slight-bodied Tamil easily dies.

"I dare say 3*d.* a day seems a very small wage to you," said the planter youth, "but it is really surprising how little these fellows will live on."

"It is surprising, indeed, when you see their thin frames, that they live at all."

"Ah, but they are much worse off at home; you should see them when they come from India." And so the conversation ended.

And this is how our tea, which we set so much store by, is produced in Ceylon and elsewhere. These places are sad-looking places. Commercialism somehow has a way of destroying all natural beauty in those regions where it dwells. Here the mountain sides are torn up, the immense and beautiful forests ravaged from base to summit, and the shaly escarpments that remain, planted in geometrical lines with tea-shrubs. You may walk for miles through such weary lands, extending rapidly now all over the mountain region from the base to near the tops of the highest mountains, the blackened skeletons of half-burnt trees alone remaining to tell of the old forests, of which before long there will be but a memory left.

It is curious, when one comes to think of it, that such huge spaces of the earth are devastated, such vast amounts of human toil expended, in the production of two things—tea and wine—which, to say the least, are not necessaries, and which certainly in the quantities commonly consumed are actually baneful. If their production simply ceased, what a gain it might seem! Yet the commercial policies of the various nations stimulate these, and always to the neglect of the necessaries of life. They stimulate the stimulants. We need not be hypercritical, but there must be something peculiar in the temper of the modern nations that they make such tremendous sacrifices in order to act in this way.

On each tea-plantation there are the "lines" (rows of huts) in which the coolies live, and the "factory"—a large wooden building, with rows of windows, a steam engine, and machinery for the various processes concerned—withering, fermenting, rolling, firing, sorting, packing, etc. The tea-bushes (a variety of the camellia) are not allowed to grow more than three or four feet high. In Ceylon the plucking goes on almost all the year round. As soon as the young shoots, with five or six leaves, have had time to form since the last plucking, a gang of workers comes round—mostly girls and women for this job—each with a basket, into which they pluck the young leaves and the little rolled-up leaf-bud, most precious of all. When taken to the factory the leaves are first spread out to wither, then rolled by machinery (to look like buds), then dried or baked by artificial heat. After this they

Tamil Girl Coolie plucking Tea

are sorted through a huge sieve, and the finest quality, consisting of the small leaf-bud, is called Flowery Pekoe; the next size, including some of the young leaf, is called Broken Pekoe; and the coarser leaves come out as Pekoe Souchong,

Souchong, etc. The difficulty with tea, as with wine, is that no two yields are alike; the conditions of plucking, fermenting, firing, etc., all make a difference in the resultant flavor. Hence a dealer, say in London, who reckons to supply his customers with tea of a certain constant flavor, has simply to *make* such tea as best he can—namely by "blending" any teas which he can lay hold of in the market, and which will produce the desired result. The names given in these cases are of course mostly fictitious.

I may as well insert here one or two extracts from letters since received from our friend "Ajax," which will perhaps help to show the condition of the coolies in the tea-gardens where he is now working. He says:

"One gets very fond of the coolies, they are so much like children; they bring all their little grievances to one to settle. A man will come and complain that his wife refuses to cook his food for him; the most minute details of family affairs are settled by the sahib of the garden. The coolies have a hard time, and are treated little better than slaves; most willing workers they are. Still all I can say is that they have a much better time than the very poor at home, such as the factory girls, tailoresses, etc., and laborers. On this garden they have met with exceptionally hard lines; the manager being an ill-bred man has had no consideration for his men, and they have died in hundreds from exposure to weather in the garden and houses, which had all crumbled away from neglect. Many families of ten or eleven in number have dwindled away to one or two. In one case, two little fellows of eight and nine, living together on five rupees a month, are the only representatives (of a former family). . . .

"I was sorry to leave (the former garden), very; I had got to know the coolies, 300 of them at anyrate who were under my charge, and they had got to know me. Many of them wanted to come with me here, but that is not allowed. Some said they would 'cut their names,' that is, take their names off the garden labor-register, and go wherever I went, but of course they could not do that. I don't know why they were so anxious to come, because I know I worked them very hard all the time I was there. I think my predecessor used to fine them and thrash them a good deal, often because he did not know what they said, and could not make them understand. I like the coolies very much, and one gets quite attached to some of them; they seem instinctively polite; and if you are ill, they tend you just like a woman—never leave one in fact. The higher and more respectable class of Baboos are just as objectionable, I think."

CHAPTER V

BRITISH LAW-COURTS AND BUDDHIST TEMPLES

Kurunégala.—I have come to the conclusion that the courts and judicial proceedings out here are a kind of entertainment provided for the "oysters" at the expense of the British Government, and that the people really look upon these institutions very much in that light. Poor things! their ancient communal life and interests, with all the local questions and politics which belonged thereto, and even to a great extent the religious festivals, have been improved away; they have but few modern joys—no votes and elections such as would delight our friend Monerasingha — no circuses, theatres, music-halls. What is there left for them but the sensations of the police-courts? The district court here is, I find, the one great centre of interest in the town. Crowds collect in the early morning, and hang about all day in its vicinity, either watching the cases or discussing the judgments delivered, till sunset, when they disperse homeward again. Cooling drinks are sold, beggars ply their trade, the little bullock-hackeries trot up and down, and the place is as busy as a fair. There is no particular stigma in conviction by an alien authority; there is a happy uncertainty in the judgments delivered by the representatives of a race that has difficulty in understanding the popular customs and language; and the worst that can happen—namely, relegation to prison life—affords a not unpleasant prospect. Besides, these institutions can be used to gratify personal spleen ; cases can be, and frequently are, cooked up in the most elaborate manner. Damages can be claimed for a fictitious assault ; and when an injury has really been done, the plaintiff (and this I find is a constantly recurring

Bullock-Hackery, Colombo

difficulty) will accuse not only the author of the mischief, but Tom, Dick, and Harry besides, who have had nothing whatever to do with it, but who are the objects of personal spite, in the hope of getting them, too, into trouble. The Cinghalese, as I have said before, are a very sensitive people. Any grievance rankles in their bosom, and in revenge they will not unfrequently use the knife. An Eurasian friend, a doctor, says that he quite thinks cases might occur in which a man who had been wounded or assaulted by another would *die out of spite* in order to get the other hanged!—would connive with his relations and starve himself, and not try to heal the wound. He says however that the cases of ruptured spleen—of which we so frequently hear—are genuine, as frequent fevers often cause immense enlargement of the spleen, which then bursts for a comparately slight cause —*e.g.* a planter and a stick.

The courts in this country are generally large thatched or tiled halls, sometimes with glass sides, but often open to the wind, with only a low wall running round, over which, as you sit inside, a crowd of bare arms and heads and bodies appears. At one end sits the English official, dutifully but wearily going through his task, a big punkah waving over his head and helping to dispel the slumbrous noon-tide heat; below him stands the *mudaliar*, who acts as interpreter—for the etiquette properly enough requires that the transactions of the court shall be given in both languages, even though the official be a native or an Englishman knowing the native language perfectly; at the table in the centre are seated a few reporters and proctors, and at the other end are the prisoners in the dock, and the policemen in their boots.

The cases are largely quarrels, and more or less unfounded accusations arising out of quarrels, thefts of bullocks or of coco-nuts, and so forth. The chief case when I was in court some days ago was rather amusing. A few days before, three or four men, having been accused, possibly wrongfully, of burglary, and having (on account of insufficient evidence) been acquitted, went off straight from the court to an arrack shop and got drunk. They then made it up between them that they would rob the man thoroughly that evening, even if they had not done so before, and give him a good hiding into the bargain; and taking to themselves some other congenial spirits went off on their errand. They found the man asleep in the verandah of his cabin, and tying him down gave him some blows. But—as it came out in the evidence with regard to the very slight marks on the body—before they could have hurt him much, the man, with great presence of mind, died, and left them charged with the crime of murder! An old woman—the man's mother—with a beautiful face, but palsied with age, came forward to give evidence. She said she was nearly 100 years old, though the evidence on this point was not very clear. Anyhow, her head was remarkably clear, and she gave her testimony well; identified several of the prisoners, said they had broken into the cabin and carried off valuables, and that one, the leader, had motioned her into a corner of the cabin, saying: "Stand aside, old mother, or you'll get hurt," while another had come up to her and said: "I think I had better take those bangles from you, as they are no good to you now, you know." There were *nine* men charged with the offence, and they were committed for trial in a higher court—very decent-looking scaramouches on the whole, just about average types of humanity.

The English officials that I have seen here and at other places strike me as remarkably good-hearted, painstaking men; but one feels the gulf between them and the people—a gulf that can never be bridged. Practically all that a Government like ours does, or can do, is to make possible the establishment of our social institutions in the midst of an alien people—our railways, education, Bible missions, hospitals, law-courts, wage-slavery, and profit-grinding, and all the rest of it, in the midst of a people whose whole life springs from another root, namely, religious feeling. The two will never blend, though the shock produced by the contact of two such utterly different civilisations may react on both, to the production of certain important results. Anyhow, for a well-meaning official it must be depressing work; for though he may construct a valuable tank, or what not, from the highest motives according to his own light—*i.e.* for the material welfare of the people and the realisation of a five per cent. profit to Government—still he never comes near touching the hearts of the millions, who would probably pay much more respect to a half-luny *yogi* than to him and all his percentages.

A.'s friend, Sámanáthan, comes to read English with me every day, and teaches me a little Tamil in return. He is something of a dandy, with his green silk coat and hair plaited down his back, and delicate hands and manners—a fellow over thirty, with a wife and children, and yet not earning any livelihood, but remaining on at home with his parents, and dependent on them! And what seems to us most strange, this is quite an admitted and natural thing to do—such is the familial communism which still prevails. He is very much of a student by nature, and in his native town (in India) gives lectures, philosophical and theological, free of charge, and which are quite popular. He is reading S. Mark with me, and reads it pretty well, being evidently familiar even with the more philosophical words, though doubtful about the pronunciation of some. He is interested in the story of Jesus, and thinks Jesus was no doubt a "sage"—*i.e.* an adept —or at anyrate versed in the arcane lore of the East. But he is much amused at the Christian doctrine of the redemption, which I suppose he has got hold of, not from Mark, but the missionaries.

On the 10th of this month (January), F. Modder and I went off on an excursion from here to Dambulla (35 miles), and thence to Anurádhapura (42 miles). Dambulla is celebrated for its Buddhist rock-temples, and Anurádhapura is the site of a very ancient city, now in ruins amid the jungle.

Despite all sorts of reports about the length of the journey and its difficulty—the chief difficulty being that of getting any exact information—M. managed to secure a bullock-cart *with springs*, and two pairs of bullocks; and we made a start about 6.30 P.M. A mattress in the cart and a pillow or two made all comfortable. We sat and talked for a couple of hours, then walked, and then went to sleep. With an average speed of *two* miles an hour we reached the rest-house at Gokarella at midnight, changed bulls, and immediately went on. Another six hours brought us to the house of a Government medical practitioner—a Cinghalese—where we got an early breakfast, and finally we reached Dr Devos' house, at Dambulla, about mid-day.

The little bulls went patiently on during the night, the Tamil driver chirruping "Jack" and "Pitta" to them (corresponding to our carters'

"Orve" and "Gee"), which some cheerful English traveller is said to have interpreted into the statement that the natives of Ceylon call all their cattle either Jack or Peter; the stars shone bright—the Milky Way innumerable. The road was bad, with occasional descents into dry sandy torrent beds; jungle stretched all around (with here and there, M.

Cinghalese Country-Cart
(Thatched with palm-branches)

says, the remains of some town buried in undergrowth); but we slept—M. slept, I slept, the driver slept, and occasionally even the good little bulls slept. Once or twice we came thus to a total stoppage, all sleeping, and then woke up at the unwonted quiet.

Just the first light of dawn, and a few strange bird-calls in the bush; the great *ficus* trees, with their mighty buttresses stretching white stems up into the yet ghostly light; ant-hills, conical and spired, all along the road-side; tangles of creepers, and then, as the sun rose, quantities of butterflies. I know nothing of butterflies, but the kinds in this country are very various and beautiful. There is one which is very common, about four inches across, black and white, with body a bright red, and under-wing spotted with the same colour—very handsome; and one day, when taking a sun-bath in the woods, an immense swallow-tail hovered round me, fully ten inches across from tip to tip of wings.

Modder is a cheerful fellow, of Dutch descent probably, of about thirty years of age, a proctor or solicitor for native cases, well up in Cinghalese and Tamil, and full of antiquarian knowledge, yet can troll a comic song nicely with a sweet voice. I find he is a regular democrat, and hates the whole caste system in which he lives embedded—thinks the U.S. must be "a glorious country." He says he has often talked to the Tamil and Cinghalese people about the folly of caste. At first they can't understand what he means—are completely at a loss to imagine anything different, but after a time the idea seems to take hold on them.

Found Devos at Dambulla—a fine clear-faced man of about thirty-three, genuine, easy-going, carrying on a hospital in this slightly populated district—just a large native village, no more—but the mails come through this way, and a few English on their way to Anurádhapura, and other places. Gangs of Tamil coolies, also, from the mainland of India, pass through Dambulla in going up country, and have to be medically examined here, for fear of cholera, etc. Living with Devos are two younger fellows, Percy Carron, who is also an Eurasian, and a Cinghalese youth, both foresters—a small easy-going bachelors' household, and all very chummy together. Thought they also treated their Tamil "boy" John well—actually called him by his name, and did not shout at him. These fellows all talk English among themselves, in a close-lipped, rapid, rather neat way. The other two chaffed the Cinghalese a good deal, who was of the usual sensitive clinging type.

In the afternoon we went up the rock to see the temples. A great rock, 500 or 600 feet high, similar to that at Kurunégala. Half-way up stretches a broad ledge, 100 yards long, commanding a fine view over hill and dale, and between this ledge and an overhanging layer of rock above are niched five temples all in a row. No façade to speak of, mere stucco walling, but within you pass into large caverns full of rude statues. The largest of the temples is 150 feet long, 40 deep, and 23 high in front—a great dark space with perhaps fifty colossal images of Buddha sitting round in the gloom with their sickly smile of Nirvana, and one huge figure, 30 or 40 feet long, lying down in illumined sleep; all crudely done, and painted bright yellows and reds, yet rather impressive. The sides too and roof of the cavern are frescoed in the same crude manner with stories from the life of Buddha, and with figures of the Hindu gods. Withal, a fusty smell, a thousand years old, of priests none too clean, of flaring oil-lamps, of withered flowers and stale incense, oppressed us horribly, and it was the greatest relief to get out again into the open.

Devos says the scene is very striking at the great festivals, when multitudinous pilgrims assemble and offer their lights and their flowers and their money, on benches, each before the figure they affect. Tom-toms beat, worshippers recite their prayers, lights twinkle, and, outside, the light of the full moon pours down upon the rock. Monkeys native to the rock are fed on this ledge in hundreds by the priests.

Ceylon is, of course, mainly Buddhist, and all over the hilly part of the island rock-temples of this sort, though smaller, are scattered—some mere shrines with a single seated or recumbent image of Buddha. They are commonly built among the woods, under some overhanging brow of rock, and the story generally runs that the cavern had in earlier times been occupied by some hermit-saint, or *yogi*, and that the temple was built in remembrance of him. There is a little one of this kind half-way up the rock at Kurunégala, and it is tended by a boy priest of about thirteen years of age, who, barehead and barefoot, but with his yellow priest-robe wound gracefully about him, attends in a dignified manner to the service of the shrine. He is generally followed by a little attendant (every one has an attendant in the East)—a small boy of about nine—who turns out to be his *khoki*, or cook! This sounds luxurious, but by rule the Buddhist priests should live the most abstemious lives. They are supposed to have no money or possessions of their own, and to be entirely celibate. Each morning they go out with their begging bowls on their arm to get their daily food. They go to a house and stand near the door, asking nothing. Then presently the woman comes out and puts a little rice in the bowl, and the priest goes on to the next house. When he has got sufficient he returns, and his attendant cooks the food (if not already cooked) and he eats it. For each priest has the privilege to choose a boy or youth to be his attendant, whom he trains up to the priesthood, and who takes his place after him. This perhaps explains the presence of the small boy *khoki* above.

The Buddhist priests, like the Hindu priests, are drawn mostly from the comparatively uneducated masses, but there is no need in their case that they should be Brahmins. A vast tolerance, and gentleness towards all forms of life, characterises the Buddhist institutions; but in the present day in Ceylon the institutions are decadent, and the priests, with a few exceptions, are an ignorant and incapable set. The efforts of Colonel Olcott however, on behalf of the Theosophical Society, and of Sumángala, the present high priest of the island, a man of great learning and gentleness, have done something in latest years to infuse a new spirit into the Buddhism of Ceylon and to rehabilitate its esoteric side.

At Kandy in one of the Buddhist temples outside the town there is a *standing* figure of Buddha twenty-seven feet high, carved in the face of the solid rock, and the temple built round it—rather fine—though with the usual crude red and yellow paint. It belongs to the time of the kings of Kandy, and is only about 150 years old. Many of the ordinary cave-temples are extremely old, however—as old as Buddhism in the island, 2000 years or more—and likely were used for religious purposes even before that.

After looking at the Dambulla temples, which are said to have been constructed by the king Walagambahu about 100 B.C., we gained the summit of the rock, whence you have a view over plains towards the sea and of ranges of hills inland, not unlike that from the rock at Kurunégala; and then descended, not without difficulty, the precipitous side. Evening fell, and darkies came out with lamps to our aid.

The same night I pushed on by mail-coach to Anurádhapura, leaving Modder behind, as he unfortunately had to return to Kurunégala the next day.

Jetawanarama Dágoba, Anurádhapura
(Ruins of a temple in foreground)

CHAPTER VI

ANURADHAPURA: A RUINED CITY OF THE JUNGLE

THE remains of this ancient city lie near the centre of the great plain which occupies the north end of the island of Ceylon. To reach them, even from Dambulla, the nearest outpost of civilisation, one has to spend a night in the "mail-coach," which in this case consists of a clumsy little cart drawn at a jog-trot through the darkness by bullocks, and generally full of native passengers. Six times in the forty-two miles the little humped cattle are changed, and at last—by the time one has thoroughly convinced oneself that it is impossible to sleep in any attainable position—one finds oneself, about 6 A.M., driving through woods full of ruins.

Here, on the site of a once vast and populous town, stands now a small village. The care of Government has cleared the jungle away from the most important remains and those lying just around the present site, so that the chief feature is a beautiful park-like region of grass and scattered trees, in which stand out scores, and even hundreds, of columns, with statues, huge dágobas, fragments of palaces, and innumerable evidences of ancient building. It is a remarkable scene. The present cutcherry stands on the shore of one of the large reservoirs which used to supply the city and neighborhood, but which at present, owing to want of rain and deficiencies of channels, is nearly dry. On climbing the embankment the bed of the lake stretches before one, with hundreds of tame buffaloes and other cattle grazing on its level meadows; a few half-naked darkies are fishing in a little water which remains in one corner; on either hand the lake-bottom is bounded by woods, and out of these woods, and out of the woods behind one, high above the trees loom green and overgrown masses of masonry, while below and among them labyrinths of unexplored ruins are hidden in thick dark tangle. It is as if London had again become a wilderness, above which the Albert Memorial and S. Paul's and the Tower still reared confused heaps of grassy stone and brickwork, while sheep and oxen browsed peacefully in the bed of the Thames, now diverted into another channel.

Here, for instance, still standing in a great square, on a piece of ground over an acre in extent, are sixteen hundred rough-hewn columns, solid granite, projecting about ten feet out of the ground, and arranged in parallel rows at right angles to each other. They are supposed to form the foundation storey of a building nine storeys high, no doubt built of wood, but according to the ancient chronicles of the Mahawanso gorgeously decorated, with its resplendent brass-covered roof and central hall of golden pillars and ivory throne, erected in the second century B.C., occupied by the royal folk and the priests, and called the Brazen Palace.

Close by is the glory of Buddhism and of Ceylon, the oldest historical tree in the world, the celebrated bo-tree of Anurádhapura, planted 245 years before the Christian era (from a slip, it is said, of the tree under which Buddha sat when the great illumination came to him), and now more than twenty-one centuries old. Extraordinary as the age is, yet the chronicles of this tree's life have been so carefully kept (see Emerson Tennent's *Ceylon*, where twenty-five references from the Mahawanso and other chronicles are given, covering from B.C. 288 to A.D. 1739), that there is at least fair reason for supposing that the story is correct. The bo-tree, though belonging to the fig family, has a leaf strongly resembling that of an aspen. The mid-rib of the leaf is, however, prolonged some two inches into a narrow point, which is sometimes curved into quite a hook. The tremulous motion of the leaf and the general appearance of the tree also resemble the aspen, though the growth is somewhat sturdier. Thousands of bo-trees are planted all over India and Ceylon in memory of Buddha (though the tree was probably an object of veneration before his time); the ground is sacred where they stand, and a good Buddhist will on no account cut one down, however inconveniently it may be growing. This particular tree, it must be confessed, is somewhat disappointing. It is small, and though obviously old, does not suggest the idea of *extreme* antiquity. It springs from the top of a mound some fifteen feet high, and the probability, I think, is that this mound has in the course of centuries been thrown up round the original trunk to support and protect it—just as has happened to Milton's mulberry-tree at Cambridge, and to others—and thus has gradually hidden a great part of the tree from view. And this idea seems to be supported by the fact that six or seven other and lesser stems branch out from neighbouring parts of the same mound, the terraces and shrines which occupy the mound helping to conceal the fact that these also are, or were at one time, really all parts of one tree. Anyhow the whole enclosure, which is about an acre in extent and is surrounded by an ancient wall, is thickly planted with bo-trees, some of really fine dimensions, so that the pious pilgrim need have no difficulty in securing a leaf, without committing the sacrilege of robbing the venerable plant.

Here, to this sacred enclosure, and to deposit flowers and offerings within it, come at certain festivals thousands of Buddhist pilgrims. Trudging in on foot or driving by bullock-cart, they camp out in the park-like grounds in the immediate neighborhood of the present village, and after paying their respects to the holy tree go to visit the dágobas and other monuments which enshrine a bone or a tooth or a hair from the brow of their great teacher. For the rest of the year these places are left almost unvisited. There are no guides to importune the rare tourist or traveller, and one wanders alone through the woods for a whole day and sees no one, except it be a troop of monkeys, with tails erect, playing leap-frog over the stumps of fallen columns, as if in ridicule of the old priests, or sitting like fakirs on the tops of those still standing.

The dágobas, which are by far the most important remains here, are bell-shaped structures mostly of solid brick, originally built to enshrine some relic. They might ingeniously be mistaken for ornamental candle-extinguishers made on a vast scale, and have mostly in their time been coated with a white plaster and decorated here and there with gold or brass. Round them have been courts supported on stone columns; and generally at the four points—North, East, West, and South—have been placed little shrines with well-cut steps and ornamental balustrades leading up to them. The interiors of these dágobas—such as they may have been—have never been accessible except to the priests; sometimes, no doubt, treasures have been concealed within them, but for the most part probably they have concealed nothing except the supposed relic, and have been built to gratify the pride and add to the popularity of the monarch of the day.

The Thuparama Dágoba, which stands at the northern extremity of the park-like clearings above mentioned, is supposed by Fergusson (*Handbook to Architecture*, vol. i. p. 41) to be older than any monument now existing on the continent of India. It was built by King Dewanipiatissa in B.C. 307 to enshrine the right collar-bone of Buddha, and was restored some years ago by the pious, so that one gets a good idea from it of the general appearance these objects originally presented. It is white, bell-shaped, and some sixty-five feet high, with a brass pinnacle on the top; and some elegant columns about eighteen feet high stand yet in admired disorder in the court below. In the accompanying illustration the dágoba and surrounding columns appear some distance in the background, and the stone pillars and steps in the foreground are the remains of the Dalada Maligawa—a temple which was built to receive the sacred tooth of Buddha when it was first brought over to Ceylon from the mainland. Round this tooth battles raged, and in the struggle for its possession dynasties rose and fell. The enormous saurian fang, which purports to be the same tooth, is now preserved in great state in the well-known Buddhist temple at Kandy, as I have already mentioned. The little figure of a gate-keeper or *dhworpal* at the foot of the steps is

Thuparama Dágoba, Anurádhapura
(With Ruins of Daladā Maligawa in foreground)

an excellent specimen of early Buddhist sculpture, and is very graceful and tender. It is given on a larger scale in a separate illustration (page 111).

The Ruanweli (or Gold-dust) Dágoba, which rears its unshapely form close to the present village, gives one a notion of the massiveness of these ancient structures, and at the same time of the ravages which lapse of years has wrought upon them. In outline it resembles a gigantic but ill-made circular haystack, 150 feet high. All the upper part of it is covered with thick grass, except where recent lapses have exposed the close yet rather soft brickwork of which the whole is compacted. The more accessible lower parts and surrounding terraces have lately been cleaned of undergrowth; and at the foot, among some well-executed carvings, stand four or five fine statues, about eight feet high—one of King Dutugemunu, who is said to have begun the building about B.C. 161, the others apparently of Buddha, and all dignified and noble in conception, if not anatomically perfect in execution.

But the dágobas which best show the gradual effacement of human handiwork by Nature are the Jetawanarama and the Abhayagiria, both of which stand some distance out in the woods, and tower above the foliage to the heights of 250 feet and 300 feet respectively. The former of these (see plate at beginning of this chapter) presents a vast cone of brickwork some 200 feet high, surmounted by a cylindrical column of the same; and the conical portion is simply overgrown by dense masses of trees, which inserting their roots into the crevices of the bricks are continually dislodging portions of this artificial mountain. Cactuses, varieties of fig, and other trees climb to the very base of the column, and here, where the brickwork is too steep to be covered with foliage, the omnipresent *wanderoo* monkey may be seen disporting itself on the very summit.

The Abhayagiria is of similar shape, but only

covered at present with a shrub-like growth. Originally it was the largest dágoba in Ceylon, being 405 feet high—or as high as S. Paul's—but time has reduced it to somewhere about 300 feet. A rather precipitous path leads from the base to the summit, which has recently been restored in some fashion, and from thence a fine view may be obtained.

As you roam through the woods by jungle paths, or along the two or three roads which have been made in late years to open up the ruins, you come upon innumerable smaller remains. Most frequent among these are groups of columns still standing, twenty or thirty together, sometimes only rough-hewn, sometimes elegantly shaped, with carven capitals, which either formed the foundation storeys of wooden buildings, or being themselves covered with roofs constituted porticoes for the resting-places of the gods in their processions, or habitations for the use of the priests. There are very few remains of walled buildings, stone or brick, but plentiful foundation outlines of what may have been public or sacred enclosures of one kind or another—some with handsome flights of steps and balustrades leading up to them, and for the lowest step the frequent half-moon stone carved with elegant devices of the elephant, the lion, the horse, the Brahmin bull, the goose, and the lotus-flower. Here among the tangle is a flight of half-a-dozen steps, springing from nowhere and apparently leading nowhither. There is a gigantic stone trough, sixty-two feet long by four feet four inches wide, over which the learned are in doubt whether it was used to contain food for the royal elephants or boiled rice for the priests!

Here at anyrate is a cistern ten feet long by five wide, elegantly carved out of a single block of granite, which, tradition says, served for the priests' rice-dish; and which only a few years ago was, by the subscription of a neighboring countryside, filled full of food (see S. M. Burrows' *Buried Cities of Ceylon*; London, Trübner & Co., 1885) for the pilgrims of the June full moon. There again is one of the numerous flat slabs which may be found, bearing an ancient inscription on its face; and in almost every direction are solid stone swimming baths or tanks, ten, twenty, or thirty yards up to (in one case) fully 100 yards in length. Two of these *pókunas*, so called—the twin *pókunas*—stand near the northern circular road, and are still in good preservation; the one given in the illustration on next page is forty-four yards long, the other about thirty, and both have handsome flights of steps at each end by which to descend to the water, and step-like tiers of stonework round the sides. They were of course not covered, but open to the sun and air.

As you go along the road after leaving these tanks, at a turn you suddenly come upon a seated image of Buddha—by the wayside, under the trees. The figure is about seven feet high as it sits. It is of dark-coloured granite, and though slightly defaced is still by far the best thing of its kind in the place. Most of the images of Buddha in the present temples of Ceylon are painfully crude productions; but this has caught something of the grace of the great Guru. The eyelids are just shut, yet so slightly as to suggest that the figure is not lost in the ordinary material sleep, but only in that luminous slumber which, while closing itself to the outward and transitory world, opens on the eternal and steadfast consciousness behind. A deep calm overspreads the face—so deep that it insensibly affects the passer-by. He involuntarily stops and gazes, surrendering himself to its influence, and to that of the silent

A Ruined Bathing Tank, Anurádhapura

forest. His thoughts subside, like waves on water when the wind ceases. He too for a moment touches the well-spring of being—he swims into identity with the universe; the trees flicker in the evening light, the Buddha just gives the slightest nod, as much as to say, "That's it"; and then—he is but stone again, and the road stretches beyond.

Curious that one man should so affect the world that he should leave his bo-trees and his dágobas and his images in thousands over half a continent; that he should gather vast cities round his name, and still, when they have perished and passed away, should remain the most glorious thing connected with them; yet Buddha could not have had this ascendancy had not other people in their thousands and hundreds of thousands experienced in greater or less degree the same facts that he experienced. We must forgive, after all, the dirty, yellow-robed priests, with their greedy claws and stinking shrines. It was Buddha's fault, not theirs, when he explored poor human nature so deeply as to invest even its lowest manifestations with sanctity.

Where this image now sits perhaps once it looked down upon the busy turmoil of a great street. The glories of the capital of the Cinghalese kingdom unrolled before and beneath it. Hear how the chronicler of the seventh century (quoted by Emerson Tennent) describes—with justifiable pride—the splendor of the city in his day: "The temples and palaces whose golden pinnacles glitter in the sky, the streets spanned by arches bearing flags, the ways strewn with sand, and on either side vessels containing flowers, and niches with statues holding lamps. Here are multitudes of men armed with swords and bows and arrows. Elephants, horses, carts, and myriads of people pass and repass—jugglers, dancers, and musicians of all nations, with chank shells and other instruments ornamented with gold. The distance from the principal gate to the east gate is four gows,* and the same from

* 16 miles.

the north to the south gate. The principal streets are Moon Street, Great King Street, Hinguruwak, and Mahawelli Street—the first containing 11,000 houses, many of them two storeys in height. The smaller streets are innumerable. The palace has large ranges of buildings, some of them two and three storeys high, and its subterranean apartments are of great extent."

Fa Hian, the Chinese traveller, who visited Ceylon about 413 A.D., also says: "The city is the residence of many magistrates, grandees, and foreign merchants; the mansions beautiful, the public buildings richly adorned, the streets and highways straight and level, and houses for preaching built at every thoroughfare." Nor was the civilisation of Anurádhapura merely material in its scope, for Tennent tells us that beside public gardens and baths, halls for music and dancing, rest-houses for travellers, almhouses, etc., they had hospitals in which *animals* as well as men were tenderly cared for. "The corn of a thousand fields was set apart by one king for their use; another put aside rice to feed the squirrels which frequented his gardens; and a third displayed his surgical skill in treating the diseases of elephants, horses, and snakes."

Founded by Cinghalese invaders of the island somewhere in the fifth or sixth centuries B.C., the city attained its first splendor under King Dewanipiatissa, who came to the throne in B.C. 306. "It was in his reign," says Burrows, "that the royal missionary Mahindo, son of the Indian king Dharmasoka, landed in Ceylon, and either introduced or regenerated Buddhism. The monarch and all his court, his consort and her women, became ready converts to the new tenets; the arrival of Mahindo's sister, Sanghamitta, with a branch of the identical tree under which Gautama obtained Buddha-hood, consummated the conversion of the island; and the king devoted the rest of his reign to the erection of enormous monuments, rock temples, and monasteries, to mark his zeal for the new faith."

After him troubles began. The Tamils of Southern India—whose history has been for so long entangled with that of the Cinghalese—or some branch of the race, attracted probably by the wealth of the new city, landed in Ceylon about 200 B.C. And from that time forward the history of Anurádhapura is the record of continual conflict between the races. There was a second great invasion in B.C. 104, and a third about A.D. 106, in which the Tamils are said to have carried back to the mainland 12,000 Cinghalese captives, as well as great quantities of treasure. But the peaceful, quiet-loving Cinghalese, whose chief talents lay in the direction of agricultural pursuits and the construction of those enormous tanks and irrigation works which still form one of the most remarkable features of the country, were no match in the arts of wars for the enterprising genius of the Tamils. The latter gradually pushed their way in more and more, dissensions between the two peoples more and more disorganised the city, till at last, for some reason not very clearly explained, in A.D. 769 the then king (Aggrabodhi IV.) evacuated his capital and established himself at Pollanarua, now also a buried city of the jungle.

From that time, it may be supposed, Anurádhapura rapidly dwindled away; the streets were no more filled with gay crowds, the slight habitations of the populace soon fell to pieces, leaving no trace behind (except a soil impregnated for miles and miles with the *débris* of bricks); the stone palaces and temples lapsed into decay. And now Buddha sits in the silence of the forest, folded in the ancient calm, just as he sat centuries and centuries ago in the tumult and roar of the city; night falls, and the elephant and the bear roam past him through the brushwood, the herds of spotted deer are startled for a moment by his lonely form in the moonlight.

If one ascends the Abhayagiria dágoba, from its vantage height of 300 feet he has a good bird's-eye view of the region. Before him to the west and north stretches as far as the eye can see a level plain almost unbroken by hills. This plain is covered, except for a few reservoirs and an occasional but rare oasis of coco-nut palm, by dense woods. On all sides they stretch, like a uniform grey-green carpet over the earth; even the present village of Anurádhapura hardly makes a break,—so small is it, and interspersed with trees. Through these woods run narrow jungle paths, and among them, scattered at intervals for miles and miles, are ruins similar to those I have described. And this is all that is left to-day of the ancient city.

I suppose the temptation to make moral reflections on such subjects is very strong! For myself I can only say that I have walked through these and other such scenes with a sense of unfeigned gratitude that they belong to a past which is dead and done with. That Time sweeps all these efforts of mortality (and our own as well) in due course into his dust-bin is a matter for which we can never be sufficiently thankful. Think, if all the monuments of human pride and folly which have been

Small Guardian Figure, or Dhworpal
(At entrance to Dalada Maligawa)

created were to endure indefinitely,—if even our own best and most useful works were to remain, cumbering up the earth with their very multitude, what a nuisance it would be! The great kings caused glorious palaces and statues and temples to be made, thinking to outvie all former and paralyse all future efforts of mankind, perpetuating their names to the end of the years. But Time, wiser, quickly removed all these things as soon as their authors were decently out of the way, leaving us just as much of them as is sufficient to convey the ideas which underlay them, and no more. As a vast dágoba, containing bricks enough to build a good-sized town, is erected to enshrine a single hair from the head of a great man, so the glorious temples and statues and pictures and palaces of a whole epoch, all put together, do but enshrine a tiny atom of the eternal beauty. Let them deliver that, and go their way.

What a good thing even that our bodies die! How thankful we ought to be that they are duly interred and done with in course of time. Fancy if we were condemned always to go on in the same identical forms, each of us, repeating the same ancient jokes, making the same wise remarks, priding ourselves on the same superiorities over our fellows, enduring the same insults from them, wearing the same fusty garments, ever getting raggeder and raggeder through the centuries—what a fate! No; let us know there is something better than that. These swarms of idle priests who ate rice out of troughs at the public expense; these endless mumbo-jumbo books that they wrote; these mighty kings with their royal finery, their harlots, and their insane battles; these animal hospitals; these ruins of great cities lost in thickets; these Alexandrian libraries burnt to ashes; these Greek statues broken and buried in the earth—all that is really durable in them has endured and will endure, the rest is surely well out of the way.

Certainly, as one jogs through the mortal hours of the night in that said mail-cart, returning the forty-two miles from Anurádhapura to Dambulla (where one meets with the nearest horse coach), wedged in with five or six other passengers, and trying in vain to find a place for one's feet amid the compacted mass of baggage that occupies the bottom of the cart, or to avoid the side-rails and rods that impinge upon one's back and head—kept well awake by the continual jingling of bells and the yells and thwacks of the driver, as he urges his active little Brahminy bulls through the darkness, or stopping to change team at wayside cabins where long conversations ensue, between dusky figures bearing lamps, on the state of the road and the probabilities of an encounter with the rogue-elephant who is supposed to haunt it—all those twelve long hours one has ample time to make suitable reflections of some kind or other on the transitory and ineffectual nature of our little human endeavor.

CHAPTER VII

A NIGHT-FESTIVAL IN A HINDU TEMPLE

THE festival of Taypusam is one of the more important among the many religious festivals of the Hindus, and is celebrated with great rejoicings on the night of the first full moon in January each year. In the case of the great temples of Southern India, some of which are so vast that their enclosures are more than a mile in circumference, enormous crowds—sometimes 20,000 people or more—will congregate together to witness the ceremonials, which are elaborately gorgeous. There are a few Hindu temples of smaller size in Ceylon, and into one of these I had the good fortune to be admitted, on the occasion of this year's festival (1891), and at the time when the proceedings were about to commence.

It was nine o'clock, the full moon was shining in the sky, and already the blaring of trumpets and horns could be heard from within as I stood at the gate seeking admittance. At first this was positively denied; but my companion, who was a person of some authority in the temple, soon effected an entrance, and we presently stood within the precincts. It must be understood that these temples generally consist of a large oblong enclosure, more or less planted with palms and other trees, within which stands the sanctuary itself, with lesser shrines, priests' dwellings, and other buildings grouped round it. In the present case the enclosure was about one hundred yards long by sixty or seventy wide, with short grass under foot. In the centre stood the temple proper—a building without any pretensions to architectural form, a mere oblong, bounded by a wall ten or twelve feet high; unbroken by any windows, and rudely painted in vertical stripes, red and white. At the far end, under trees, were some low priests' cottages; and farther on a tank or reservoir, not very large, with a stone balustrade round it. Coming round to the front of the temple, which was more ornamented, and where the main doorway or entrance was, we found there a considerable crowd assembled. We were in fact just in time to witness the beginning of the ceremony; for almost immediately a lot of folk came rushing out through the doorway of the temple in evident excitement; torches were lighted, consisting of long poles, some surmounted with a flaming ring of rags dipped in coco-nut oil, others with a small iron crate in which lumps of broken coco-nut burned merrily. In a few moments there was a brilliant light; the people arranged themselves in two lines from the temple door; sounds of music from within got louder; and a small procession appeared, musicians first, then four nautch girls, and lastly a small platform supported on the shoulders of men, on which was the great god Siva.

At first I could not make out what this last-named object was, but presently distinguished two rude representations of male and female figures, Siva and his consort Sakti, apparently cut out of one block, seated, and about three feet high, but so bedone with jewels and silks that it was difficult to be sure of their anatomy! Over them was held a big ornamental umbrella, and behind followed the priest. We joined the procession, and soon arrived at the edge of the reservoir which I have already mentioned, and on which was floating a strange kind of ship. It was a raft made of bamboos lashed to empty barrels, and on it a most florid and brilliant canopy, covered with cloths of different colors and surmounted by little scarlet pennants. A flight of steps down to the water occupied the whole of one side of the tank, the other three sides were surrounded by the stone balcony, and on these steps and round the balcony the crowd immediately disposed itself, while the procession went on board. When the god was properly arranged under his canopy, and the nautch girls round about him, and when room had been found for the crew, who with long poles were to propel the vessel, and for as many musicians as convenient—about a dozen souls in all—a bell rang, and the priest, a brown-bodied young Brahmin with the sacred thread over his shoulders and a white cloth edged with red round his loins, made an offering of flame of camphor in a five-branched lamp. A hush fell upon the crowd, who all held their hands, palms together, as in the attitude of prayer (but also symbol of the desire to be joined together and to the god)—some with their arms high above their head; a tray was placed on the raft, of coco-nuts and bananas, which the priest opening deposited before the image; the band burst forth into renewed uproar, and the ship went gyrating over the water on her queer voyage.

What a scene! I had now time to look around

a little. All round the little lake, thronging the steps and the sides in the great glare of the torches, were hundreds of men and boys, bare-bodied, barehead and barefoot, but with white loin-cloths—all in a state of great excitement—not religious so much as spectacular, as at the commencement of a theatrical performance, myself and companion about the only persons clothed,—except that in a corner and forming a pretty mass of color were a few women and girls, of the poorer class of Tamils, but brightly dressed, with nose-rings and ear-rings profusely ornamented. On the water, brilliant in scarlet and gold and blue, was floating the sacred canopy, surrounded by musicians yelling on their various horns, in the front of which—with the priest standing between them—sat two little naked boys holding small torches; while overhead through the leaves of plentiful coconut and banana palms overhanging the tank, in the dim blue sky among gorgeous cloud-outlines just discernible, shone the goddess of night, the cause of all this commotion.

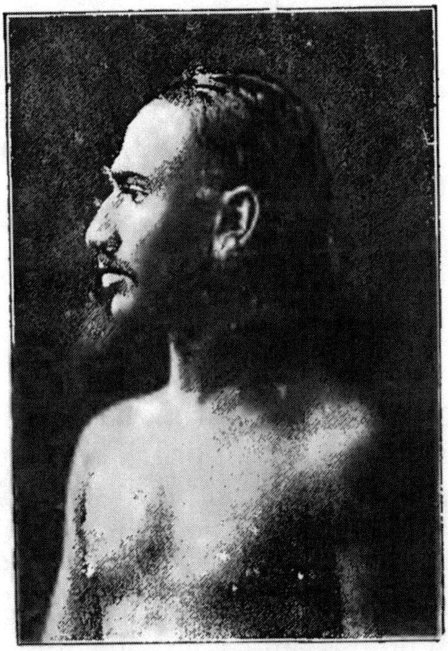

Tamil Man

Such a blowing up of trumpets in the full moon!

For the first time I gathered some clear idea of what the ancient festivals were like. Here was a boy blowing two pipes at the same time, exactly as in the Greek bas-reliefs. There was a man droning a deep bourdon on a reed instrument, with cheeks puffed into pouches with long-sustained effort of blowing; to him was attached a shrill flageolet player—the two together giving much the effect of Highland bagpipes. Then there were the tom-toms, whose stretched skins produce quite musical and bell-like though monotonous sounds; and lastly two old men jingling cymbals and at the same time blowing their terrible chank-horns or conches. These chanks are much used in Buddhist and Hindu temples. They are large whorled sea-shells of the whelk shape, such as sometimes ornament our mantels. The apex of the spiral is cut away and a mouthpiece cemented in its place, through which the instrument can be blown like a horn. If, then, the fingers be used to partly cover and vary the mouth of the shell, and at the same time the shell be vibrated to and fro in the air—what with its natural convolutions and these added complications, the most ear-rending and diabolically wavy bewildering and hollow sounds can be produced, such as might surely infect the most callous worshiper with a proper faith in the supernatural.

The temper of the crowd, too, helped one to understand the old religious attitude. It was thoroughly *whole-hearted*—I cannot think of any other word. There was no piety—in our sense of the word—or very little, observable. They were just thoroughly enjoying themselves—a little excited, no doubt, by chanks and divine possibilities generally, but not subdued by awe; talking freely to each other in low tones, or even indulging occasionally —the younger ones—in a little bear-fighting; at the same time proud of the spectacle and the presence of the divinity, heart and soul in the ceremony, and anxious to lend hands as torch-bearers or image-bearers, or in any way, to its successful issue. It is this temper which the wise men say is encouraged and purposely cultivated by the ceremonial institutions of Hinduism. The temple services are made to cover, as far as may be, the whole ground of life, and to provide the pleasures of the theatre, the art-gallery, the music-hall, and the concert-room in one. People attracted by these spectacles—which are very numerous and very varied in character, according to the different feasts—presently remain to inquire into their meaning. Some like the music, others the bright colors. Many men come at first merely to witness the dancing of the nautch girls, but afterwards and insensibly are drawn into spheres of more spiritual influence. Even the children find plenty to attract them, and the temple becomes their familiar resort from early life.

The theory is that all the ceremonies have inner and mystic meanings—which meanings in due time are declared to those who are fit—and that thus the temple institutions and ceremonies constitute a great ladder by which men can rise at last to those inner truths which lie beyond all formulas and are contained in no creed. Such is the theory, but like all theories it requires large deductions before acceptance. That such theory was one of the formative influences of the Hindu ceremonial, and that the latter embodies here and there important esoteric truths descending from Vedic times, I hardly doubt; but, on the other hand, time, custom, and neglect, different streams of tradition blending and blurring each other, reforms and a thousand influences have—as in all such cases—produced a total concrete result which no one theory can account for or co-ordinate.

Such were some of my thoughts as I watched the crowd around me. They, too, were not uninterested in watching me. The appearance of an Englishman under such circumstances was perhaps a little unusual, and scores of black eyes were turned inquiringly in my direction; but covered as I was by the authority of my companion no one seemed to resent my presence. A few, I thought, looked shocked, but the most seemed rather pleased, as if proud that a spectacle so brilliant and impressive should be witnessed by a stranger—besides there were two or three among the crowd whom I happened to have met before and spoken with, and whose friendly glances made me feel at home.

Meanwhile, the gyrating raft had completed two or three voyages round the little piece of water. Each time it returned to the shore fresh offerings were made to the god, the bell was rung again, a moment of hushed adoration followed, and then with fresh strains of mystic music a new start for the deep took place. What the inner signification of these voyages might be I had not and have not the faintest idea; it is possible even that no one present knew. At the same time, I do not doubt that the drama was originally instituted in order to commemorate some actual event, or to symbolise some doctrine. On each voyage a hymn was sung or recited. On the first voyage the Brahmin priest declaimed a hymn from the Vedas—a hymn that may have been written 3000 years ago—nor was there anything in the whole scene which appeared to me discordant with the notion that the clock had been put back 3000 years (though, of course, the actual new departure in the Brahminical rites which we call Hinduism does not date back anything like so far as that). On the second voyage a Tamil hymn was sung by one of the youths trained in the temples for this purpose; and on the third voyage another Tamil hymn, with interludes of the most ecstatic caterwauling from chanks and bagpipes! The remainder of the vogages I did not witness, as my conductor now took me to visit the interior of the temple.

That is, as far as it was permissible to penetrate. For the Brahmin priests who regulate these things, with far-sighted policy make it one of their most stringent rules that the laity shall not have access beyond a short distance into the temple, and heathen like myself are, of course, confined to the mere forecourts. Thus the people feel more awe and sanctity with regard to the holy place itself and the priests who fearlessly tread within than they do with regard to anything else connected with their religion.

Having passed the porch, we found ourselves in a kind of entrance hall with one or two rows of columns supporting a flat wooden roof—the walls adorned with the usual rude paintings of various events in Siva's earthly career. On the right was a kind of shrine with a dancing figure of the god in relief—the perpetual dance of creation; but unlike some of the larger temples, in which there is often most elaborate and costly stonework, everything here was of the plainest, and there was hardly anything in the way of sculpture to be seen. Out of this forecourt opened a succession of chambers into which one might not enter; but the dwindling lights placed in each served to show distance after distance. In the extreme chamber farthest removed from the door, by which alone daylight enters—the rest of the interior being illumined night and day with artificial lights—is placed, surrounded by lamps, the most sacred object, the lingam. This, of course, was too far off to be discerned—and indeed it is, except on occasions, kept covered—but it appears that instead of being a rude image of the male organ (such as is frequently seen in the outer courts of these temples), the thing is a certain white stone, blue-veined and of an egg-shape, which is mysteriously fished up—if the gods so will it—from the depths of the river Nerbudda, and only thence. It stands in the temple in the hollow of another oval-shaped object which represents the female *yoni*; and the two together, emblemising Siva and Sakti, stand for the sexual energy which pervades creation.

Thus the worship of sex is found to lie at the root of the present Hinduism, as it does at the root of nearly all the primitive religions of the world. Yet it would be a mistake to conclude that such worship is a mere deification of material functions. Whenever it may have been that the Vedic prophets descending from Northern lands into India first discovered within themselves that capacity of spiritual ecstasy which has made them even down till to-day one of the greatest religious forces in the world, it is certain that they found (as indeed many of the mediæval Christian seers at a later time also found) that this ecstasy had a certain similarity to the sexual rapture. In their hands, therefore, the rude phallic worships, which their predecessors had with true instinct celebrated, came to have a new meaning; and sex itself, the most important of earthly functions, came to derive an even greater importance from its relation to the one supreme and heavenly fact, that of the soul's union with God.

In the middle line of all Hindu temples, between the lingam and the door, are placed two other very sacred objects—the couchant bull Nandi and an upright ornamented pole, the Kampam, or as it is sometimes called, the flagstaff. In this case the bull was about four feet in length, carved in one block of stone, which from continual anointing by pious worshippers had become quite black and lustrous on the surface. In the great temple at Tanjore there is a bull twenty feet long cut from a single block of syenite, and similar bull-images are to be found in great numbers in these temples, and of all sizes down to a foot in length, and in any accessible situation are sure to be black and shining with oil. In Tamil the word *pasu* signifies both *ox*—*i.e.* the domesticated ox—and the *soul.* Siva is frequently represented as riding on a bull; and the animal represents the human soul which has become subject and affiliated to the god. As to the flagstaff, it was very plain, and appeared to be merely a wooden pole nine inches or so thick, slightly ornamented, and painted a dull red color. In the well-known temple at Madura the kampam is make of teak plated with gold, and is encircled with certain rings at intervals, and at the top three horizontal arms project, with little bell-like tassels hanging from them. This curious object has, it is said, a physiological meaning, and represents a nerve which passes up the median line of the body from the genital organs to the brain (? the great sympathetic). Indeed, the whole dispositions of the parts in these temples is supposed (as, of course, also in the Christian churches) to represent the human body, and so also the universe of which the human body is only the miniature. I do not feel myself in a position, however, to judge how far these correspondences are exact. The inner chambers in this particular temple were, as far as I could see, plain and unornamented.

On coming out again into the open space in front of the porch, my attention was directed to some low buildings which formed the priests' quarters. Two priests were attached to the temple, and a separate cottage was intended for any travelling priest or lay benefactor who might want accommodation within the precincts.

And now the second act of the sacred drama was commencing. The god, having performed a sufficient number of excursions on the tank, was being carried back with ceremony to the space in front of the porch—where for some time had been standing, on portable platforms made of poles, three strange animal figures of more than life-size—a bull, a peacock, and a black creature somewhat resembling a hog, but I do not know what it was meant for. On the back of the bull, which was evidently itself in an amatory and excited mood, Siva and Sakti were placed ; on the hog-like animal was mounted another bejewelled figure—that of Ganésa, Siva's son ; and on the peacock again the figure of his other son, Soubramánya. Camphor flame was again offered, and then a lot of stalwart and enthusiastic worshippers seized the poles, and mounting the platforms on their shoulders set themselves to form a procession round the temple on the grassy space between it and the outer wall. The musicians, as usual, went first, then came the dancing girls, and then after an interval of twenty or thirty yards the three animals abreast of each other on their platforms, and bearing their respective gods upon their backs. At this point we mingled with the crowd and were lost among the worshipers. And now again I was reminded of representations of antique religious processions. The people, going in front or following behind, or partly filling the space in front of the gods—though leaving a lane clear in the middle—were evidently getting elated and excited. They swayed their arms, took hands or rested them on each other's bodies, and danced rather than walked along ; sometimes their shouts mixed with the music ; the tall torches swayed to and fro, flaring to the sky and distilling burning drops on naked backs in a way which did not lessen the excitement ; the smell of hot coco-nut oil mingling with that of humanity made the air sultry ; and the great leaves of bananas and other palms leaning over and glistening with the double lights of moon and torch flames gave a weird and tropical beauty to the scene.*

* Mrs Speir, in her *Life in Ancient India*, p. 374, says that we first hear of Siva worship about B.C. 300, and that it is described

In this rampant way the procession moved for a few yards, the men wrestling and sweating under the weight of the god-images, which according to orthodox ideas are always made of an alloy of the five metals known to the ancients — an alloy called *panchaloka*—and are certainly immensely heavy; and then it came to a stop. The bearers rested their poles on strong crutches carried for the purpose, and while they took breath the turn of the nautch girls came.

Cinghalese Girl

Most people are sufficiently familiar nowadays, through Oriental exhibitions and the like, with the dress and bearing of these Devadásis, or servants of God. "They sweep the temple," says the author of *Life in an Indian Village*, "ornament the floor with quaint figures drawn in rice flour, hold the sacred light before the god, fan him, and dance and

by Megasthenes as "celebrated in tumultuous festivals, the worshippers anointing their bodies, wearing crowns of flowers, and sounding bells and cymbals. From which," she adds, "the Greeks conjectured that Siva worship was derived from Bacchus or Dionysos, and carried to the East in the traditionary expedition which Bacchus made in company with Hercules."

sing when required." "In the village of Kélambakam," he continues, "there are two dancing girls, Kanakambujam and Minakshi. K. is the concubine of a neighboring Mudelliar, and M. of Appalacharri the Brahmin. But their services can be obtained by others." I will describe the dress of one of the four present on this occasion. She had on a dark velveteen tunic with quite short gold-edged sleeves, the tunic almost concealed from view by a very handsome scarf or *sari* such as the Indian women wear. This sari, made of crimson silk, profusely ornamented with gold thread, was passed over one shoulder, and having been wound twice or thrice round the waist was made to hang down like a petticoat to a little below the knee. Below this appeared silk leggings of an orange colour; and heavy silver anklets crowned the naked feet. Handsome gold bangles were on her arms (silver being usually worn below the waist and gold above), jewels and bell-shaped pendants in her nose and ears, and on her head rose-colored flowers pinned with gold brooches and profusely inwoven with the plaited black hair that hung down her back. The others with variations in color had much the same costume.

To describe their faces is difficult. I think I seldom saw any so inanimately sad. It is part of the teaching of Indian women that they should never give way to the expression of feeling, or to any kind of excitement of manner, and this in the case of better types leads to a remarkable dignity and composure of bearing, such as is comparatively rare in the West, but in more stolid and ignorant sorts produces a most apathetic and bovine mien. In the case of these nautch women, circumstances are complicated by the prostitution which seems to be the inevitable accompaniment of their profession. One might, indeed, think that it was distinctly a *part* of their profession—as women attached to the service of temples whose central idea is that of sex; but some of my Hindu friends assure me that this is not so: that they live where they like, that their dealings with the other sex are entirely their own affair, and are not regulated or recognised in any way by the temple authorities, and that it is only, so to speak, an accident that these girls enter into commercial relations with men—generally, it is admitted, with the wealthier of those who attend the services—an accident, of course, quite likely to occur, since they are presumably good-looking, and are early forced into publicity and out of the usual routine of domestic life. All the same, though doubtless these things are so now, I think it may fairly be supposed that the sexual services of these nautch girls *were* at one time a recognised part of their duty to the temple to which they were attached. Seeing, indeed, that so many of the religions of antiquity are known to have recognised services of this kind, seeing also that Hinduism did at least incorporate in itself primitive sexual worships, and seeing that there is no reason to suppose that such practices involved any slur in primitive times on those concerned in them—rather the reverse—I think we have at any rate a strong *primâ-facie* case. It is curious too, that, even to-day, notwithstanding the obvious drawbacks of their life, these girls are quite recognised and accepted in Hindu families of high standing and respectability. When marriages take place they dress the bride, put on her jewels; and, generally speaking, are much referred to as authorities on dress. Whatever, however, may have been the truth about the exact duties and position of the Devadásis in old times, the four figuring away there before their gods that night seemed to me to present but a melancholy and effete appearance. They were small and even stunted in size, nor could it be said that any of them were decently good-looking. The face of the eldest—it was difficult to judge their age, but she might have been twenty—was the most expressive, but it was thin and exceedingly weary; the faces of the others were the faces of children who had ceased to be children, yet to whom experience had brought no added capacity.

These four waifs of womanhood, then, when the procession stopped, wheeled round, and facing the god approached him with movements which bore the remotest resemblance to a dance. Stretching out their right hands and right feet together (in itself an ungraceful movement) they made one step forward and to the right; then doing the same with left hands and feet, made a step in advance to the left. After repeating this two or three times they then, having first brought their finger points to their shoulders, extended their arms forward towards the deity, inclining themselves at the same time. This also was repeated, and then they moved back much as they had advanced. After a few similar evolutions, sometimes accompanied by chanting, they wheeled round again, and the procession moved forwards a few yards more. Thus we halted about half-a-dozen times before we completed the circuit of the temple, and each time had a similar performance.

On coming round to the porch what might be called the third act commenced. The platform of the bull and the god Siva was—not without struggles—lowered to the ground so as to face the porch, the other two gods being kept in the background; and then the four girls, going into the temple and bringing forth little oil-lamps, walked in single file round the image, followed by the musicians also in single file. These latter had all through the performance kept up an almost continuous blowing; and their veined, knotted faces and distended cheeks bore witness to the effort, not to mention the state of our own ears! It must, however, in justice be said that the drone, the flageolet, and the trumpets were tuned to the same keynote, and their combined music alone would not have been so bad; but a chank-shell can no more be tuned than a zebra can be tamed, and when *two* of these instruments together, blown by two wiry old men obdurately swaying their heads, were added to the tumult, it seemed not impossible that one might go giddy, and perhaps become *theopneustos*, at any moment.

The show was now evidently culminating. The entry of the musicians into the temple, where their reverberations were simply appalling, was the signal for an inrush of the populace. We passed in with the crowd, and almost immediately Siva, lifted from the bull, followed, borne in state under his parasol. He was placed on a stand in front of the side shrine in the forecourt already mentioned; and a curtain being drawn before him, there was a momentary hush and awe. The priest behind the curtain (whom from our standpoint we could see) now made the final offerings of fruit, flowers, and sandalwood, and lighted the five-branched camphor lamp for the last time. This burning of camphor is, like other things in the service, emblematic. The five lights represent the five senses. As camphor consumes itself and leaves no residue behind, so should the five senses, being offered to God, consume themselves and disappear. When this is done, that happens in the soul which was now figured in the temple service; for as the last of the camphor burned itself away the veil was swiftly drawn aside—and there stood the image of Siva revealed in a blaze of light.

The service was now over. The priest distributed the offerings among the people; the torches were put out; and in a few minutes I was walking homeward through the streets and wondering if I were really in the modern world of the nineteenth century.

A VISIT TO A GÑÁNI

The Gñáni

CHAPTER VIII

A VISIT TO A GNANI

During my stay in Ceylon I was fortunate enough to make the acquaintance of one of the esoteric teachers of the ancient religious mysteries. These Gurus or Adepts are to be found scattered all over the mainland of India; but they lead a secluded existence, avoiding the currents of Western civilisation—which are obnoxious to them—and rarely come into contact with the English or appear on the surface of ordinary life. They are divided into two great schools, the Himalayan and South Indian—formed probably, even centuries back, by the gradual retirement of the Adepts into the mountains and forests of their respective districts before the spread of foreign races and civilisations over the general continent. The Himalayan school has carried on the more democratic and progressive Buddhistic tradition, while the South Indian has kept more to caste and to the ancient Brahminical and later Hindu lines. This separation has led to divergences in philosophy, and there are even (so strong is sectional feeling in all ranges of human activity) slight jealousies between the adherents of the two schools; but the differences are probably after all very superficial; in essence their teaching and their work may, I think, be said to be the same.

The teacher to whom I allude belongs to the

South Indian school, and was only sojourning for a time in Ceylon. When I first made his acquaintance he was staying in the precincts of a Hindu temple. Passing through the garden and the arcade-like porch of the temple with its rude and grotesque frescoes of the gods—Siva astride the bull, Sakti, his consort, seated behind him, etc.—we found ourselves in a side-chamber, where, seated on a simple couch, his bed and day-seat in one, was an elderly man (some seventy years of age, though he did not look nearly as much as that) dressed only in a white muslin wrapper wound loosely round his lithe and even active dark brown form: his head and face shaven a day or two past, very gentle and spiritual in expression, like the best type of Roman Catholic priest—a very beautiful, full, and finely-formed mouth, straight nose and well-formed chin, dark eyes, undoubtedly the eyes of a seer, dark-rimmed eyelids, and a powerful, prophetic, and withal childlike manner. He soon lapsed into exposition, which he continued for an hour or two with but few interjections from his auditors.

At a later time he moved into a little cottage where, for several weeks, I saw him nearly every day. Every day the same—generally sitting on his couch, with bare arms and feet, the latter often coiled under him—only requiring a question to launch off into a long discourse—fluent, and even rapt, with ready and vivid illustration and long digressions, but always returning to the point. Though unfortunately my knowledge of Tamil was so slight that I could not follow his conversation and had to take advantage of the services of a friend as interpreter, still it was easy to see what a remarkable vigor and command of language the man had, what power of concentration on the subject in hand, and what a wealth of reference—especially citation from ancient authorities—wherewith to illustrate his discourse.

Everything in the East is different from the West, and so are the methods of teaching. Teaching in the East is mainly authoritative and traditional. That is its strong point and also its defect. The pupil is not expected to ask questions of a sceptical nature or expressive of doubt; the teacher does not go about to "prove" his thesis to the pupil, or support it with arguments drawn from the plane of the pupil's intelligence; he simply redelivers to the pupil, in a certain order and sequence, the doctrines which were delivered to him in his time, which have been since verified by his own experience, and which he can illustrate by phrases and metaphors and citations drawn from the sacred books. He has, of course, his own way of presenting the whole, but the body of knowledge which he thus hands down is purely traditional, and may have come along for thousands of years with little or no change. Originality plays no part in the teaching of the Indian Sages. The knowledge which they have to impart is of a kind in which invention is not required. It purports to be a knowledge of the original fact of the universe itself—something behind which no man can go. The West may originate, the West may present new views of the prime fact—the East only seeks to give to a man that fact itself, the supreme consciousness, undifferentiated, the key to all that exists.

The Indian teachers, therefore, say there are as a rule three conditions of the attainment of Divine knowledge or *gñánam*—(1) The study of the sacred books; (2) the help of a Guru; and (3) the verification of the tradition by one's own experience. Without this last the others are, of course, of no use; and the chief aid of the Guru is directed to the instruction of the pupil in the methods by which he may attain to personal experience. The sacred books give the philosophy and some of the experiences of the *gñáni* or illuminated person, but they do not, except in scattered hints, give instruction as to how this illumination is to be obtained. The truth is, it is a question of evolution; and it would neither be right that such instruction should be given to everybody, nor indeed possible, since even in the case of those prepared for it the methods must differ, according to the idiosyncrasy and character of the pupil.

There are apparently isolated cases in which individuals attain to *Gñánam* through their own spontaneous development, and without instruction from a Guru, but these are rare. As a rule, every man who is received into the body of Adepts receives his initiation through another Adept who himself received it from a forerunner, and the whole constitutes a kind of church or brotherhood with genealogical branches so to speak—the line of Adepts from which a man descends being imparted to him on his admission into the fraternity. I need not say that this resembles the methods of the ancient mysteries and initiations of classic times; and, indeed, the Indian teachers claim that the Greek and Egyptian and other Western schools of arcane lore were merely branches, more or less degenerate, of their own.

The course of preparation for Gñánam is called

yogam, and the person who is going through this stage is called a *yogi*—from the root *yog*, to join—one who is seeking junction with the universal spirit. Yogis are common all over India, and exist among all classes and in various forms. Some emaciate themselves and torture their bodies, others seek only control over their minds, some retire into the jungles and mountains, others frequent the cities and exhibit themselves in the crowded fairs, others again carry on the avocations of daily life with but little change of outward habit. Some are humbugs, led on by vanity or greed of gain (for to give to a holy man is highly meritorious); others are genuine students or philosophers; some are profoundly imbued with the religious sense; others by mere distaste for the world. The majority probably take to a wandering life of the body, some become wandering in mind; a great many attain to phases of clairvoyance and abnormal power of some kind or other, and a very few become Adepts of a high order.

Anyhow, the matter cannot be understood unless it is realised that this sort of religious retirement is thoroughly accepted and acknowledged all over India, and excites no surprise or special remark. Only some five or six years ago a relative * of the late Rajah of Tanjore—a man of some forty or fifty years of age, and one of the chief native personages in that part of India—made up his mind to become a devotee. He one day told his friends he was going on a railway journey, sent off his servants and carriages from the palace to the station, saying he would follow, gave them the slip, and has never been heard of since! His friends went to the man who

* Panjali Karana Sahib.

was known to have been acting as his Guru, who simply told them, "You will never find him." Supposing the G.O.M. or the Prince of Wales were to retire like this—how odd it would seem!

To illustrate this subject I may tell the story of Tilleináthan Swámy, who was the teacher of the Guru whose acquaintance I am referring to in this chapter. Tilleináthan was a wealthy shipowner of high family. In 1850 he devoted himself to religious exercises, till 1855, when he became "emancipated." After his attainment he felt sick of the world, and so he wound up his affairs, divided all his goods and money among relations and dependants, and went off stark naked into the woods. His mother and sisters were grieved, and repeatedly pursued him, offering to surrender all to him if he would only return. At last he simply refused to answer their importunities, and they desisted. He appeared in Tanjore after that in '57, '59, '64, and '72, but has not been seen since. He is supposed to be living somewhere in the Western Ghauts.

In '58 or '59, at the close of the Indian Mutiny, when search was being made for Nana Sahib, it was reported that the Nana was hiding himself under the garb (or no garb) of an "ascetic," and orders were issued to detain and examine all such people. Tilleináthan was taken and brought before the sub-magistrate at Kumbakónam, who told him the Government orders, and that he must dress himself properly. At the same time the sub-magistrate, having a friendly feeling for T. and guessing that he would refuse obedience, had brought a wealthy merchant with him, whom he had persuaded to stand bail for Tilleináthan in such emergency. When, however, the merchant saw Tilleináthan, he expressed his doubts about standing bail for him—whereupon T. said, "Quite right, it is no good your standing bail for me; the English Government itself could not stand bail for one who creates and destroys Governments. I will be bail for myself." The sub-magistrate then let him go.

But on the matter being reported at headquarters the sub. was reprimanded, and a force, consisting of an inspector and ten men (natives of course), was sent to take Tilleináthan. He at first refused and threatened them, but on the inspector pleading that he would be dismissed if he returned with empty hands T. consented to come "in order to save the inspector." They came into full court—as it happened—before the collector (Morris), who immediately reprimanded T. for his mad costume! "It is you that are mad," said the latter, "not to know that this is my right costume,"—and he proceeded to explain the four degrees of Hindu probation and emancipation. (These are, of course, the four stages of student, householder, yogi, and gñáni. Every one who becomes a gñáni must pass through the other three stages. Each stage has its appropriate costume and rules; the yogi wears a yellow garment; the gñáni is emancipated from clothing, as well as from all other troubles.)

Finally, T. again told the collector that he was a fool, and that he, T., would punish him. "What will you do?" said the collector. "If you don't do justice I will burn you," was the reply! At this the mass of the people in court trembled, believing, no doubt, implicitly in T.'s power to fulfil his threat. The collector, however, told the inspector to read the Lunacy Act to Tilleináthan, but the inspector's hand shook so that he could hardly see the words—till T. said, "Do not be afraid—I will explain it to you." He then gave a somewhat detailed account of the Act, pointed out to the collector that it did not apply to his own case, and ended by telling him once more that he was a fool. The collector then let him go!

Afterwards Morris—having been blamed for letting the man go—and Beauchamp (judge), who had been rather impressed already by T.'s personality, went together and with an escort to the house in Tanjore in which Tilleináthan was then staying—with an undefined intention, apparently, of arresting him. T. then asked them if they thought he was under their Government—to which the Englishmen replied that they were not there to argue philosophy but to enforce the law. T. asked how they would enforce it. "We have cannons and men behind us," said Morris. "And I," said T., "can also bring cannons and forces greater than yours." They then left him again, and he was no more troubled.

This story is a little disappointing in that no miracles come off, but I tell it as it was told to me by the Guru, and my friend A. having heard it substantially the same from other and independent witnesses at Tanjore, it may be taken as giving a fairly correct idea of the kind of thing that occasionally happens. No doubt the collector would look upon Tilleináthan as a "luny"—and from other stories I have heard of him (his utter obliviousness of ordinary conventionalities and proprieties, that he would lie down to sleep in the middle of the street to the great inconvenience of traffic, that he would sometimes keep on repeating a single vacant phrase over and over again for half a day, etc.), such an opinion might, I should say, fairly be justified. Yet, at the same time, there is no doubt he was a very remarkable man, and the deep reverence with which our friend the Guru spoke of him was obviously not accorded merely to the abnormal powers which he seems at times to have manifested, but to the profundity and breadth of his teaching and the personal grandeur which prevailed through all his eccentricities.

It was a common and apparently instinctive practice with him to speak of the great operations of Nature, the thunder, the wind, the shining of the sun, etc., in the first person, "I"—the identification with, or non-differentiation from, the universe (which is the most important of esoteric doctrines) being in his case complete. So also the democratic character of his teaching surpassed even our Western records. He would take a pariah dog—the most scorned of creatures—and place it round his neck (compare the pictures of Christ with a lamb in the same attitude), or even let it eat out of one plate with himself! One day, in Kumbakónam, when importuned for instruction by five or six disciples, he rose up, and saying, "Follow me" went through the streets to the edge of a brook which divided the pariah village from the town—a line which no Hindu of caste will ever cross—and stepping over the brook bade them enter the defiled ground. This ordeal, however, his followers could not endure, and—except one—they all left him.

Tilleináthan's pupil, the teacher of whom I am presently speaking, is married, and has a wife and children. Most of these "ascetics" think nothing of abandoning their families when the call comes to them and going to the woods, perhaps never to be seen again. He, however, has not done this, but lives on quietly at home at Tanjore. Thirty or forty years ago he was a kind of confidential friend and adviser to the then reigning prince of Tanjore, and was well up in traditional state-craft and politics; and even only two or three years ago took quite an active interest in the National Indian Congress. His own name was Ramaswámy, but he acquired the name Ilákkanam, "the Grammarian," on account of his proficiency in Tamil grammar and philosophy, on which subject he was quite an authority, even before his initiation.

Tamil is a very remarkable, and, indeed, complex language—rivaling the Sanskrit in the latter respect. It belongs to the Dravidian group, and has few Aryan roots in it except what have been borrowed from Sanskrit. It contains, however, an extraordinary number of philosophical terms, of which some are Sanskrit in their origin, but many are entirely its own; and, like the people, it forms a strange blend of practical qualities with the most inveterate occultism. "Tamil," says the author of an article in the *Theosophist* for November '90, "is one of the oldest languages of India, if not of the world. Its birth and infancy are enveloped in mythology. As in the case of Sanskrit, we cannot say when Tamil became a literary language. The oldest Tamil works extant belong to a time, about 2000 years ago, of high and cultured refinement in Tamil poetic literature. All the religious and philosophical poetry of Sanskrit has become fused into Tamil, which language contains a larger number of popular treatises in occultism, alchemy, etc., than even Sanskrit; and it is now the only spoken language of India that abounds in occult treatises on various subjects." Going on to speak of the Tamil Adepts, the author of this article says: "The popular belief is that there were eighteen brotherhoods of Adepts scattered here and there, in the mountains and forests of the Tamil country, and presided over by eighteen Sadhoos; and that there was a grand secret brotherhood composed of the eighteen Sadhoos, holding its meetings in the hills of the Agasthya Kútam in the Tinnevelly district. Since the advent of the English and their mountaineering and deforestation, these occultists have retired far into the interior of the thick jungles on the mountains; and a large number have, it is believed, altogether left these parts for more congenial places in the Himalayan ranges. It is owing to their influence that the Tamil language has been inundated, as it were, with a vast number of works on esoteric philosophy. The works of Agasthya Muni alone* would fill a whole library. The chief and only object of these brotherhoods has been to popularise esoteric truths and bring them home to the masses. So great and so extensive is their influence that the Tamil literature is permeated with esoteric truths in all its ramifications." In fact, the object of this article is to point out the vast number of proverbs and popular songs, circulating among the Tamils to-day, which conceal under frivolous guise the

* Or those ascribed to him.

K

most profound mystic truths. The grammar, too—as I suppose was the case in Sanskrit—is linked to the occult philosophy of the people.

To return to the Teacher, besides state-craft and grammar he is well versed in matters of law, and not unfrequently tackles a question of this kind for the help of his friends; and has some practical knowledge of medicine, as well as of cookery, which he considers important in its relation to health (the divine health, *Sukham*). It will thus be seen that he is a man of good practical ability and acquaintance with the world, and not a mere dreamer, as is too often assumed by Western critics to be the case with all those who seek the hidden knowledge of the East. In fact, it is one of the remarkable points of the Hindu philosophy that practical knowledge of life is expressly inculcated as a preliminary stage to initiation. A man must be a householder before he becomes a yogi; and familiarity with sexual experience is sometimes encouraged rather than reprobated, in order that having experienced one may in time pass beyond it. Indeed, it is not unfrequently maintained that the early marriage of the Hindus is advantageous in this respect, since a couple married at the age of fifteen or sixteen have, by the time they are forty, a grown-up family launched in life, and having circled worldly experience, are then free to dedicate themselves to the work of "emancipation."

During his *yoga* period, which lasted about three years, his wife was very good to him, and assisted him all she could. He was enjoined by his own teacher to refrain from speech, and did so for about a year and a half, passing most of his time in fixed attitudes of meditation, and only clapping his hands when he wanted food, etc. Hardly anything shows more strongly the hold which these religious ideas have upon the people than the common willingness of the women to help their husbands in works of this kind, which, beside the sore inconvenience of them, often deprive the family of its very means of subsistence and leave it dependent on the help of relations and others. But so it is. It is difficult for a Westerner even to begin to realise the conditions and inspirations of life in the East.

Refraint from speech is not a necessary condition of initiation, but it is enjoined in some cases. (There might be a good many cases among the Westerners where it would be very desirable—with or without initiation!) "Many practising," said the Guru one day, "have not spoken for twelve years—so that when freed they had lost the power of speech—babbled like babies—and took some time to recover it. But for two or three years you experience no disability." "During my initiation," he added, "I often wandered about the woods all night, and many times saw wild beasts, but they never harmed me—as, indeed, they cannot harm the initiated."

At the present time he lives (when at home) a secluded life, mostly absorbed in trance conditions—his chief external interest, no doubt, being the teaching of such people as are led to him, or he is led to instruct. When, however, he takes up any practical work he throws himself into it with that power and concentration which is peculiar to a "Master," and which is the natural corollary of the power of abstraction when healthily used.

Among their own people these Gurus often have

small circles of disciples, who receive the instruction of their master, and in return are ever ready to attend upon his wants. Sometimes such little parties sit up all night alternately reading the sacred books and absorbing themselves in meditation. It appears that Ilákkanam's mother became his pupil and practised according to instruction, making good progress. One day, however, she told her son that she should die that night.* "What, are you ill?" he said. "No," she replied, "but I feel that I shall die." Then he asked her what she desired to be done with her body. "Oh, tie a rope to it and throw it out into the street," was her reply—meaning that it did not matter—a very strong expression, considering caste regulations on the subject. Nothing more was said, but that night at 3 A.M., as they and some friends were sitting up (cross-legged on the floor as usual) reading one of the sacred books, one of those present said, "But your mother does not move,"—and she was dead.

When in Ceylon our friend was only staying temporarily in a cottage, with a servant to look after him, and though exceedingly animated and vigorous as I have described, when once embarked in exposition — capable of maintaining his discourse for hours with unflagging concentration—yet the moment such external call upon his faculties was at an end, the interest that it had excited seemed to be entirely wiped from his mind; and the latter returned to that state of interior meditation and absorption in the contemplation of the world disclosed to the inner sense, which had apparently become his normal condition.

* "Go to the feet of the goddess Minakshi."

I was, in fact, struck, and perhaps a little shocked, by the want of interest in things and persons around him displayed by the great man—not that, as I have said, he was not very helpful and considerate in special cases—but evidently that part of his nature which held him to the actual world was thinning out; and the personalities of attendants and of those he might have casual dealings with, or even the scenes and changes of external nature, excited in him only the faintest response.

As I have said, he seemed to spend the greater part of the twenty-four hours wrapt in contemplation, and this not in the woods, but in the interior of his own apartment. As a rule, he only took a brief half-hour's walk mornings and evenings, just along the road and back again, and this was the only time he passed out of doors. Certainly this utter independence of external conditions—the very small amount of food and exercise and even of sleep that he took, combined with the great vigour that he was capable of putting forth on occasion both bodily and mentally, and the perfect control he had over his faculties—all seemed to suggest the idea of his having access to some interior source of strength and nourishment. And, indeed, the general doctrine that the gñáni can thus attain to independence and maintain his body from interior sources alone (eat of the "hidden manna") is one much cherished by the Hindus, and which our friend was never tired of insisting on.

Finally, his face, while showing the attributes of the seer, the externally penetrating quick eye, and the expression of *illumination*—the deep mystic light within—showed also the prevailing sentiment of happiness behind it. *Sandósham, Sandósham eppótham* —"Joy, always joy"—was his own expression, oft repeated.

Perhaps I have now said enough to show—what, of course, was sufficiently evident to me—that, however it may be disguised under trivial or even in some cases repellent coverings, there *is* some reality beneath all these—some body of real experience, of no little value and importance, which has been attained in India by a portion at any rate of those who have claimed it, and which has been handed down now through a vast number of centuries among the Hindu peoples as their most cherished and precious possession.

CHAPTER IX

CONSCIOUSNESS WITHOUT THOUGHT

THE question is, What is this experience? or rather—since an experience can really only be known to the person who experiences it—we may ask, "What is the nature of this experience?" And in trying to indicate an answer of some kind to this question I feel considerable diffidence, just for the very reason (for one) already mentioned—namely, that it is so difficult or impossible for one person to give a true account of an experience which has occurred to another. If I could give the exact words of the teacher, without any bias derived either from myself or the interpreting friend, the case might be different; but that I cannot pretend to do; and if I could, the old-world scientific forms in which his thoughts were cast would probably only prove a stumbling-block and a source of confusion, instead of a help, to the reader. Indeed, even in the case of the sacred books, where we have a good deal of accessible and authoritative information, Western critics, though for the most part agreeing that there *is* some real experience underlying, are sadly at variance as to what that experience may be.

For these reasons I prefer not to attempt or pretend to give the exact teaching, unbiassed, of the Indian Gurus, or their experiences; but only to indicate as far as I can, in my own words, and in modern thought-forms, what I take to be the direction in which we must look for this ancient and world-old knowledge which has had so stupendous an influence in the East, and which, indeed, is still the main mark of its difference from the West.

And first let me guard against an error which is likely to arise. It is very easy to assume, and very frequently assumed, in any case where a person is credited with the possession of an unusual faculty, that such person is at once lifted out of our sphere into a supernatural region, and possesses every faculty of that region. If, for instance, he or she is or is supposed to be clairvoyant, it is assumed that *everything* is or ought to be known to them ; or if the person has shown what seems a miraculous power at any time or in any case, it is asked by way of discredit why he or she did not show a like power at other times or in other cases. Against all such hasty generalisations it is necessary to guard ourselves. If there is a higher form of consciousness attainable by man than that which he for the most part can claim at present, it is probable, nay certain, that it is evolving and will evolve but slowly, and with many a slip and hesitant pause by the way. In the far past of man and the animals consciousness of sensation and consciousness of self have been successively evolved—each of these mighty growths with innumerable branches and branchlets continually spreading. At any point in this vast experience, a new growth, a new form of consciousness, might well have seemed miraculous. What could be more marvelous than the first revealment of the sense of sight, what more inconceivable to those who had not experienced it, and what more certain than that the first use of this faculty must have been fraught with delusion and error? Yet there may be an inner vision which again transcends sight, even as far as sight transcends touch. It is more than probable that in the hidden births of time there lurks a consciousness which is not the consciousness of sensation and which is not the consciousness of self—or, at least, which includes and entirely surpasses these—a consciousness in which the contrast between the *ego* and the external world, and the distinction between subject and object, fall away. The part of the world into which such a consciousness admits us (call it *supramundane* or whatever you will) is probably at least as vast and complex as the part we know, and progress in that region at least equally slow and tentative and various, laborious, discontinuous, and uncertain. There is no sudden leap out of the back parlor onto Olympus; and the routes, when found, from one to the other, are long and bewildering in their variety.

And of those who do attain to some portion of this region, we are not to suppose that they are at once demi-gods, or infallible. In many cases, indeed, the very novelty and strangeness of the experiences give rise to phantasmal trains of delusive speculation. Though we should expect, and though it is no doubt true on the whole; that what we should call the higher types of existing humanity are those most likely to come into possession of any new faculties which may be flying about, yet it is not always so; and there are cases, well recognised, in which persons of decidedly deficient or warped moral nature attain powers which properly belong to a high grade of evolution, and are correspondingly dangerous thereby.

All this, or a great part of it, the Indian teachers insist on. They say—and I think this commends the reality of their experience—that there is nothing abnormal or miraculous about the matter; that the faculties acquired are, on the whole, the result of long evolution and training, and that they have distinct laws and an order of their own. They recognise the existence of persons of a demoniac faculty, who have acquired powers of a certain grade without corresponding moral evolution; and they admit the rarity of the highest phases of consciousness and the fewness of those at present fitted for its attainment.

With these little provisos then established, I think we may go on to say that what the Gñáni seeks and obtains is a new order of consciousness—to which for want of a better we may give the name *universal* or *cosmic* consciousness, in contradistinction to the individual or special bodily consciousness with which we are all familiar. I am not aware that the *exact* equivalent of this expression "universal consciousness" is used in the Hindu philosophy; but the *Sat-chit-ánanda Brahm* to which every yogi aspires indicates the same idea: *sat*, the reality, the all pervading; *chit*, the knowing, perceiving; *ánanda*, the blissful—all these united in one manifestation of Brahm.

The West seeks the individual consciousness—the enriched mind, ready perceptions and memories, individual hopes and fears, ambitions, loves, conquests—the self, the local self, in all its phases and forms—and sorely doubts whether such a thing as an universal consciousness exists. The East seeks the universal consciousness, and, in those cases where its quest succeeds, individual self and life thin away to a mere film, and are only the shadows cast by the glory revealed beyond.

The individual consciousness takes the form of *Thought*, which is fluid and mobile like quicksilver, perpetually in a state of change and unrest, fraught with pain and effort; the other consciousness is *not* in the form of Thought. It touches, sees, hears, and *is* those things which it perceives—without motion, without change, without effort, without distinction of subject and object, but with a vast and incredible Joy.

The individual consciousness is specially related to the body. The organs of the body are in some degree its organs. But the *whole* body is only as one organ of the cosmic consciousness. To attain this latter one must have the power of knowing one's self separate from the body, of passing into a state of *ecstasy* in fact. Without this the cosmic consciousness cannot be experienced.

It is said: "There are four main experiences in initiation—(1) the meeting with a Guru; (2) the consciousness of Grace, or *Arul* (which may perhaps be interpreted as the consciousness of a change—even of a physiological change—working within one); (3) the vision of Siva (God), with which the knowledge of one's self as distinct from the body is closely connected; (4) the finding of the universe within." "The wise," it is also said, "when their thoughts cease to move perceive within themselves the Absolute consciousness, which is *Sarva sakshi*, Witness of all things."

Great have been the disputes among the learned as to the meaning of the word Nirwana—whether it indicates a state of no-consciousness or a state of vastly enhanced consciousness. Probably both views have their justification: the thing does not admit of definition in the terms of ordinary language. The important thing to see and admit is that under cover of this and other similar terms there does exist a real and recognisable fact (that is, a state of consciousness in some sense), which has been experienced over and over again, and which to those who have experienced it in ever so slight a degree has appeared worthy of lifelong pursuit and devotion. It is easy, of course, to represent the thing as a mere word, a theory, a speculation of the dreamy Hindu; but people do not sacrifice their lives for empty words, nor do mere philosophical abstractions rule the destinies of continents. No, the word represents a reality, something very basic and inevitable in human nature. The question really is not to define the fact—for we cannot do that—but to get at and experience it.

It is interesting at this juncture to find that modern Western science, which has hitherto—without much result—been occupying itself with mechanical theories of the universe, is approaching from its side this idea of the existence of another form of consciousness. The extraordinary phenomena of hypnotism—which, no doubt, are in some degree related to the subject we are discussing, and which have been recognised for ages in the East—are forcing Western scientists to assume the existence of the so-called *secondary consciousness* in the body. The phenomena seem really inexplicable without the assumption of a secondary agency of some kind, and it every day becomes increasingly difficult *not* to use the word consciousness to describe it.

Let it be understood that I am not for a moment assuming that this secondary consciousness of the hypnotists is in all respects identical with the cosmic consciousness (or whatever we may call it) of the Eastern occultists. It may or may not be. The two kinds of consciousness may cover the same ground, or they may only overlap to a small extent. That is a question I do not propose to discuss. The point to which I wish to draw attention is that Western science is envisaging the possibility of the existence in man of another consciousness of some kind, beside that with whose working we are familiar. It quotes (A. Moll) the case of Barkworth, who "can add up long rows of figures while carrying on a lively discussion, without allowing his attention to be at all diverted from the discussion"; and asks us how Barkworth can do this unless he has a secondary consciousness which occupies itself with the figures while his primary consciousness is in the thick of argument. Here is a lecturer (F. Myers) who for a whole minute allows his mind to wander entirely away from the subject in hand, and imagines himself to be sitting beside a friend in the audience and to be engaged in conversation with *him*, and who wakes up to find himself still on the platform lecturing away with perfect ease and coherency. What are we to say to such a case as that? Here again is a pianist who recites a piece of music by heart, and finds that his recital is actually hindered by allowing his mind (his primary consciousness) to dwell upon what he is doing. It is sometimes suggested that the very perfection of the musical performance shows that it is mechanical or unconscious, but is this a fair inference? and would it not seem to be a mere contradiction in terms to speak of an unconscious lecture or an unconscious addition of a row of figures?

Many actions and processes of the body—*e.g.* swallowing, are attended by distinct personal consciousness; many other actions and processes are quite unperceived by the same; and it might seem reasonable to suppose that these latter at anyrate were purely mechanical and devoid of any mental substratum. But the later developments of hypnotism in the West have shown—what is well known to the Indian fakirs—that under certain conditions consciousness of the internal actions and processes of the body can be obtained; and not only so, but consciousness of events taking place at a distance from the body and without the ordinary means of communication.

Thus the idea of another consciousness, in some respects of wider range than the ordinary one, and having methods of perception of its own, has been gradually infiltrating itself into Western minds.

There is another idea, which modern science has been familiarising us with, and which is bringing us towards the same conception—that, namely, of the fourth dimension. The supposition that the actual world has four space-dimensions instead of three makes many things conceivable which otherwise would be incredible. It makes it conceivable that apparently separate objects—*e.g.* distinct people—are really physically united; that things apparently sundered by enormous distances of space are really quite close together; that a person or other object might pass in and out of a closed room without disturbance of walls, doors, or windows, etc.; and if this fourth dimension were to become a factor of our consciousness it is obvious that we should have means of knowledge which to the ordinary sense would appear simply miraculous. There is much apparently to suggest that the consciousness attained to by the Indian gñánis in their degree, and by hypnotic subjects in theirs, is of this fourth-dimensional order.

As a solid is related to its own surfaces, so, it would appear, is the cosmic consciousness related to the ordinary consciousness. The phases of the personal consciousness are but different facets of the other consciousness; and experiences which seem remote from each other in the individual are perhaps all equally near in the universal. Space itself, as we know it, may be practically annihilated in the consciousness of a larger space of which it is but the superficies; and a person living in London may not unlikely find that he has a backdoor opening quite simply and unceremoniously out in Bombay.

"The true quality of the soul," said the Guru one day, "is that of space, by which it is at rest, everywhere. But this space (Akása) within the soul is far above the ordinary material space. The whole of the latter, including all the suns and stars, appears to you then, as it were, but an atom of the former"—and here he held up his fingers as though crumbling a speck of dust between them.

"At rest everywhere," "Indifference," "Equality."

This was one of the most remarkable parts of the Guru's teaching. Though (for family reasons) maintaining many of the observances of caste himself, and though holding and teaching that for the mass of the people caste rules were quite necessary, he never ceased to insist that when the time came for a man (or woman) to be "emancipated" all these rules must drop aside as of no importance—all distinction of castes, classes, all sense of superiority or self-goodness—of right and wrong even—and the most absolute sense of Equality must prevail towards every one, and determination in its expression. Certainly it was remarkable (though I knew that the sacred books contained it) to find this germinal principle of Western democracy so vividly active and at work deep down beneath the innumerable layers of Oriental social life and custom. But so it is; and nothing shows better the relation between the West and the East than this fact.

This sense of Equality, of Freedom from regulations and confinements, of Inclusiveness, and of the Life that "rests everywhere," belongs, of course, more to the cosmic or universal part of man than to the individual part. To the latter it is always a stumbling-block and an offence. It is easy to show that men are not equal, that they cannot be free, and to point the absurdity of a life that is indifferent and at rest under all conditions. Nevertheless, to the larger consciousness these are basic facts, which underlie the common life of humanity, and feed the very individual that denies them.

Thus repeating the proviso that in using such terms as cosmic and universal consciousness we do not commit ourselves to the theory that the instant a man leaves the personal part of him he enters into absolutely unlimited and universal knowledge, but only into a higher order of perception—and admitting the intricacy and complexity of the region so roughly denoted by these terms, and the microscopical character of our knowledge about it—we may say once more, also as a roughest generalisation, that the quest of the East has been this universal consciousness, and that of the West the personal or individual consciousness. As is well known, the East has its various sects and schools of philosophy, with subtle discriminations of qualities, essences, godheads, devilhoods, etc., into which I do not propose to go, and which I should feel myself quite incompetent to deal with. Leaving all these aside, I will keep simply to these two rough Western terms, and try to consider further the question of the *methods* by which the Eastern student sets himself to obtain the cosmic state, or such higher order of consciousness as he does encompass.

Paramaguru Swami

(Lived many years in the forests of S. India and Ceylon)

CHAPTER X

METHODS OF ATTAINMENT

THE subject of the methods used by the yogis for the attainment of another order of consciousness has its physical, its mental, and its moral sides—and doubtless other sides as well.

Beginning with the physical side, it is probable that the discounting or repression of the physical brain—or of that part of it which is the seat of the primary consciousness—is the most important: on the theory that the repression of the primary consciousness opens the way for the manifestation of any other consciousness that may be present. Thus hypnotism lulls or fatigues the ordinary brain into a complete torpor—so allowing the phenomena connected with the secondary consciousness to come out into the greater prominence. It need not be supposed that hypnotism *induces* the secondary consciousness, but only that it removes that other consciousness which ordinarily conceals or hinders its expression. Some of the methods adopted by the yogis are undoubtedly of this hypnotic character, such as the sitting or standing for long periods absolutely fixed in one position; staring at the sun or other object; repeating a word or phrase over and over again for thousands of times, etc.; and the clairvoyant and other results produced seem in many respects very similar to the results of Western hypnotism. The yogi, however, by immense persistence in his practices, and by using his own will to effect the change of consciousness, instead of surrendering himself into the power of another person, seems to be able to transfer his "I" or *ego* into the new region, and to remember on his return to ordinary consciousness what he has seen there; whereas the hypnotic subject seems to be divided into a double *ego*, and as a rule remembers nothing in the primary state of what occurred to him in the secondary.

Others of the yogis adopt prolonged fasting, abstinence from sleep, self-torture, and emaciation, with the same object—namely, the reduction of the body, and apparently with somewhat similar results—though in these cases not only insight is supposed to be gained, but added powers over nature, arising from the intense forces of control put forth and educed by these exercises. The fact that the *Siddhi* or miraculous powers can be gained in this way is so universally accepted and taken for granted in India that (even after making all allowances) it is difficult not to be carried away on the stream of belief. And, indeed, when one considers the known powers of the will—cultivated as it is to but a feeble degree amongst most of us—there seems to be an inherent probability in the case. The Adepts, however, as a rule, though entirely agreeing that the attainment of the Siddhi powers is *possible*, strongly condemn the quest of them by these methods—saying with great justice that the mere fact of a quest of this kind is a breach of the law of Indifference and Trust, and that the quest being instigated by some desire—ambition, spiritual pride, love of gain, or what not—necessarily ends either by stultifying itself, or by feeding the desire, and, if some powers are gained, by the devotion of them to evil ends.

Thus the methods that are mainly physical produce certain results—clairvoyances and controls—which are largely physical in their character, and are probably for the most part more or less morbid and dangerous. They are, however, very widely spread among the inferior classes of yogis all over India, and the performances which spring from them, by exciting the fear and wonder of the populace, often become—as in the case of mesmeric performances in the West—a source of considerable gain to the chief actor.

There remain two other classes of methods—the mental and the moral.

Of the mental no doubt the most important is the Suppression of Thought—and it is not unlikely that this may have, when once understood, a far-reaching and important influence on our Western life—overridden and dominated as it is by a fever of Thought which it can by no means control. Nothing, indeed, strikes one more as marking the immense contrast between the East and the West than, after leaving Western lands, where the ideal of life is to have an almost insanely active brain and to be perpetually on the war-path with fearful and wonderful projects and plans and purposes, to come to India and to find its leading men—men of culture and learning and accomplishment—deliberately passing beyond all these and addressing themselves to the task of effacing their own thoughts, effacing all their own projects and purposes in order that the diviner consciousness may enter in and occupy the room so prepared.

The effacement of projects and purposes—which comes to much the same thing as the control of desire—belongs more properly to the *moral* side of the question, and may be considered later on. The subjection of Thought—which obviously is very closely connected with the subjection of Desire—may, however, be considered here.

The *Gñana-yogis* (so called to distinguish them from the *Karma-yogis*, who rely more upon the external and physical methods) adopt two practices—(1) that of intense concentration of the thoughts on a fixed object; (2) that of the effacement of thought altogether.

(1) The thoughts may be fixed on a definite object—for instance, on one's own breathing—the inflow and outflow of the atmosphere through the channels of the physical body. The body must be kept perfectly still and motionless for a long period—so that it may pass entirely out of consciousness—and the thoughts fixed on the regulated calm tide of respiration, to the complete exclusion of every other subject. Or the name of an object—a flower, for instance—may be repeated incessantly—the image of the object being called up at the same time—till at last the name and the image of the object blend and become indistinguishable in the mind.

Such practices have their literal and their spiritual sides. If carried out merely as formulæ, they evidently partake of a mesmeric (self-mesmeric) character, and ultimately induce mesmeric states of consciousness.* If carried out with a strong sense of

* The Rev. H. Callaway, in a paper on "Divination among

their inner meaning—the presence of the vast cosmic life in the breathing, the endeavor to realise Brahma himself in the flower or other object contemplated—they naturally induce a deeper sense of the universal life and consciousness than that which belongs to the mesmeric state. Anyhow, they teach a certain power and control over the thoughts; and it is a doctrine much insisted on by the Gurus that in life generally the habit of the undivided concentration of the mind on that which one is doing is of the utmost importance. The wandering of the mind, its division and distraction, its openness to attack by brigand cares and anxieties, its incapacity to heartily enjoy itself in its work, not only lame and cripple and torment it in every way, but are a mark of the want of that faith which believes in the Now as the divine moment, and takes no thought for the Morrow. To concentrate at all times wholly and unreservedly in what you are doing at the moment is, they say, a distinct step in Gñánam.

(2) The next step, the effacement of Thought, is a much more difficult one. Only when the power of concentration has been gained can this be attempted with any prospect of success. The body must be kept, as before, perfectly motionless, and in a quiet place, free from disturbance; not in an attitude of ease or slumber, but sitting or standing erect with muscles tense. All will-power is required, and the greatest vigilance. Every thought must be de-

the Natives of Natal" (*Journal of the Anthropological Institute*, vol. i. p. 176), says that the natives, "in order to become clairvoyant, attempt to effect intense concentration and abstraction of the mind—an abstraction even from their own thoughts." And this is done by herdsmen and chiefs alike—though, of course, with varying success.

stroyed on the instant of its appearance. But the enemy is subtle, and failure—over a long period—inevitable. Then when success seems to be coming and Thought is dwindling, Oblivion, the twin-foe, appears and must also be conquered. For if Thought merely gives place to Sleep, what is there gained? After months, but more probably years, of intermittent practice the power of control grows; curious but distinct physiological changes take place; one day the student finds that Thought has gone: he stands for a moment in Oblivion; then *that* veil lifts, and there streams through his being a vast and illumined consciousness, glorious, that fills and overflows him, "surrounding him so that he is like a pot in water, which has the liquid within it and without." In this consciousness there is divine knowledge but no thought. It is *Samádhi*, the universal "I Am."

Whatever people may think of the reality of this "Samádhi," of the genuineness or the universality of the consciousness obtained in it, etc. (and these are questions which, of course, require examination), it is incontestable that for centuries and centuries it has been an object of the most strenuous endeavor to vast numbers even of the very acutest and most capable intellects of India. Earthly joys paled before this ecstasy; the sacred literatures are full of its praise. That there lurks here some definite and important fact of experience is, I think, obvious—though it is quite probable that it is not yet really understood, either by the East that discovered it or the West that has criticised it.

Leaving, however, for the present the consideration of this ultimate and transcendent result of the effacement of Thought, and freely admitting that the

Eastern devotees have in the ardor of their pursuit of it been often led into mere absurdities and excesses—that they have in some cases practically mutilated their thinking powers—that they have refrained from speech for such prolonged years that at last not only the tongue but the brain itself refused to act—that they have in instances reduced themselves to the condition of idiots and babbling children, and rendered themselves incapable of carrying on any kind of work ordinarily called useful—admitting all this, it still remains true, I think, that even in its lower aspects this doctrine is of vast import to-day in the West.

For we moderns, while we have dominated Nature and external results in the most extraordinary way through our mechanical and other sciences, have just neglected this other field of mastery over our own internal mechanism. We pride ourselves on our athletic feats, but some of the performances of the Indian fakirs in the way of mastery over the *internal* processes of the body—processes which in ordinary cases have long ago lapsed into the region of the involuntary and unconscious—such as holding the breath over enormous periods, or reversing the peristaltic action of the alimentary canal throughout its entire length—are so astonishing that for the most part the report of them only excites incredulity among us, and we can hardly believe—what I take it is a fact—that these physiological powers have been practised till they are almost reduced to a science.

And if we are unwilling to believe in this internal mastery over the body, we are perhaps almost equally unaccustomed to the idea of mastery over our own inner thoughts and feelings. That a man should be a prey to any thought that chances to take possession of his mind is commonly among us assumed as unavoidable. It may be a matter of regret that he should be kept awake all night from anxiety as to the issue of a lawsuit on the morrow, but that he should have the power of determining whether he be kept awake or not seems an extravagant demand. The image of an impending calamity is no doubt odious, but its very odiousness (we say) makes it haunt the mind all the more pertinaciously—and it is useless to try to expel it.

Yet this is an absurd position for man, the heir of all the ages, to be in: hag-ridden by the flimsy creatures of his own brain. If a pebble in our boot torments us we expel it. We take off the boot and shake it out. And once the matter is fairly understood it is just as easy to expel an intruding and obnoxious thought from the mind. About this there ought to be no mistake, no two opinions. The thing is obvious, clear, and unmistakable. It should be as easy to expel an obnoxious thought from your mind as to shake a stone out of your shoe; and till a man can do that, it is just nonsense to talk about his ascendancy over Nature, and all the rest of it. He is a mere slave and a prey to the bat-winged phantoms that flit through the corridors of his own brain.

Yet the weary and careworn faces that we meet by thousands, even among the affluent classes of civilisation, testify only too clearly how seldom this mastery is obtained. How rare, indeed, to meet a *man*! How common rather to discover a creature hounded on by tyrant thoughts (or cares or desires), cowering, wincing under the lash—or perchance priding himself to run merrily in obedience to a driver that rattles the reins and persuades him that he is free—whom we cannot converse with in careless *tête-à-tête* because that alien presence is always there, on the watch.

It is one of the most prominent doctrines of the Gñánis that the power of expelling thoughts, or if need be, of killing them dead on the spot, *must* be attained. Naturally the art requires practice; but like other arts, when once acquired, there is no more mystery or difficulty about it. And it is worth practice. It may, indeed, fairly be said that life only begins when this art has been acquired. For obviously, when instead of being ruled by individual thoughts, the whole flock of them in their immense multitude and variety and capacity is ours to direct and despatch and employ where we list ("for He maketh the winds his messengers and the flaming fire his minister"), life becomes a thing so vast and grand compared with what it was before that its former condition may well appear almost antenatal.

If you can kill a thought dead, for the time being, you can do anything else with it that you please. And therefore it is that this power is so valuable. And it not only frees a man from mental torment (which is nine-tenths at least of the torment of life), but it gives him a concentrated power of handling mental work absolutely unknown to him before. The two things are correlative to each other. As already said, this is one of the principles of Gñánam. While at work your thought is to be absolutely concentrated in it, undistracted by anything whatever irrelevant to the matter in hand—pounding away like a great engine, with giant power and perfect economy—no wear and tear of friction, or dislocation of parts, owing to the working of different forces at the same time. Then, when the work is finished, if there is no more occasion for the use of the machine, it must stop equally absolutely—stop entirely—no *worrying* (as if a parcel of boys were allowed to play their devilments with a locomotive as soon as it was in the shed)—and the man must retire into that region of his consciousness where his true self dwells.

I say the power of the thought-machine itself is enormously increased by this faculty of letting it alone on the one hand and of using it singly and with concentration on the other. It becomes a true tool, which a master-workman lays down when done with, but which only a bungler carries about with him all the time to show that he is the possessor of it.

Then on and beyond the work turned out by the tool itself is the knowledge that comes to us apart from its use: when the noise of the workshop is over, and mallet and plane laid aside—the faint sounds coming through the open window from the valley and the far seashore: the dim fringe of diviner knowledge, which begins to grow, poor thing, as soon as the eternal click-clack of thought is over—the extraordinary intuitions, perceptions, which, though partaking in some degree of the character of thought, spring from entirely different conditions, and are the forerunners of a changed consciousness.

At first they appear miraculous, but it is not so. They are not miraculous, for they are always there.

(The stars are always there.) It is we who are miraculous in our inattention to them. In the systemic or secondary or cosmic consciousness of man (I daresay all these ought to be distinguished, but I lump them together for the present) lurk the most minute and varied and far-reaching intuitions and perceptions—some of them in their swiftness and subtlety outreaching even those of the primary consciousness—but to them we do not attend, because Thought, like a pied piper, is ever capering and fiddling in front of us. And when Thought is gone, lo! we are asleep. To open your eyes in that region which is neither Night nor Day is to behold strange and wonderful things.

As already said, the subjection of Thought is closely related to the subjection of Desire, and has consequently its specially moral as well as its specially intellectual relation to the question in hand. Nine-tenths of the scattered or sporadic thought with which the mind usually occupies itself when not concentrated on any definite work is what may be called self-thought—thought of a kind which dwells on and exaggerates the sense of self. This is hardly realised in its full degree till the effort is made to suppress it; and one of the most excellent results of such an effort is that with the stilling of all the phantoms which hover round the lower self, one's relations to others, to one's friends, to the world at large, and one's perception of all that is concerned in these relations, come out into a purity and distinctness unknown before. Obviously, while the mind is full of the little desires and fears which concern the local self, and is clouded over by the thought-images which such desires and fears evoke, it is impossible that it should see and understand the greater facts beyond and its own relation to them. But with the subsiding of the former the great Vision begins to dawn; and a man never feels less alone than when he has ceased to think whether he is alone or not.

It is in this respect that the subjection of desire is really important. There is no necessity to suppose that desire, in itself, is an evil; indeed, it is quite conceivable that it may fall into place as a useful and important element of human nature—though certainly one whose importance will be found to dwindle and gradually disappear as time goes on. The trouble for us is, in our present state, that desire is liable to grow to such dimensions as to overcloud the world for us, emprison, and shut us out from inestimable Freedom beneath its sway. Under such circumstances it evidently is a nuisance, and has to be dominated. No doubt certain sections of the Indian and other ascetic philosophies have taught the absolute extinction of desire, but we may fairly regard these as cases—so common in the history of all traditional teaching—of undue prominence given to a special detail, and of the exaltation of the letter of the doctrine above the spirit.

The moral element (at which we have now arrived) in the attainment of a higher order of consciousness is, of course, recognised by all the great Indian teachers as of the first importance. The sacred books, the sermons of Buddha, the discourses of the present-day Gurus, all point in the same direction. Gentleness, forbearance towards all, abstention from giving pain, especially to the animals, the recognition of the divine spirit in every creature down to the lowest, the most absolute sense of equality and the most absolute candor, an undisturbed serene mind, free from anger, fear, or any excessive and tormenting desire — these are all insisted on.

Thus though physical and mental conditions are held—and rightly—to be important, the moral conditions are held to be at least equally important. Nevertheless, in order to guard against misconception, which in so complex a subject may easily arise, it is necessary to state here—what I have hinted before—that different sections and schools among the devotees place a very different respective value upon the three sets of conditions—some making more of the physical, others of the mental, and others again of the moral—and that, as may be easily guessed, the results attained by the various schools differ considerably in consequence.

The higher esoteric teachers naturally lay the greatest stress on the moral, but any account of their methods would be defective which passed over or blinked the fact that they go *beyond* the moral—because this fact is in some sense of the essence of the Oriental inner teaching. Morality, it is well understood, involves the conception of oneself as distinct from others, as distinct from the world, and presupposes a certain antagonism between one's own interests and those of one's fellows. One "sacrifices" one's own interests to those of another, or "goes out of one's way" to help him. All such ideas must be entirely left behind if one is to reach the central illumination. They spring from ignorance, and are the products of darkness. On no word did the "Grammarian" insist more strongly than on the word Non-differentiation. You are not even to differentiate yourself in thought from others; you are not to begin to regard yourself as separate from them. Even to talk about helping others is a mistake; it is vitiated by the delusion that you and they are twain. So closely does the subtle Hindu mind go to the mark! What would our bald commercial philanthropy, our sleek æsthetic altruism, our scientific isophily, say to such teaching? All the little self-satisfactions which arise from the sense of duty performed, all the cheese-parings of equity between oneself and others, all the tiny wonderments whether you are better or worse than your neighbour, have to be abandoned; and you have to learn to live in a world in which the chief fact is *not* that you are distinct from others, but that you are a part of and integral with them. This involves, indeed, a return to the communal order of society, and difficult as this teaching is for us in this day to realise, yet there is no doubt that it must lie at the heart of the Democracy of the future, as it has lain, germinal, all these centuries in the hidden womb of the East.

Nor from Nature. You are not to differentiate yourself from Nature. We have seen that the Guru Tilleináthan spoke of the operations of the external world as "I," having dismissed the sense of difference between himself and them. It is only under these, and such conditions as these, that the little mortal creature gradually becomes aware of What he is.

This non-differentiation is the final deliverance. When it enters in the whole burden of absurd cares, anxieties, duties, motives, desires, fears, plans, purposes, preferences, etc., rolls off and lies like mere lumber on the ground. The winged spirit is free, and takes its flight. It passes through the veil of mortality and leaves that behind. Though I say this non-differentiation is the final deliverance (from the bonds of illusion), I do not say it is the final experience. Rather I should be inclined to think it is only the beginning of many experiences. As, in the history of man and the higher animals, the consciousness of self—the local self—has been the basis of an enormous mass of perceptions, intuitions, joys, sufferings, etc., incalculable and indescribable in multitudinousness and variety, so, in the history of man and the angels, will the consciousness of the cosmic and universal life—the true self underlying—become the basis of another and far vaster knowledge.

There is one respect in which the specially Eastern teaching commonly appears to us Westerners—and on the whole I am inclined to think justly—defective; and that is in its little insistence on the idea of Love. While, as already said, a certain gentleness and forbearance and passive charity is a decided feature of Indian teaching and life, one cannot help noting the absence—or less prominence, at anyrate—of that positive spirit of love and human helpfulness which in some sections of Western society might almost be called a devouring passion. Though with plentiful exceptions, no doubt, yet there is a certain quiescence and self-inclusion and absorbedness in the Hindu ideal, which amounts almost to coldness; and this is the most curious, because Hindu society—till within the last few years at anyrate—has been based upon the most absolutely communal foundation. But perhaps this fact of the communal structure of society in India is just the reason why the social sentiment does not seek impetuously for expression there: while in Europe, where existing institutions are a perpetual denial of it, its expression becomes all the more determined and necessary. However that may be, I think the fact may be admitted of a difference between the East and West in this respect. Of course, I am not speaking of those few who may attain to the consciousness of non-differentiation, because in their case the word love must necessarily change its meaning; nor am I speaking of the specially individual and sexual and amatory love, in which there is no reason to suppose the Hindus deficient; but I am rather alluding to the fact that in the West we are in the habit of looking on devotion to other humans (widening out into the social passion) as the most natural way of losing one's self-limitations and passing into a larger sphere of life and consciousness: while in the East this method is little thought of or largely neglected, in favor of the concentration of oneself in the divine, and mergence in the universal in that way.

I think this contrast—taking it quite roughly—may certainly be said to exist. The Indian teachers, the sacred books, the existing instruction, centre consciously or unconsciously round the development of Will-power. By will to surrender the will; by determination and concentration to press inward and upward to that portion of one's being which belongs to the universal, to conquer the body, to conquer the thoughts, to conquer the passions and emotions; always will, and will-power. And here again we have a paradox, because in their quiescent, gentle, and rather passive external life—so different from the push and dominating energy of the Western nations—there is little to make one expect such force. But while modern Europe and America has spent its Will in the mastery of the external world, India has reserved hers for the conquest of inner and spiritual kingdoms. In their hypnotic phenomena, too, the yogis exhibit the force of will, and this differentiates their hypnotism from that of the West, in which the patient is operated upon by another person. In the latter there is a danger of loss of will-power, but in the former (auto-hypnotism) will-power is no doubt gained, while at the same time hypnotic states are induced. Suggestion, which is such a powerful agent in hypnotism, acts here too, and helps to knit the body together, pervading it with a healing influence, and bringing the lower self under the direct domination of the higher; and in this respect the Guru to some extent stands in the place of the operator, while the yogi is his subject.

Thus in the East the Will constitutes the great path; but in the West the path has been more specially through Love—and probably will be. The great teachers of the West—Plato, Jesus, Paul—have indicated this method rather than that of the ascetic will; though, of course, there have not been wanting exponents of both sides. The one method means the gradual dwindling of the local and external self through inner concentration and aspiration, the other means the enlargement of the said self through affectional growth and nourishment, till at last it can contain itself no longer. The bursting of the sac takes place; the life is poured out, and, ceasing to be local, becomes universal. Of this method Whitman forms a signal instance. He is egotistic enough in all conscience; yet at last, through his immense human sympathy, and through the very enlargement of his *ego* thus taking place, the barriers break down and he passes out and away.

> "O Christ! This is mastering me!
> In at the conquered doors they crowd. I am possessed.
>
> . . . .
>
> I embody all presences outlawed or suffering;
> See myself in prison shaped like another man,
> And feel the dull unintermitted pain.
>
> . . . .
>
> Enough! enough! enough!
> Somehow I have been stunned. Stand back!
> Give me a little time beyond my cuffed head, slumbers, dreams, gaping;
> I discover myself on the verge of a usual mistake.
> That I could forget the mockers and insults!
> That I could forget the trickling tears, and the blows of bludgeons and hammers!
> That I could look with a separate look on my own crucifixion and bloody crowning."

But such expressions as these—in which the passion of humanity wraps the speaker into another sphere of existence—are *not* characteristic of the East, and are not found in the Indian scriptures. When its time comes the West will probably adopt this method of the liberation of the human soul—through love—rather than the specially Indian method—of the Will; though doubtless both have to be, and will be, in the future to a large extent concurrently used. Different races and peoples incline according to their idiosyncrasies to different ways; each individual even—as is quite recognised by the present-day Gurus—has his special line of approach to the supreme facts. It is possible that when the Western races once realise what lies beneath this great instinct of humanity, which seems in some ways to be their special inspiration, they will outstrip even the Hindus in their entrance to and occupation of the new fields of consciousness.

CHAPTER XI

TRADITIONS OF THE ANCIENT WISDOM-RELIGION

I HAVE dwelt so far on the nature of certain experiences (which I have not, however, attempted to describe) and on the methods by which, specially in India, they are sought to be obtained; and I have done so in general terms, and with an endeavor to assimilate the subject to Western ideas and to bring it into line with modern science and speculation. I propose in this chapter to dwell more especially on the formal side of our friend's teaching, which will bring out into relief the special character of Eastern thought and its *differences* from our present-day modes of thought.

I must, however, again warn the reader against accepting anything I say, except with care and reserve, and especially not to broaden out into sweeping generalities any detailed statement I may happen to make. People often ask for some concise account of Indian teaching and religion. Supposing someone were to ask for a concise account of the Christian teaching and religion, which of us, with all our familiarity with the subject, could give an account which the others would accept? From the question whether Jesus and Paul were initiates in the Eastern mysteries—as the modern Gurus claim that they were, and as I think there can be no doubt that they were—either by tradition or by spontaneous evolution; through the question of the similarity and differences of their teaching; the various schools of early Christianity; the Egyptian influences; the Gnostic sects and philosophy; the formation and history of the Church, its organisations, creeds, and doctrines; mediæval Christianity and its relation to Aristotle; the mystic teachers of the thirteenth and fourteenth centuries; the ascetic and monastic movements; the belief in alchemy and witchcraft; the miracles of the Saints; the Protestant movement and doctrines, etc. etc.; down to the innumerable petty sects of to-day and all their conflicting views on the Atonement and the sacraments and the inspiration of the Bible, and all the rest of it—who would be so bold as to announce the gist and *résumé* of it all in a few brief sentences? Yet the great Indian evolution of religious thought—while historically more ancient—is at least equally vast and complex and bewildering in its innumerable ramifications. I should feel entirely incompetent to deal with it as a whole—and here, at anyrate, am only touching upon the personality and utterances of one teacher, belonging to a particular school, the South Indian.

This Guru was, as I have said, naturally one of those who insisted largely—though not by any means exclusively—on the moral and ultra-moral sides of the teaching; and from this point of view his personality was particularly remarkable. His gentleness and kindliness, combined with evident power; and inflexibility and intensity underlying; his tense eyes, as of the seer, and gracious lips and expression, and ease and dignity of figure; his entire serenity and calm—though with lots of vigor when needed — all these were impressive. But perhaps I was most struck—as the culmination of character and manhood—by his perfect simplicity of manner. Nothing could be more unembarrassed, unselfconscious, direct to the point in hand, free from kinks of any kind. Sometimes he would sit on his sofa-couch in the little cottage, not unfrequently, as I have said, with bare feet gathered beneath him; sometimes he would sit on a chair at the table; sometimes in the animation of discourse his muslin wrap would fall from his shoulder, unnoticed, showing a still graceful figure, thin, but by no means emaciated; sometimes he would stand for a moment, a tall and dignified form; yet always with the same ease and grace and absence of self-consciousness that only the animals and a few among human beings show. It was this that made him seem very near to one, as if the ordinary barriers which divide people were done away with; and if this was non-differentiation working within, its external effect was very admirable.

I dwell perhaps the more on these points of character, which made me feel an extraordinary *rapprochement* and unspoken intimacy to this man, because I almost immediately found on acquaintance that on the plane of ordinary thought and scientific belief we were ever so far asunder, with only a small prospect, owing to difficulties of language, etc., of ever coming to an understanding. I found—though this, of course, gave a special interest to his conversation—that his views of astronomy, physiology, chemistry, politics, and the rest, were entirely unmodified by Western thought and science—and that they had come down through a long line of oral tradition, continually reinforced by references to the sacred books, from a most remote antiquity. Here was a man who, living in a native principality under an Indian rajah, and skilled in the learning of his own country, had probably come across very few English at all till he was of mature years, had not learned the English language, and had apparently troubled himself but little about Western ideas of any kind. I am not a stickler for modern science myself, and think many of its conclusions very shaky; but I confess it gave me a queer feeling when I found a man of so subtle intelligence and varied capacity calmly asserting that the earth was the centre of the physical universe and that the sun revolved about it! With all seriousness he turned out the theory (which old Lactantius *Indicopleustes* introduced from the East into Europe about the third century A.D.)—namely, that the earth is flat, with a great hill, the celebrated Mount Meru, in the north, behind which the sun and moon and other heavenly bodies retire in their order to rest. He explained that an eclipse of the moon (then going on) was caused by one of the two "dark planets," Raku or Kètu (which are familiar to astrology), concealing it from view. He said (and this is also an ancient doctrine) that there were 1008 solar or planetary systems similar to ours, some *above* the earth, some *below*, and some on either hand. As to the earth itself, it had been destroyed and re-created many times in successive æons, but there had never been a time when the divine knowledge had not existed on it. There had always been an Indian (*gñána bhumi*, or Wisdom-land, in contra-distinction to the Western *bhoga bhumi*, or land of pleasure), and always Vedas or Upanishads (or books corresponding) brought by divine teachers. (About modern theories of submerged continents and lower races in the far past he did not appear to know anything or to have troubled his head, nor did he put forth any views on this subject of the kind mentioned by Sinnett in his *Esoteric Buddhism.* Many of his views, however, were very similar to those given in that book.)

His general philosophy appeared to be that of the Siddhantic system, into which I do not propose to go in any detail, as it may be found in the books; and all such systems are hopelessly dull, and may be said to carry their own death-warrants written on their faces. The Indian systems of philosophy bear a strong resemblance to the Gnostic systems of early Christian times, which latter were no doubt derived from the East. They all depend upon the idea of emanation, which is undoubtedly an important idea, and corresponds to some remarkable facts of consciousness; but the special forms in which the idea is cast in the various systems are not very valuable.

The universe in the Siddhantic system is composed of five elements—(1) ether; (2) air; (3) fire; (4) water; and (5) earth; and to get over the obvious difficulties which arise from such a classification, it is explained that these are not the *gross* ether, air, fire, water, and earth that we know, but *subtle* elements of the same name, which are themselves perfectly pure, but by their admixture produce the gross elements. Thus the air we know is not a true element, but is formed by a mixture of the subtle air, with small portions of the subtle ether, subtle fire, subtle water, and subtle earth, and so on. This explains how it is there may be various kinds of air or of water or of earth. Then the five subtle elements give rise to the five forms of sensation in the order named—(1) Sound; (2) Touch; (3) Form; (4) Taste; (5) Smell; and to the five corresponding organs of sense. Also, there are five intellectual faculties evolved by admixture from the subtle elements, namely—(1) the inner consciousness, which has the quality of ether or space; (2) the organ of perception and Thought (*manas*), which has the quality of aërial agitation and motion; (3) Reason (*buddhi*), which has the quality of light and fire; (4) Desire (*chittam*), which has the emotional rushing character of water; (5) the I-making faculty (*ahankâra*), which has the hardness and resistance of the earth. Also the five organs of action—the voice, the hands, the feet, the anus, and the penis—in the same order; and the five vital airs which are supposed to pervade the different parts of the body and to impel their action.

This is all very neat and compact. Unfortunately, it shares the artificial character which all systems of philosophy have, and which makes it quite impossible to accept any of them. I think our friend quite recognised this, for more than once he said, and quoted the sacred books to the same effect, that "Everything which can be thought is untrue." In this respect the Indian philosophy altogether excels our Western systems (except the most modern). It takes the bottom out of its own little bucket in the most impartial way.

Nevertheless, whatever faults they may have, and however easy it may be to attack their thought-forms, the great Indian systems (and those of the West the same) are no doubt based upon deep-lying facts of consciousness, which it must be our business some time to disentangle. I believe there are facts of consciousness underlying such unlikely things as the evolution of the five subtle elements, even though the *form* of the doctrine may be largely fantastic. The primal element, according to this doctrine, is the ether or *space* (*Akása*), the two ideas of space and ether being curiously identified, and the other elements—air, fire, etc.—are evolved in succession from this one by a process of thickening or condensation. Now this consciousness of space—not the material space, but the space within the soul—is a form of the supreme consciousness in man, the *sat-chit-ánanda* Brahm—Freedom, Equality, Extension, Omnipresence—and is accompanied by a sense which has been often described as a combination of all the senses—sight, hearing, touch, etc.—in one, so that they do not even appear differentiated from each other. In the course of the descent of the consciousness from this plane to the plane of ordinary life (which may be taken to correspond to the creation of the actual world) the transcendent space-consciousness goes through a sort of obscuration or condensation, and the senses become differentiated into separate and distinct faculties. This—or something like it—is a distinct experience. It may well be that the formal doctrine about the five elements is merely an attempt necessarily very defective, since these things *cannot* be adequately expressed in that way—to put the thing into a form of thought. And so with other doctrines: some may contain a real *inhalt*, others may be merely ornamental thought-fringes, put on for the sake of logical symmetry, or what not. In its *external* sense the doctrine of the evolution of the other elements successively by condensation from the ether is after all not so far removed from our modern scientific ideas. For the chief difference between the air, and other such gases, and the ether is supposed by us to be the closeness of the particles in the former; then in the case of fire, the particles come into violent contact, producing light and heat; in fluids their contact has become continuous though mobile; and in the earth and other solids their contact is fixed.

However, whatever justification the formal analysis of man and the external world into their constituent parts may have or require, the ultimate object of the analysis in the Indian philosophy is to convince the pupil that He is a being apart from them all. "He whose perception is obscured mistakes the twenty-six *tatwas* (categories or 'thats') for himself, and is under the illusions of 'I' and 'mine.' To be liberated by the grace of a proper spiritual teacher from the operation of this obscuring power, and to realise that these are not self, constitute 'deliverance.'" Here is the ultimate fact of consciousness, which is the same, and equally true, whatever the analysis of the *tatwas* may be.

"The true quality of the Soul is that of space, by which it is at rest, everywhere. Then," continued the Guru, "comes the Air-quality, by which it moves with speed from place to place; then the Fire-quality, by which it discriminates; then the Water-quality, which gives it emotional flow; and then the Earth or self-quality, rigid and unyielding.

As these things evolve out of the soul, so they must involve again, into it and into Brahm."

To go with the five elements, etc., the system expounded by the Guru supposes five shells enclosing the soul. These, with the soul itself, and Brahm, the undifferentiated spirit lying within the soul, form seven planes or sections, as in the Esoteric Buddhism of Sinnett and the Theosophists. The divisions, however, are not quite identical in the two systems, which appear to be respectively North Indian and South Indian. In the North Indian we have (1) the material body; (2) the vitality; (3) the astral form; (4) the animal soul; (5) the human soul; (6) the soul proper; and (7) the undifferentiated spirit. In the South Indian we have (1) the material shell; (2) the shell of the vital airs; (3) the sensorial shell; (4) the cognitional shell; (5) the shell of oblivion and bliss in sleep; (6) the soul; and (7) the undifferentiated spirit. The two extremes seem the same in the two systems, but the intermediate layers differ. In some respects the latter system is the more effective; it has a stronger practical bearing than the other, and appears to be specially designed as a guide to action in the work of emancipation. In some respects the other system has a wider application. Neither, of course, have any particular value except as convenient forms of thought for their special purposes, and as very roughly embodying in their different degrees various experiences which the human consciousness passes through in the course of its evolution. "It is not till all the five shells have been successively peeled off that consciousness enters the soul, and it sees itself and the universal being as one. The first three are peeled off at each bodily death of the man, but they grow again out of what remains. It is not enough to pass beyond these, but beyond the other two also. Then when that is done the student enters into the fulness of the whole universe ; and with that joy no earthly joy can for a moment be compared."

"Death," he continued, "is usually great agony, as if the life were being squeezed out of every part—like the juice out of a sugar-cane—only for those who have already separated their souls from their bodies is it not so. For them it is merely a question of laying down the body at will, when its *karma* is worked out, or of retaining it, if need be, to prolonged years." It is commonly said that Vasishta, who first gave the sacred knowledge to mankind, is still living and providing for the earth ; and Tilleináthan Swamy is said to have seen Tiruválluvar, the pariah priest who wrote the *Kurral* over 1000 years ago. "In ordinary cases the last thoughts that cling to the body ('the ruling passion strong in death') become the seed of the next ensuing body."

In this system the outermost layer of that portion of the human being which survives death is the shell of thought (and desire). As the body is modified in every-day life by the action of the thought-forms within, and grows out of them, so the new body at some period after death grows out of the thought-forms that survive. "The body is built up by your thought, and not by your thought in this life only, but by the thought of previous lives."

Of the difficult question about hereditary likeness, suggesting that the body is also due to the thought of the parents, he gave no very detailed account,—only that the atomic soul is carried at some period after death by universal laws, or by its own affinities into a womb suitable for its next incarnation, where, finding kindred thought-forms and elements, it assimilates and grows from them, with the result of what is called family likeness.

Some of his expositions of Astrology were very interesting to me—particularly to find this world-old system with all its queer formalities and deep underlying general truths still passively (though I think not actively) accepted and handed down by so able an exponent—but I cannot record them at any length. The five operations of the divine spirit, namely—(1) Grace; (2) Obscuration; (3) Destruction; (4) Preservation; and (5) Creation, correspond to the five elements—space, air, fire, water, and earth—and are embodied in the nine planets, thus—(1) Raku and Kètu; (2) Saturn; (3) the Sun and Mars; (4) Venus, Mercury, and the Moon; (5) Jupiter. It is thus that the birth of a human being is influenced by the position of the planets—*i.e.* the horoscope. The male semen contains the five elements, and the composition of it is determined by the attitude of the nine planets in the sky! There seems here to be a glimmering embodiment of the deep-lying truth that the whole universe conspires in the sexual act, and that the orgasm itself is a flash of the universal consciousness; but the thought-forms of astrology are as indigestible to a mind trained in Western science as I suppose the thought-forms of the latter are to the philosopher of the East!

When I expostulated with the Guru about these, to us, crudities of Astrology, and about such theories as that of the flat earth, the cause of eclipses, etc., bringing the most obvious arguments to attack his position—he did not meet me with any arguments, being evidently unaccustomed to deal with the matter on that plane at all; but simply replied that these things had been seen "in pure consciousness," and that they *were* so. It appeared to me pretty clear, however, that he was not speaking authentically, as having seen them so himself, but simply recording again the tradition delivered in its time to him. And here is a great source of difficulty; for the force of tradition is so tremendous in these matters, and blends so, through the intimate relation of teacher and pupil, with the pupil's own experience, that I can imagine it difficult in some cases for the pupil to disentangle what is authentically his own vision from that which he has merely heard. Besides—as may be easily imagined—the whole system of teaching tends to paralyse activity on the thought-plane to such a degree that the spirit of healthy criticism has been lost, and things are handed down and accepted in an otiose way without ever being really questioned or properly envisaged. And, lastly, there is a cause which, I think, acts sometimes in the same direction—namely, that the *yogi* learns—either from habit or from actual experience of a superior order of consciousness—so to despise matters belonging to the thought-world, that he really does not care whether a statement is true or false, in the mundane sense—*i.e.* consistent or inconsistent with other statements belonging to the same plane. All these causes make it extremely difficult to arrive at what we should call truth as regards matters of fact—appearances alleged to have been seen, feats performed, or the occurrence of past events; and though there may be no prejudice against the *possibility* of them, it is wise—in cases where definite and unmistakable evidence is absent, to withhold the judgment either way, for or against their occurrence.

With regard to these primitive old doctrines of Astronomy, Astrology, Philology, Physiology, etc., handed down from far-back times and still embodied in the teaching of the Gurus, though it is impossible to accept them on the ordinary thought-plane, I think we may yet fairly conclude that there is an element of cosmic consciousness in them, or at any-rate in many of them, which has given them their vitality and seal of authority so to speak. I have already explained what I mean, in one or two cases. Just as in the old myths and legends (Andromeda, Cupid and Psyche, Cinderella and a great many more) an effort was made to embody indirectly, in ordinary thought-forms, things seen with the inner eye and which could not be expressed directly—so was the same process carried out in the old science. Though partly occupied with things of the thought-plane, it was also partly occupied in giving expression to things which lie behind that plane—which we in our Western sciences have neither discerned nor troubled ourselves about. Hence, though confused and defective and easily impugnable, it contains an element which is yet of value. Take the theory of the flat earth for instance, already mentioned, with Mount Meru in the north, behind which the sun and moon retire each day. At first it seems almost incredible that a subtle-brained, shrewd people should have entertained so crude a theory at all. But it soon appears that while being a rude explanation of external facts, and one which might commend itself to a superficial observer, it is also and in reality a description of certain internal phenomena seen. There are a sun and moon within, and there is a Mount Meru (so it is said) within, by which they are obscured. The universe within the soul and the universe without correspond and are the similitudes of each other, and so (theoretically at anyrate) the language which describes one should describe the other.

It is well known that much of the mediæval alchemy had this double signification—the terms used indicated two classes of facts. Sometimes the inner meaning preponderated, sometimes the outer; and it is not always easy to tell in the writings of the alchemists which is specially intended. This alchemical teaching came into Europe from the East—as we know; yet it was not without a feeling of surprise that I heard the Guru one day expounding as one of the ancient traditions of his own country a doctrine that I seemed familiar with as coming from Paracelsus or some such author—that of the transmutation of copper into gold by means of solidified mercury. There is a method, he explained, preserved in mystic language in some of the ancient books by which mercury can be rendered *solid.* This solid mercury has extraordinary properties: it is proof against the action of fire; if you hold a small piece of it in your mouth, arrows and bullets cannot harm you; and the mere touch of it will turn a lump of copper into gold.

Now this doctrine has been recognised by students of the mediæval alchemy to have an esoteric meaning. Quicksilver or mercury—as I think I have already mentioned—is an image or embodiment of thought itself, the ever-glancing, ever shifting; to render quicksilver solid is to fix thought, and so to enter into the transcendent consciousness. He who does that can be harmed neither by arrows nor by bullets; a touch of that diviner principle turns the man whose nature is but base copper into pure gold. The Guru, however, expounded this as if in a purely literal and external sense; and on my questioning him it became evident that he believed in some, at anyrate, of the alchemical transmutations in this sense—though what evidence he may have had for such belief did not appear.

I remember very well the evening on which this conversation took place. We were walking along an unfrequented bit of road or by-lane; the sky was transparent with the colors of sunset, the wooded hills a few miles off looked blue through the limpid air. He strode along—a tall dark figure, with coal-black eyes—on raised wooden sandals or clogs—his white wrapper loosely encircling him—with so easy and swift a motion that it was quite a consideration to keep up with him—discoursing all the while on the wonderful alchemical and medical secrets preserved from ages back in the *slokas* of the sacred books—how in order to safeguard this arcane knowledge, and to render it inaccessible to the vulgar, methods had been adopted of the transposition of words, letters, etc., which made the text mere gibberish except to those who had the key; how there still existed a great mass of such writings inscribed on palm and other leaves, and stored away in the temples and monasteries—though much had been destroyed—and so forth; altogether a strange figure—something uncanny and superhuman about it.

I found it difficult to believe that I was in the end of the nineteenth century, and not three or four thousand years back among the sages of the Vedic race; and indeed the more I saw of this Guru the more I felt persuaded (and still feel) that in general appearance, dress, mental attitude, and so forth, he probably resembled to an extraordinary degree those ancient teachers whose tradition he still handed down. The more one sees of India the more one learns to appreciate the enormous tenacity of custom and tradition there, and that the best means to realise its past may be to study its present life in the proper quarters.

His criticisms of the English, of English rule in India, and of social institutions generally, were very interesting—to me at anyrate—as coming from a man so perfectly free from Western "taint" and modern modes of thought, and who yet had had considerable experience of state policy and administration in his time, and who generally had circled a considerable experience of life. He said—what was quite a new idea to me, but in the most emphatic way—that the rule of the English in the time of the East India Company had been much better than it had become since under the Crown. Curiously enough, his charge was that "the Queen" had made it so entirely commercial. The sole idea now, he said, is money. Before '57 there had been some kind of State policy, some idea of a large and generous rule, and of the good of the people, but in the present day the rule was essentially feeble, with no defined policy of any kind except that of the money bag. This criticism impressed me much, as corroborating from an entirely independent source the growth of mere commercialism in Britain during late years, and of the nation-of-shopkeepers theory of government.

Going on to speak of government generally, his views would, I fear, hardly be accepted by the schools—they were more Carlylean in character. "States," he said, "must be ruled by Justice, and then they will succeed." (An ancient doctrine this, but curiously neglected all down history.) "A king should stand, and did stand in old times, as the representative of Siva (God). He is nothing in himself—no more than the people—his revenue is derived from them—he is elected by them—and he is in trust to administer justice—especially criminal justice. In the courtyard of the palace of Chola-King, near Tanjore, there hung at one time a bell which the rajah placed there in order that anyone feeling himself aggrieved might come and ring it, and so claim redress or judgment. 'Justice or Equality," he continued, "is the special attribute of God; and he who represents God, *i.e.* the king, must consider this before all things. The same with rich people—they are bound to serve and work for the poor, from whom their riches come."

This last sentence he repeated so often, at different times and in different forms, that he might almost have been claimed as a Socialist—certainly was a Socialist in the heart of the matter; and at anyrate this teaching shows how near the most ancient traditions come to the newest doctrines in these respects, and how far the unclean commercialism out of which we are just passing stands from either.

As to the English people, he seemed to think them

hopelessly plunged into materialism, but said that if they did turn to "sensible pursuits" (*i.e.* of divine knowledge) their perseverance and natural sense of justice and truth would, he thought, stand them in good stead. The difficulties of the gnosis in England were, however, very great; "those who do attain some degree of emancipation there do not know that they have attained; though having experience they lack knowledge." "You in the West," he continued, "say *O God, O God!* but you have no *definite* knowledge or methods by which you can attain to see God. It is like a man who knows there is *ghee* (butter) to be got out of a cow (*pasu*, metaph. for soul). He walks round and round the cow and cries, *O Ghee, O Ghee!* Milk pervades the cow, but he cannot find it. Then when he has learned to handle the teat, and has obtained the milk, he still cannot find the ghee. It pervades the milk and has also to be got by a definite method. So there is a definite method by which the divine consciousness can be educed from the soul, but it is only in India that complete instruction exists on this point—by which a man who is 'ripe' may systematically and without fail attain the object of his search, and by which the mass of the people may ascend as by a ladder from the very lowest stages to such 'ripeness.'"

India, he said, was the divine land, and the source from which the divine knowledge had always radiated over the earth. Sanskrit and Tamil were divine languages—all other languages being of lower caste and origin. In India the conditions were in every way favorable to attainment, but in other lands not so. Some Mohammedans had at different times adopted the Indian teaching and become Gñánis, but it had always been in India, and not in their own countries, that they had done so. Indeed, the Mohammedan religion, though so different from the Hindu, had come from India, and was due to a great Rishi who had quarrelled with the Brahmins and had established forms and beliefs in a spirit of opposition to them. When I asked him what he thought of Christ, he said he was probably an adept in gñánam, but his hearers had been the rude mass of the people and his teaching had been suited to their wants.

Though these views of his on the influence of India and its wisdom-religion on the world may appear, and probably are in their way, exaggerated, yet they are partly justified by two facts which appear to me practically certain: (1) that in every age of the world and in almost every country there has been a body of doctrine handed down, which, with whatever variations and obscurations, has clustered round two or three central ideas, of which, perhaps, that of emancipation from self through repeated births is the most important; so that there has been a kind of tacit understanding and freemasonry on this subject between the great teachers throughout history—from the Eastern sages, down through Pythagoras, Plato, Paul, the Gnostic schools, the great mediæval alchemists, the German mystics and others, to the great philosophers and poets of our own time; and that thousands of individuals on reaching a certain stage of evolution have corroborated, and are constantly corroborating, from their own experience the main points of this doctrine; and (2) that there must have existed in India, or in some neighboring region from which India drew its tradition, *before all history*, teachers who saw these occult facts and understood them well, probably better than the teachers of historical times, and who had themselves reached a stage of evolution at least equal to any that has been attained since.

If this is so then there is reason to believe that there is a distinct body of experience and knowledge into which the whole human race is destined to rise, and which there is every reason to believe will bring wonderful and added faculties with it. From whatever mere formalities or husks of tradition or abnormal growths have gathered round it in India, this has to be disentangled; but it is not now any more to be the heritage of India alone, but for the whole world. If, however, anyone should seek it for the advantage or glory to himself of added powers and faculties, his quest will be in vain, for it is an absolute condition of attainment that all action for self as distinct from others shall entirely cease.

INDIA

Great Pagoda in Temple at Tanjore

(192 feet high)

CHAPTER XII

THE SOUTH INDIAN TEMPLES

LEAVING Colombo by steamer one evening in the later part of January, I landed on the sandy, flat shores of Tuticorin the next day about noon. The deck was crowded with 250 of the poorest class of Tamils, coolies mostly, with women and children, lying in decent confusion heaped upon one another, passively but sadly enduring the evil motion of the ship and the cold night air. One man, nameless, unknown, and abjectly thin, died in the night, and was cast overboard. I was the only Englishman on board beside the captain and officers. Said the second officer, "Well, I would rather have these fellows than a lot of English emigrants. The lowest class of English are the damnedest, dirtiest, etceteraest etceteras in the world."

Tuticorin is a small place with a large cotton mill, several Roman Catholic churches and chapels, relics of Portuguese times, and a semi-Christianised, semi-wage-slaving native population. From there to Madras is about two days by rail through the great plains of the Carnatic, which stretch between the seashore and the Ghauts—long stretches of sand and scrub, scattered bushes and small trees, and the kittool palm ; paddy at intervals where the land is moister, and considerable quantities of cotton on the darker soil near Tuticorin ; mud and thatch villages under clumps of coco-palm (not such fine trees as in Ceylon); and places of village worship—a portico or shrine with a great clay elephant or half-circle of rude images of horses facing it; the women working in the fields or stacking the rice-straw in stacks similar to our corn-stacks; the men drawing water from their wells to run along the irrigation channels, or in some cases actually carrying the water in pots to pour over their crops!

These plains, like the plains of the Ganges, have been the scene of an advanced civilisation from early times, and have now for two thousand years at anyrate been occupied by the Tamil populations. Fergusson in his *History of Architecture* speaks of *thirty* great Dravidian temples to be found in this region, "any one of which must have cost as much to build as an English cathedral." I visited three, those of Mádura, Tanjore, and Chidámbaram, which I will describe, taking that at Tanjore first, as having the most definite form and plan.

I have already (Chap. VII.) given some account of a smaller Hindu temple. The temples in this region are on the same general plan. There is no vast interior as in a Western cathedral, but they depend for their effect rather upon the darkness and inaccessibility of the inner shrines and passages, and upon the gorgeous external assemblage of towers and porticos and tanks and arcades brought together within the same enclosure. At Mádura the whole circumference of the temple is over 1000 yards, and at Sri Rungam each side of the enclosure is as much as half-a-mile long. In every case there has no doubt been an original shrine of the god, round which buildings have accumulated, the external enclosure being thrown out into a larger and larger circumference as time went on; and in many cases the later buildings, the handsome outlying gateways or *gopuras* and towers, have by their size completely dwarfed the shrine to which they are supposed to be subsidiary, thus producing a poor artistic effect.

In the temple at Tanjore the great court is 170

Temple at Tanjore, General View

(Portico with colossal bull on the right, priests' quarters among trees on the left)

yards long by 85 wide. You enter through a gateway forming a pyramidal structure 40 or 50 feet high, ornamented with the usual carved figures of Siva and his demon doorkeepers, and find yourself in a beautiful courtyard, flagged, with an arcade running round three sides, the fourth side being occupied by priests' quarters; clumps of coco-palms and other trees throw a grateful shade here and there; in front of you rises the great pyramidal tower or pagoda, 190 feet high, which surmounts the main shrine, and between the shrine and yourself is an open portico on stone pillars, beneath which reposes a huge couchant bull, about six yards long and four yards high, said to be cut from a solid block of syenite brought 400 miles from the quarries. This bull is certainly very primitive work, and is quite brown and saturated with constant libations of oil; but whether it is 2700 years old, as the people here say, is another question. The difficulty of determining dates in these matters is very great; historical accuracy is unknown in this land; and architectural style gives but an uncertain clue, since it has probably changed but little. Thus we have the absurdity that while natives of education and intelligence are asserting on the one hand that some of these temples are five or even ten thousand years old, the Western architects assert, equally strongly, that they can find no work in them of earlier date than 1000 A.D., while much of it belongs to the sixteenth and seventeenth centuries. Probably the architects are, in the main, right. It is quite probable, however, that the inner shrines in most of these cases *are* extremely old, much older than 1000 A.D.; but they are so buried beneath later work, and access to them is so difficult, and if access were obtained their more primitive style would so baffle chronology that the question must yet remain undetermined.

Close to the bull is the *kampam* or flagstaff, and then, beyond, a flight of steps leading up to the main sanctuary and the tower or pagoda. The sanctuary is all fine and simple work of red sandstone, in which horizontal lines predominate. At its far end, and under the pagoda, would be, no doubt, the inner shrine or holy of holies—the *vimana* or womb of the temple, a cubical chamber—in which the *lingam* would be placed. Into these mysteries we did not penetrate, but contented ourselves with looking at the pagoda from the outside. It is a very dignified and reposeful piece of work, supposed by Fergusson to belong to the early part of the fourteenth century; ninety-six feet square at the base, with vertical sides for about fifty feet, and then gradually drawing in narrower through thirteen stories to the summit (see Plate at head of this chapter). The red sandstone walls at the base are finely and quietly panelled with statues of Siva—not grotesque, but dignified and even graceful—in the niches. Higher up in the pyramidal part the statues are fewer, and are mingled with couchant bulls and flame-like designs composed of multitudinous cobras and conches and discs (symbols of the god—who is lord of Time, the revolving disc, and of Space, represented by the sounding conch) in tiers of continually diminishing size to the summit, where a small dome—said to be also a single massive block of stone—is surmounted by a golden pinnacle. The natural red of the stone which forms the lower walls is artificially deepened in the panels, and the traces of blue and green tints remaining, together with silvery and brown incrustations of lichen in the upper parts, give a wonderful richness to the whole. I am afraid, however, that the pyramidal structure is not stone, but brick covered with plaster. The frequency of the bull everywhere throughout this and other Sivaite temples reminds one of the part played by the same animal in Persian and Egyptian worship, and of the import of the Zodiacal sign Taurus as a root-element of the solar religions. The general structure and disposition of these buildings might, I should think, also recall the Jewish and Egyptian temples.

All round the base of the great sanctuary and in other parts of the temple at Tanjore are immense inscriptions—in Telugu, says one of the Brahmins, but I cannot tell—some very fresh and apparently modern, others nearly quite obliterated.

The absolute incapacity shown by the Hindus for reasoned observation in religious matters was illustrated by my guide—who did not in other respects appear to be at all a stickler for his religion. When he first called my attention to the pagoda, he said, adding to his praise of its beauty, "Yes, and it never casts a shadow, never any shadow." Of course, I did not trouble to argue such a point, and as we were standing at the time on the sunlit side of the building, there certainly was no shadow visible *there.* Presently, however—after, say, half-an-hour, —we got round to the other side, and were *actually standing in the shadow,* which was then quite extensive, it being only about 9 A.M., and the sun completely hidden from us by the pagoda; I had forgotten all about the matter, when the guide said again and with enthusiasm, "And it has no shadow." Then, seeing my face (!) he added, "No, this is not the shadow." "But," said I, "it *is.*" "No," he repeated, "this is not the shadow of the *pagoda,* for that never casts any shadow"—and then he turned for corroboration to an old, half-naked Brahmin standing by, who, of course, repeated the formula

—and with an air of mechanical conviction which made me at once feel that further parley was useless.

It might seem strange, to anyone not acquainted with the peculiarities of human nature, that people should go on, perhaps for centuries, calmly stating an obvious contradiction in terms like that without ever, so to speak, turning a hair! But so it is, and I am afraid even we Westerners can by no means claim to be innocent of the practice. Among the Hindus, however, in connection with religion this feature is really an awkward one. Acute and subtle as they are, yet when religion comes on the field their presence of mind forsakes them, and they make the most wild and unjustifiable statements. I am sorry to say I have never witnessed a real good thungeing miracle myself. We have all heard plenty of stories of such things in India, and I have met various Hindus of ability and culture who evidently quite believed them, but (although quite willing and ready-equipped to believe them myself) I have always felt, since that experience of the shadow, that one "couldn't be too careful."

On either side of the great pagoda, and standing separate in the courtyard, are two quite small temples dedicated, one to Ganésa and the other to Soubramániya, very elegant, both of them; and one or two stone *pandals* or porticos for resting-places of the gods in processions. One can imagine what splendid arenas for processions and festivals these courts must afford, in which enormous crowds sometimes assemble to take part in ceremonials similar to that which I have described in Chapter VII. Owing, however, to former desecrations by the

French (who in 1777 fortified the temple itself), and present treatment by the British Government, this Tanjore temple is not so much frequented as it used to be. The late Rajah of Tanjore, prior to 1857, supported the place, of course, with handsome funds; but the British Government only undertakes *necessary* repairs and allows a pension of four rupees a month to the existing temple servants. They are therefore in a poor way.

The arcade at the far end and down one side of the court is frescoed with the usual grotesque subjects—flying elephants trampling on unbelievers, rajahs worshipping the god, women bathing, etc., and is furnished the whole way with erect stone *lingams*—there must be at least a hundred of them. These lingams are cylindrical stones a foot and a half high or so, and eight or nine inches thick, some bigger, some smaller, standing in sort of oval troughs, which catch the oil which is constantly poured over the lingams. Women desiring children pay their offerings here, of flowers and oil, and at certain festivals these shrines are, notwithstanding their number, greatly in request.

The palace at Tanjore is a very commonplace, round-arched, whitewashed building with several courts—in part of which the women-folk of the late rajah are still living behind their bars and shutters; the whole place a funny medley of Oriental and Western influences; a court of justice opening right on to one of the quadrangles, with great oil-paintings of former rajahs; a library; a harness and dress room, with elephants' saddles, horses' head-gear, rajahs' headgear, etc.; a reception-room also quite open to a court, with sofas, arm-chairs, absurd prints, a bust of Nelson, and a clockwork ship on a troubled sea; elephants wandering about in the big court; painted figures of English officers on the sideposts of one of the gates, and so forth.

Round the palace, and at some little distance from the temple, clusters the town itself, with its narrow alleys and mostly one-storeyed cottages and cabins, in which the goldsmiths and workers in copper and silver repoussé ware carry on their elegant trades.

The ancient city of Mádura, though with a population of 60,000, is even more humble in appearance than Tanjore. At first sight it looks like a mere collection of mud cabins—though, of course, there are English bungalows on the outskirts, and a court-house and a church and an American mission-room and school, and the rest. The weavers are a strong caste here; they weave silk (and cotton) *saris*, though with failing trade as against the incoming machine-products of capitalism—and you see their crimson-dyed pieces stretched on frames in the streets.

The *choultrie* leading up to one of the temple gates is a colonnade 110 yards long, a central walk and two aisles, with carven monolithic columns—a warrior sitting on a rearing horse trampling shields of soldiers and slaying men or tigers, or a huge, seated king or god, in daring crudeness—and great capitals supporting a stone roof. Choultries were used as public feeding-halls and resting-places for Brahmins, as well as for various ceremonies, and in old days, when the Brahmins were all-powerful, such places were everywhere at their service, and they had a high old time. This choultrie has, however, been turned into a silk and cotton market, and was gay, when I saw it, with crowds of people, and goods pinned up to the columns. Emerging from it, the eastern gate of the temple stands on the opposite side of the road—a huge *gópura*, pagoda form, fifteen storeys or so high, each tier crowded with figures — Siva hideous with six arms and protruding eyes and teeth, Siva dancing, Siva contemplative, Siva and Sakti on the bull, demon doorkeepers, etc.—the whole picked out in the usual crude reds, yellows, greens, blues, and branching out at top into grotesque dragon-forms—a strange piece of work, yet having an impressive total effect, as it rises 200 feet into the resplendent sky over the little mud and thatch cottages—its crude details harmonised in the intense blaze, and its myriad nooks of shadow haunted by swallows, doves, and other birds.

There are nine such gópuras or gate-towers in all in this temple, all on much the same plan, ranging from 40 to 200 feet in height, and apparently used to some extent as dwelling-places by priests, yogis, and others. These, together with the various halls, shrines, tanks, arcades, etc., form a huge enclosure 280 yards long by nearly 250 wide.

On entering the huge doorway of the eastern gópura one finds oneself immediately in a wilderness of columns—the hall of a thousand columns—besides arcades, courts, and open and covered spaces —a labyrinth full of people (for this temple is much frequented)—many of whom are selling wares, but here more for temple use, flowers for offerings, cakes of cowdung ashes for rubbing on the forehead, embroidered bags to put these in, money-changers, elephants here and there, with bundles of green stuff among the columns, elephant-keepers, the populace arriving with offerings, and plentiful Brahmins going to and fro. The effect of the numerous columns—and there are fully a thousand of them, fifteen feet high or so—is very fine—the light and shade, glimpses of sky or trees through avenues of carved monsters, or cavernous labyrinths of the same ending in entire darkness; grotesque work, and in detail often repulsive, but lending itself in the mass to the general effect—Siva dancing again, or Ganésa with huge belly and elephant head, or Parvati with monstrous breasts—"all out of one stone, all out of one stone," the guide keeps repeating: feats of marvelous patience (*e.g.* a chain of separate links all cut from the same block), though ugly enough, very often, in themselves.

And now, skirting round the inner sanctuary to the left, we come into a sort of cloister opening on a tank some fifty yards square, from whence we get a more general view of the place, and realise its expanse. The five or six gópuras visible from our standpoint serve to indicate this—all painted in strong color but subdued by distance, roofs of various portions of the temple, clumps of palm and other trees, two gold-plated turrets shining brilliantly in the sun, the tank itself with handsome stone tiers and greenish waters where the worshipers wash their feet, the cloisters frescoed with elaborate legendary designs, and over all, in the blue sky, flocks of birds—swallows, doves, and bright green parrots chattering. Once more we plunge into dark galleries full of hungry-eyed Brahmins, and passing the shrine of Minakshi, into which we cannot gain admittance, come into the very sombre and striking corridor which runs round the entire inner shrine. The huge monoliths here are carven with more soberness and grace, and the great capitals bear cross-beams, which in their turn support projecting architraves. Hardly a soul do we meet as we make the circuit of the three sides. The last turn brings us to the entrance of the inner sanctuary itself; and here is the gold-plated *kambam* which I have already described (Chap. VII.), and close behind it the bull Nandi and the gloom of the interior lit only by a distant lamp or two. To these inner parts come only those who wish to meditate in quiet; and in some secluded corner may one occasionally be seen, seated on the floor with closed eyes and crossed legs, losing or endeavoring to lose, himself in *samádhi.*

Outside the temple in the streets of Mádura we saw three separate Juggernath cars, used on occasions in processions. These cars are common enough even in small Hindu towns. They are unwieldy, massive things, often built in several tiers, and with solid wooden wheels on lumbering wooden axles, which look as if they were put on (and probably are) in such a way as to cause the maximum of resistance to motion. At Streevelliputhur there is a car thirty feet high with wheels eight feet in diameter. The people harness themselves to these things literally in thousands; the harder the car is to move the greater, naturally, is the dignity of the god who rides upon it, and the excitement becomes intense when he is at last fairly got under weigh. But I have not witnessed one of these processions.

The temple of Chidámbaram is in some respects more interesting than those of Tanjore and Mádura. It is, in fact, more highly thought of as a goal of pilgrimage and a place of festival than any other South Indian temple, and may be said to be the Benares of South India. The word Chidámbaram means *region of pure consciousness*, and Siva is worshiped here under his most excellent name of Nádarája, *lord of the dance.* "O thou who dancest the dance of bliss in the heaven of pure consciousness."

There is a little railway station of Chidámbaram, but it is two or three miles from the temple and the town; and though the town itself numbers some 20,000 to 30,000 inhabitants, there is not a single Englishman resident in the place or within some miles of it, the only white-faced inhabitant being a Eurasian druggist who keeps a shop there. When I was there the whole temple was in course of repair, and the Brahmins were such a nuisance that I really did not get so good an idea of the place as I could have wished. These gentry swarm here, and descend upon one like birds of prey, in quest of tips; indeed, the physiognomy of a great many of them suggests the kite family—sharp eyes, rather close together, and a thin aquiline nose; this with their large foreheads, looking all the larger on account of the shaven head, does not give a very favorable impression.

The ascendency of the Brahmin caste is certainly a very remarkable historical fact. It is possible that at one time they really resembled the guardians of Plato's ideal republic—teachers and rulers who themselves possessed nothing and were supported by the contributions of the people; but before so many centuries had gone by they must have made the first part of their functions subsidiary to the last, and now—though a good many of them ply trades and avocations of one kind or another—the majority are mere onhangers of the temples, where they become sharers of the funds devoted to the temple services, and bleed the pockets of pious devotees. When a Hindu of any worldly substance approaches one of these places, he is immediately set upon by five or six loafers of this kind—each of whom claims that his is the Brahmin family which has always done the priestly services for the visitor's family (and, indeed, they do keep careful note of these matters), and that *he*, therefore, should conduct the visitor to the proper quarter of the temple, take his offerings to the god, and receive his reward accordingly.

This temple is, I should think, about the same size as that at Mádura, but more open, like the Tanjore temple. There are four gópuras of about equal size—120 feet high or so—at the four points of the compass. On entering by the eastern one the hall of a thousand columns stands away in the court to the right, and gives the idea of a complete temple in itself. The sides and back end are closed in, but the front forms a sort of portico, and columns similar to those of the portico—every one a monolith—extend through the entire interior. There is a lane or aisle down the middle, and then on each side they stand thick, in rows perhaps ten feet apart.

As you go in the gloom gets deeper and deeper. Only here and there a gap in the external wall throws a weird light. The whole suggests a rock cave cut in multitudinous pillars to support the overlying weight, or a gloomy forest of tree-trunks. But the columns are commonplace in themselves, and their number and closeness together under a flat roof of no great weight is not architecturally admirable. When you reach the interior sanctum, where you might expect to find the god at home, you discover a mere bare cavity, so dark that you cannot see the roof, and occupied by innumerable bats, who resent your intrusion with squeaks and shrieks. But my guide explained to me that twice a year the god *does* come to dwell there, and then they clean the place up and decorate it with lamps for a season.

A large tank stands just west of this hall—a tank 200 feet long, I should think—in which men (and women) were washing their feet and clothes. These tanks are attached to every temple. At Mádura there is a very beautiful one, "the golden lotus tank," two miles away from the temple, with a pagoda on an island in the midst of it—to which they resort at the Taypúsam festival. Also at Mylapore, Madras, there is a handsome tank with pagoda just outside the temple; but mostly they are within the precincts.

Entering the inner inclosure at Chidámbaram you come to various arcades and shrines, where Brahmins and chetties raged. The chetties have great influence at Chidámbaram; their caste supplies, I believe, the main funds of the temple—which is practically, therefore, in their hands. I was presented with flower garlands and a lime, and expected to make my money-offering in front of a little temple, of Vishnu, I think, which they seasonably explained to me was to be roofed with gold! On the other hand—to the left—was a temple to Siva—both these forms being worshiped here. Into the shrine of Parvati I did not penetrate, but it looked ancient and curious. Fergusson says that this shrine belongs to the fourteenth or fifteenth centuries, and the inner sanctuaries to somewhere about 1000 A.D., while the hall of the thousand columns—which shows Mohammedan influence—is as late as the seventeenth century.

An elderly stoutish man, half naked, but with some authority evidently—who proved afterwards to be the head of the chetties—announced in a loud voice that I was to be treated with respect and shown as much as possible—which only meant that I was to give as large an offering as possible. Then an excited-looking fellow came up, a medium-sized man of about forty, and began talking cockney English as fluently and idiomatically as if he had been born by the Thames, rattling off verses and nursery rhymes with absurd familiarity. The rest said he was a cranky Brahmin with an insane gift for language—knew Sanskrit and ever so many tongues.

Escaping from these I left the temple and went into the village to see the goldsmiths who are employed (by the chetties) on work connected with its restoration. Found a large workshop, where they were making brass roof-pinnacles, salvers, pedestals for images, etc., and plating the same with gold leaf or plates—also store of solid gold things—armlets and breastplates for the gods, etc.—another touch remindful of Greek life. The gold leaf was being beaten out between thin membranes, many leaves at once, with a hammer. All handwork, of course.

My guide—who is the station clerk and a Brahmin, while his station-master is a Sudra (O this steam-engine!)—told me on the way back that the others at the station often advised him to give up his caste practices; but he had plenty of time in the middle of the day, between the trains, to go through his ablutions and other ceremonies, and he did not see why he should not do so.

As we walked along the road we met two pilgrims—with orange-colored cloths—coming along. One of them, a hairy, wild, and obstinate-looking old man, evidently spotted the hated Englishman from afar, and as he passed put his tongue gently but firmly out at me!

CHAPTER XIII

MADRAS AND CALCUTTA

INDIA beggars description—the interminable races, languages, creeds, colors, manners, costumes.

The streets of Madras (Blacktown) are a blaze of color—predominant white, but red, orange, brilliant green and even blue cloths and turbans meet the eye in every direction. Blacktown reminds one of Pompeii—as it may have been in its time—mostly one-storeyed buildings, stuccoed brick with little colonnades or lean-to thatches in front, cool, dark, stone interiors with little or no furniture —a bit of a court somewhere inside, with a gleam of the relentless sun—a few mango leaves over the door in honour of the Pongal festival (now going on), and saffron smeared on door-posts; a woman standing half lost in shadow, men squatting idling in a verandah, a brahmin cow with a bright brass necklace lying down just in the street—(sometimes in the verandah itself); a Hindu temple with its queer, creepy images fronting on the street, and a Juggernath car under a tall thatch, waiting for its festival; or a white arabesqued and gimp-arched mosque with tall minarets pinnacled with gold spiring up into the blue; absurd little stalls with men squatted among their baskets and piled grains and fruits; and always this wonderful crowd going up and down between.

I should think half the people have religious marks on their foreheads—black, white, or red spots on the frontal sinus—horizontal lines (Sivaite), vertical lines (Vaishnavite)—sometimes two vertical white marks joined at the base with a red mark between, sometimes a streak of colour all down the ridge of the nose—and so forth. It is as if every little sect or schism of the Christian Church declared itself by a symbol on the brow.

How different from Ceylon! There is a certain *severity* about India, both climate and people. The dry soil, the burning sun (for though so much farther north the sun has a more *wicked* quality about it here), are matched by a certain aridity and tension in the people. Ceylon is idyllic, romantic—the plentiful foliage and shade everywhere, the easy-going nature of the Cinghalese themselves, the absence of caste—even the English are softened towards such willing subjects. But here, such barriers, such a *noli-me-tangere* atmosphere!—the latent feud between Hindu and Mussulman everywhere, *their* combined detestation of the English springing out upon you from faces passing; rigid orthodoxies and superiorities; the Mohammedans (often big and moderately well-conditioned men) looking down with some contempt upon the lean Hindu; the Hindus equally satisfied in their own superiority, comforting themselves with quotations from *Shastras* and *Puranas*.

As to the boatmen and drivers and guides and servants generally, they torment one like gadflies; not swindling one in a nice open *riant* way like the Italians of the same ilk, but with smothered dodges and obsequious craft. The last hotel I was at here was odious—a lying Indian manager, lying and cringing servants, and an idiotic old man who acted as my "boy" and tormented my life out of me, fiddling around with my slippers on pretence of doing something, or holding the towel in readiness for me while I was washing my face. On my leaving, the manager—as he presented his bill with utmost dignity and grace—asked for a tip; so did the head-waiter, and all the servants down to the bath-man; then there were coolies to carry my luggage from the hotel steps (where the servants, of course, left it) to the cab, and then, when I had started, the proprietor of the cab ran after it, stopped it, and demanded a larger fare than I had agreed to! On one occasion (in taking a boat) I counted eleven people who put in a claim for *bakshish.* Small change cannot last for ever, and even one's vocabulary of oaths is liable to be exhausted in time!

It requires a little tact to glide through all this without exposing oneself to the enemy. Good old John Bull pays through the nose for being ruler of this country. He overwhelms the people by force, but they turn upon him—as the weaker is prone to do—through craft; and truly they have their revenge. Half believing in the idea that as *sahib* and ruler of the country he must live in such and such style, have so many servants, etc., or he would lose his prestige, he acquiesces in a system of impositions; he is pestered to death, and hates it all, but he must submit. And the worst is one is conscious all the time of being laughed at for one's pains. But British visitors must not commit the mistake—so commonly made by people in a foreign country—of supposing that the classes created in India by our presence, and who in some sense are the reflection of our own sins, are or represent the normal population—even though we naturally see more of them than we do of the latter.

There are, however, in the great cities of India little hotels kept and frequented by English folk where one is comparatively safe from importunities; and if you are willing to be altogether a second-rate person, and go to these places, travel second class by train, ride in bullock-hackeries, and "undermine the empire" generally by doing other such undignified things, you may travel with comparative peace of mind and security of pocket.

Madras generally is a most straggling, dull, and (at night) ill-lighted place. Blacktown, already described, and which lies near the harbor, is the chief centre of native life; but the city generally, including other native centres, plexuses of commercial life, knots of European hotels and shops, barracks, hospitals, suburban villas and bungalows, stretches away, with great intervals of dreary roads between, for miles and miles, over a dead flat on whose shore the surf beats monotonously. Adyar, where the Theosophists have their headquarters—and which is still only a suburb of Madras—is seven miles distant from the harbor. The city, however, though shorn of its former importance as far as the British are concerned, and slumbering on its memories of a hundred years ago, is a great centre of native activity, literary and political; the National Indian Congress receives some of its strongest support from it; many influential natives reside here; papers like the *Hindu*, both in English and vernacular, are published here, and a great number of books printed, in Tamil and other South Indian languages.

At Adyar I saw Bertram Keightley and one or two others, and had some pleasant chats with them. Col. Olcott was absent just at the time. The Theosophist villa, with roomy lecture-hall and library, stands pleasantly among woods on the bank of a river and within half-a-mile of the sea. Passing from the library through sandalwood doors into an inner sanctum I was shown a variety of curios connected with Madame Blavatsky, among which were a portrait, apparently done in a somewhat dashing style—just the head of a man, surrounded with clouds and filaments—in blue pigment on a piece of white silk, which was "precipitated" by Madame Blavatsky in Col. Olcott's presence—she simply placing her two hands on the white silk for a moment. Keightley told me that Col. Olcott tested a small portion of the silk so colored, but found the pigment so fast in the fibre that it could not by any means be washed out. There were also two oil portraits—heads, well framed and reverently guarded behind a curtain—of the now celebrated Kout Houmi, Madame Blavatsky's Guru, and of another, Col. Olcott's Guru—both fine-looking men, apparently between forty and fifty years of age, with shortish beards and (as far as I could see, for the daylight was beginning to fail) dark brown hair; and both with large eyes and what might be called a spiritual glow in their faces. Madame Blavatsky knew Col. Olcott's Guru as well as her own, and the history of these two portraits (as told me by Keightley) is that they were done by a German artist whom she met in the course of her travels. Considering him competent for the work—and he being willing to undertake it—she projected the images of the two Gurus into his mind, and he painted from the mental pictures—she placing her hand on his head during the operation. The German artist-medium accounted perhaps for the decidedly mawkish expression of both faces as well as for the considerable likeness to each other—which, considering that Kout Houmi dates from Cashmere, and the other (I think) from Thibet, might not have been expected. All the same, they are fine faces, and it is not impossible that they may be, as I believe Madame Blavatsky and Col. Olcott considered them, good likenesses. Keightley was evidently much impressed by the "old lady's" clairvoyant power, saying that sometimes in her letters from England she displayed a knowledge of what was going on at Adyar, which he could not account for. Altogether I had an interesting conversation with him.

Among other places in Madras I visited one of the little Pompeiian houses in Blacktown, which I have already described—where a Hindu acquaintance, a small contractor, is living: a little office, then a big room divided in two by a curtain—parlor in front and domestic room behind—all cool and dark and devoid of furniture, and little back premises into which I did not come. He is an active-minded man, and very keen about the Indian Congress, to which he was delegate last year, sends hundreds of copies of the *Hindu* and other "incendiary" publications about the country each week, and, like thousands and hundreds of thousands of his fellow-countrymen to-day, has learnt the lessons taught him by the British Government so well that the one thing he lives for is to see electoral and representative institutions embedded into the life of the Indian peoples, and the images of Vishnu and Siva supplanted in the temples by those of John Stuart Mill and Herbert Spencer.

While I was there two elderly gentlemen of quite the old school called—innocent enough of Herbert Spencer and of cloth coats and trousers—with their white muslins round their bodies, and red shawls over their shoulders, and grey-haired, keen, narrow faces and bare shins and horny feet, which they tucked up onto their chairs as they sat; but with good, composed, unhurried manners, as all Easterns of the old school seem to have. This habit of the mild Hindu, of tucking his feet under him, is his ever-present refuge in time of trouble or weariness; at the railway station or in any public place you may see him sitting on a seat, and beneath him, in the place where his feet ought to be, are his red slippers; but of visible link between them and his body there is no sign—as if he had already severed connection with the earth and was on the way toward heaven.

Calcutta.—Arrived 6th Feb., about 4 P.M.—steaming all day since dawn up the Hooghly, 130 miles from the light-boat at its mouth to Calcutta—a dismal river, with dismal, flat shores, sandy and dry in places and only grown with scrub, in others apparently damp, to judge by the clumps of bamboo; landscape often like Lincolnshire, trees of similar shape, stacks of rice-straw looking just like our stacks, mud and thatch villages; in other places the palmyra and coco-nut palm; and doubtless in parts wild tangles and jungles haunted by tigers; aboriginal boats going up and down; and the Hooghly narrowing at last from four or five miles near its mouth to half-a-mile at the Howrah bridge of boats.

Nearing Calcutta, brick-kilns and the smoky, tall chimneys of civilisation appear along the banks, and soon we find ourselves among docks and wharfs, and a forest of shipping, alongside of a modern-looking city (that part of it).

Calcutta is built on a dead flat. There is a considerable European quarter of five-storeyed buildings, offices, warehouses, law-courts, hotels, shops, residences, wide streets and open spaces, gardens, etc.; after which the city breaks away into long straggling lines of native dwellings—small flat-roofed tenements and shops, crowded bazaars and tram-lines—embedding almost aboriginal quarters, narrow lanes with mere mud and tile cabins—labyrinths where a European is stared at.

The white dome of the Post Office, like a small St Paul's, dominates the whole riverside city with its crowded shipping and animated quays—fit symbol of modern influences. Round no temple or mosque or minster does the civilising Englishman group his city, but round the G.P.O. It would almost seem, here in Calcutta, as if the mere rush of commercial interests had smashed up the native sanctions of race and religion. The orderly rigor of caste, which is evident in Madras, is not seen; dress is untidy and unclean, the religious marks if put on at all are put on carelessly; faces are low in type, lazy, cunning, bent on mere lucre. The Bengali is, however, by nature a versatile, flexile creature, sadly wanting in backbone, and probably has succumbed easily to the new disorganising forces. Then the mere mixture of populations here may have a good deal to do with it. A huge tur moil throngs the bazaars, not only Bengalis, but Hindustanis, Mohammedans, Chinese, and seedy-looking Eurasians—in whom one can discern no organising element or seed-form of patriotism, religion, or culture (with the exception, perhaps, of the Chinese). It seems to be a case of a dirty Western commercialism taking the place of the old Pharisaism of caste and religion—and it is hard to say which may be the worst.

Sunday (the 8th) was a great day for bathing in the river. I did not know that the Hooghly was for such purposes considered to be a part of the Ganges, but it appears that it is; and owing to an important and rare astronomical conjunction, announced in the almanacs, bathing on that day was specially purificatory. In the morning the water-side was thronged with people, and groups of pilgrims from a distance could be seen coming in along the roads. Wherever the banks shelved down to the water, or the quays and river-walls allowed, huge crowds (here mostly dressed in unbleached cotton with little color) could be seen preparing to bathe, or renewing themselves afterwards—beggars at all the approaches spreading their cloths on the ground to catch the scanty handfuls of rice thrown to them; everywhere small vendors of flowers for offerings, or of oil, or sandalwood paste for smearing the body with after the bath, or of colored pigments for painting sect-marks on the forehead; strings of peasants followed by their wives and children; old, infirm people piloted by sons and daughters; here a little old woman, small like a child, drawn in a clumsy wooden barrow to the waterside; there a horrible blind man with matted hair, squatted, yelling texts from the holy books; here family groups and relatives chatting together, or cliques and clubs of young men coming up out of the water—brass pots glancing, and long hair uncurled in the wind. If you imagine all this taking place on a fine summer's day somewhere a little below London Bridge, the scene would hardly be more incongruous than it is here by the handsome wharfs of Calcutta Strand, under the very noses of the great black-hulled steamships which to-day perhaps, or to-morrow, are sailing for the West.

The evening before the festival I went with Panna Lall B. to a European circus which happened to be in the place. There one saw the same absurd incongruity—dense masses of "oysters" perched or sitting cross-legged on their benches—their wraps drawn round them, for the night was really cold—watching under the electric light the lovely and decidedly well-developed Miss Alexandra in tights performing on the trapeze, or little "Minnie" jumping through circles of flame. Considering that, except among the poorest classes (peasants, etc.), the Bengalis keep their women closely shut up, and that it is a rare thing to see a female (unless it be a child or old woman) in the streets of Calcutta—a scene of this kind at the circus must cause a sufficient sensation; and, indeed, the smile which curled the lips of some of these rather Mephistophelean spectators was something which I shall not easily forget.

But the mass of the people of India must be

wretchedly poor. These half-starved peasants from the surrounding country wandering about (their thin, thin wives and daughters trailing after them, holding on to the man's unbleached and scanty cotton cloth—over the *maidan*, through the Asiatic Museum, through the streets, by the riverside—with gaping, listless faces) are a sad and touching sight; yet it only corroborates what I have seen in other parts. "Wide and deepened poverty all over the land, such as the world has never before seen on so vast a scale," says Digby; not without testimony to show that the people in the native states are in a better condition than those under our organisation. Even if the poverty is not increasing (and this is a matter on which it is most difficult to form a definite opinion), there seems to be no evidence to show that it is decreasing. The famines go on with at least undiminished severity, and the widespread agricultural paralysis is by no means really compensated by a fallacious commercial prosperity, which in the larger centres is enriching the few at the expense of the many.*

After watching these pathetic crowds on Sunday, I went the next day to a meeting of the Countess of Dufferin's Fund for the Medical Education of Indian Women—a well-meant movement, which after being launched with all advantages and *éclat*, has only met with moderate success. A very varied spectacle of dress and nationality. Rajahs and native chiefs of all sorts of hues and costumes; yellow silk tunics figured with flowers, flowing purple robes, dainty little turbans over dark mustachioed faces, sprays and feathers of diamonds; English

* See Appendix.

ladies in the pink of fashion, military uniforms, and the Viceroy and Lady Lansdowne in the centre in quiet morning costume. The English speakers belauded the native chiefs present, and the native chiefs complimented the English ladies; but, after the spectacle of the day before, the general congratulations fell rather flat upon me, nor did they appear to be justified by the rather melancholy and inefficient appearance of the bevy of native women-students and nurses present. Sir Charles Elliott, the Lieut.-Governor, made a kindly speech, which left on one the unpleasant impression that one sometimes gets from those big-brained doctrinaire persons whose amiability is all the more hard and narrow-minded because it is so well-intentioned. Lord Lansdowne underneath an exterior (physical and mental) of decadent aristocracy seems to have just a feeble spark of the old English high-caste ruling quality about him, which may have been good in its time, but will be of little use, I fear, to the half-starved peasants of to-day.

I fancy, with all respect to the genuine good intention shown in these zenana missions, medical education funds, etc., there must be something rather comical to the natives themselves in philanthropic efforts of this kind, made by a people who understand the country so little as the English do; just as there is something rather comical to the masses at home in the toy "charities" and missions of the lady and gentleman here, and suggestive of an old parable about a mote and a beam. In a lecture given by the Maharajah of Benares, in July 1888, he chaffed these philanthropists somewhat—recounting how one such lady "actually regretted that the peasant cultivators could not provide themselves with boots! while another had a long conversation with a Rani on the ill effects of infant marriage, and was surprised to hear that the Rani had been married at the age of seven, and had sons and grandsons, all of whom were happy and contented. The Rani then turned to the lady, and observing that her hair was turning grey, inquired whether no one had ever offered her proposals of marriage, and suggested that the *English* laws required some modification to insure ladies against remaining so long in a state of single blessedness."

But the most interesting people, to me, whom I have met here, are a little *côterie* of Bengalis who live quite away in the native part of the city. Chundi Churn B. is a schoolmaster, and keeps a small school of thirty or forty boys, which lies back in a tangle of narrow lanes and alleys, but is quite a civilised little place, with benches and desks just like an English school—except that like all the schools in this part of the world it is quite open to the street (with trellised sides in this case), so that passers-by can quite easily see and be seen. Chundi Churn told me that he started the school on purely native lines, but had poor success until he introduced the English curriculum—English history, science, Euclid, Algebra, etc.—when he soon got as many boys as he wanted. As in all the Indian schools they work what appear to us frightfully long hours, 7 to 9 A.M.; then an hour for breakfast; 10 A.M. to 2 P.M., and then an hour for dinner; and again from 3 to 6. I fancy they must take it fairly easy; and then it is certain that the native boys—though they have active little brains—are much more quiescent than the English, are content to sit still, and the master has little trouble in keeping order.

I have been round several evenings after school hours and chatted with Chundi Churn and his brother and various friends that dropped in—an intelligent little community. Two of them are Brahmin fellows of about thirty, with the eager, tense look that the Brahmins mostly have, but good, imaginative faces. We discuss the Indian Congress, English and Indian customs, the child-marriage question (which is raging just now), and the great question of Caste. They insist on my eating various sweet cakes of native preparation, but will not eat with me; and they smoke hubble-bubble pipes, which they pass round—but the Brahmins must have a hubble-bubble to themselves! At the same time they are careful to explain that "no one believes in all this now"; but as they are at home, and only trellis-work between us and the lane, it would not do to violate the rules. And this, I believe, is largely the state of affairs. The anglicising population, for the sake of parents' feelings (and they are tender on this point), or respectability, or commercial connection, keep up a show of caste rules which they have ceased, or are ceasing, to believe in; and it is an open secret that Brahmin gentlemen of high standing in their caste, not unfrequently when travelling, or in places where they are not known, resort to British hotels and have a high feed of beefsteaks and champagne!

One of the Brahmins is clerk in a mercantile establishment in the English part of Calcutta, and some of the others are students at the Metropolitan College. Western education is going on at a tremendous rate—so much so that there will soon be an educated proletariat (what Grant Duff calls "the worst of evils") in the great cities of India. Two or three of the party are very quick at mathematics—which seems to be a subject in which the Bengalis excel—and readily picked up the key to one or two little problems which I presented to them. They all seem to be much impressed with the greatness of Western civilisation—for the present at anyrate—though they will suffer a reaction probably before very long. Finding I knew something of astronomy they pelted me with questions about the stars, and insisted on going out at night and trying to hunt up the ecliptic among the constellations! Then, after a time, they would relapse into tale-telling and music. The fellows still show a truly Oriental love of long stories, and would listen with rapt attention to one of their party relating some ancient yarn about the child of a king who was exposed in the woods and ultimately came back after many convolutions of adventure and claimed his kingdom—just as if they had not heard it before; or about the chaste Draupatha (in the Mahabhárata) who—when Duriyodhana, desiring to insult her before a large assembly, gave orders that she should be stripped of her cloth—thought of Vishnu, and her cloth went on lengthening and unwinding indefinitely—their stories lengthening and unwinding like Draupatha's cloth, in a way that would have delighted the heart of William Morris.

Panna Lall, Chundi Churn's brother, is a bright-mannered youth of about twenty, of a modest, affectionate disposition, and with a certain grace and dignity of bearing, He doesn't care about books, but has a good ear, and plays one or two musical instruments in an easy, unstudied way; lives in quite primitive style with his father down in one of these back lanes, but has a tiny little room of his own, where he takes me to sit and chat with friends. There is *no* furniture, but you squat cross-legged on

Panna Lall B.

the floor—so there is plenty of room for quite a party. There may be a box or two in a corner, and on the walls some shelves and a few prints. Indeed it gives one a curious sensation to see crude-colored woodcuts, framed under glass, and exactly resembling the pictures of the Virgin or of Christ common in Catholic countries, and then on nearer approach to find that they represent Siva or Parvati, or among the Bengalis Chaitanya, or some other incarnation of the divinity, standing or seated on a lotus flower and with benign head encircled by an aureole. These pictures are printed in Calcutta.

Panna Lall is quite an athlete, and interested in anything in that line. He took me one day to a little bit of ground where he and some friends have their horizontal bars, etc.; they did some good tumbling and tight-rope walking, and with their golden-brown skins and muscular bodies looked well when stripped. The Bengali Babu is often of a lightish-brown colour. The people generally wear more clothing than in South India, and at this time of year throw a brown woollen shawl over their shoulders *toga* fashion; their heads are almost always bare, but they have taken a great fancy lately in Calcutta to wearing narrow-toed patent-leather shoes, which look sufficiently absurd, and must be fearfully uncomfortable, on their well-developed broad feet. Only it is a mark of distinction and civilisation! Panna Lall every now and then, when walking, entreats me to stop and rest under a tree, and then takes off his shoes and waggles his toes about to soothe and refresh them! I am never tired of admiring the foot in its native state. It is so broad and free and full and muscular, with a good concave curve on the inner line, and the toes standing well apart from each other—so different from the ill-nourished, unsightly thing we are accustomed to. I sometimes think we can never attain to a broad, free and full life on our present understandings in the West.

Another absurd custom of the young Babus here (I am speaking of the mass of the people) is that of putting on a Manchester cotton shirt, pure and simple, when they wish to appear in full dress! As they do not wear trousers, the effect (combined with the patent-leather shoes) is very naïve and touching.

On the whole, Calcutta does not impress me very favorably. There is the official society, and the trading and commercial ditto, and the educational and legal sections, and a considerable racing population, including a great number of jockeys and horse-trainers who come over with their girls from Australia for the season; there is a fine zoological garden and a botanic garden, and the Asiatic Museum, and various public buildings, and two or three colleges, including a college for native women; but all these interests seem to serve chiefly in the direction of *disorganising* the mass of the people and the primitive sanctions of their life. Taking it at its worst, the general population is dirty, lazy, and rapacious. As in our slums, a kind of listlessness and despair marks the people in the poorest quarters, who, instead of congregating as with us round a beershop, may be seen perching about on doorsteps and even on the tops of walls, sitting on their heels with knees drawn up to the chin, and a draggled garment about them—looking painfully like vultures, and generally chewing betel, that common resource against hunger. One notes, however, even here, a few fine faces, and a good many very pathetic ones, of old people.

Chundi Churn plays a little on the *sitar*—the original of our *guitar*, I suppose—an instrument with a long neck, and small belly made of a pumpkin shell, and four or five wires (originally three wires, from *si*, three, and *tar*, string). The frets are movable, so that keeping the same key-note you can play in major, minor, or other modes. I am beginning to understand the Indian music better now, after having heard a little in different places, but have not very much systematic knowledge about it. It appears that they divide the octave into twenty-two exactly equal parts, called *sruti*—each part having its own special name. An interval of four *srutis* may then be said to constitute a major tone, three *srutis* a minor tone, and two a semitone—though this is not *quite* exact; and out of these three intervals, major tone, minor tone, and semitone—a seven-step scale is constituted very nearly similar to ours, and having the semitones in the same places. The key-note of this scale is called *Sa* or *Ansa*, and corresponds to our *Do*, and though not exactly a key-note in the modern sense of the word, it is the most accentuated note and "rules the others." By adopting any of the other six notes as key-note scales are got very nearly corresponding to the seven Gregorian scales of the old church music; and one very commonly in use, if I am not mistaken, corresponds to the Phrygian mode—*i.e.* that which we produce on the piano by using E as tonic and playing all the white keys.

These seven scales constituted the first system of Hindu music; but they had a second system in which the notes, though preserving their names, could be, any of them, raised or dropped by a *sruti*; and a third system in which one or two notes being omitted, five or six step scales were produced.

Out of the hundreds (or thousands) of possible scales thus producible, the Oriental mind, unable to find the scientific root of the whole business, made a fantastic selection. There were six sons of Brahma and Saráswati called Rágas—the genii of the passions. Six principal scales were named after these genii and call *Rags*, and then each of these had five feminine sub-scales or *Raginas* attached to it; and so forth. Then the numbers five, six, and seven became typical of divisions of the year, days of the week, the number of planets, etc., and very soon a most fanciful system was elaborated—the remains only of which have lingered to the present day. The old notation appears to have died out; but a vast number of time-honored melodies, or rather phrases, in the different modes and scales, have been preserved by tradition—and are now called *rags* and *raginas*, though these names were formerly applicable to the scales only. These *rags* and *raginas* are not what we should call tunes, but are brief or extended phrases, which have been classified as suitable for various occasions, emotions, festivals, times of day, seasons of the year, and the like; and these the musician uses and combines, within limits, to his taste; and in the hands of a skilful person they are very effective, but become abominably insipid and conventional if treated in a mechanical way.

Besides the regular notes belonging to any given scale, the Hindus use the quarter tones, or *srutis*, a good deal in the little turns and twanks of which they are so fond; and sometimes by slurring they pass through every intermediate gradation of tone. The slur, which is congenial to the mystic, vague melody of the East, and so foreign to the distinct articulation of Western music, is often used in singing; and on the *sítar* a slight slurring rise of tone is produced by drawing the string sideways along the fret—a device which recalls the clavichord of which Sebastian Bach was so fond, in which instrument the hammer which struck the string was also the bridge which defined its length, so that an increased pressure by the finger on the key, after the first striking of the note, raised the bridge a little, tightened the string, and so produced a plaintive rise of tone.

All this gives the idea of a complicated system of music; and it will be seen that in the range of mere melody the Hindu music has really a greater capacity of subtle expression than ours. But in harmony it is deficient—the ground idea of their harmony being the use of a drone bass—which bass, though it may change not unfrequently, always seems to preserve the drone character. And, of course, the deficiency in harmony reacts on and limits the play of melody.

The general character of the music, like that of much of the Indian life, reminds one of our own mediæval times. The monkish plain-song and the early minstrel music of Europe were probably very similar to this. There was the same tendency to work from a droning bass, rather than from a keynote in our sense of the word, the same tendency to subordinate the music to the words, causing vague, and not always balanced, flights of intricate melody, the same love of ornamental kinks, and the same want of absolute definition in the matter of time.

The instruments most commonly used, besides the

Sítar and its relative the *Vina*, are the *Manda*, a horizontal harp, somewhat resembling the Tyrolese *zither*; the *Sigara*, a small clarionet; a bamboo flageolet, which has a very sweet and mellow tone;

Woman playing Sítar

the *Tabala*, a small kettledrum; and the *Taus*, a four-stringed fiddle played with a bow. This last is a very curious instrument. Beneath the four main strings are stretched a number of other fine wires, which, by their vibration, lightly reinforce and sustain the notes played. The effect, when not played too fast, is very graceful and clinging, with subtle harmonics; and I have heard some most bewitching phrasing on this instrument—a dialogue, one might say, between it and the voice—with accompaniment of the little Tabala. The Tabala itself is very charming, with its gurgling and bell-like sounds and sudden explosions and chattering accompaniments, executed by the fingers and the butt end of the hand on two drums simultaneously. The great effect of the *sítar*, whose tone on the whole is thin, is undoubtedly the side tension of the strings, which gives much expression to it.

At its best, the Indian music seems to me to produce a powerful impression—though generally either plaintive or frenzied. On the deep background of the drone are wrought these (Wagnerian) phrases, which are perfectly fluent and variable according to the subject conveyed, which are extraordinarily subtle in expression, and which generally rise in intensity and complexity as the piece progresses, till the hearers are worked into a state of cumulated excitement. When there are several instruments and voices thus figuring together over the same bass, the effect is fine. The little tambours, with their gurgling notes, record the time in a kind of unconscious way, and keep the musicians together. The big drums and the lower strings of the *vina* give the required basses, the *taus* and *sítars* and voices fly up and down in delightful intricacy, quarter notes touched here and there create a plaintive discord, and even the slur, judiciously used, adds a weird effect as of the wind in the forest.

When not at its very best, however, it is certainly

(to me) damnably rambling, monotonous, and wearisome—notwithstanding chromatic effects of admitted elegance and occasional passages of great tenderness. What the music most seems to want is distinct form and contrast, and the ruder rockier elements—nor is their time-system sufficiently developed to allow change of accent in successive bars, etc. They all say, however, that the art is not cultivated to-day, and, indeed, is greatly decadent and to some extent actually lost. Like all branches of learning in India, and the caste-system itself, it has been subject to intense pedantry and formalism, and has become nearly stifled amid the otiose rules which cumber it. On the other hand, it is interesting to find that the Hindus call our music not only monotonous (as we call theirs, and which may be accounted for, by mere unfamiliarity—as a town-bred man thinks all sheep alike), but also coarse and rude—by which, I fancy, they mean that our intervals are all very obvious and commonplace, and the time-system rigid—while probably our sequences of harmony are lost upon them. Panna Lall, I find, picks up our tunes quite easily, and seems to like them fairly, but always adds a lot of little kinks and twanks of his own.

After all, though the vaguely-floating, subtle, recitative style of the Indian music has its drawbacks, and makes one crave for a little more definition and articulateness, it presses upon one as possible that *our* music might gain something by the adoption and incorporation of some of these more subtle Eastern elements—if only at times, and as an enhancement of our range of expression by contrast with our own generic style.

CHAPTER XIV

BENARES

THE great plains of the Ganges are very impressive; so vast—with a stretch, roughly speaking, of a thousand miles, and breadth from 200 to 300 miles—so populous,* yet with such an ancient world-old village life; and dominated always by these tremendous powers of sun and sky. All the way from Calcutta to Delhi (and beyond) this immense plain, absolutely flat, spreads in every direction, as far as eye can see, the same—dotted, park-like, with trees (mangos many of them) which, thickening here and there into a clump of palmyra palms, indicate the presence of a village. The long stretches of bare land with hardly a blade of grass, shimmering in the noonday heat; oases of barley and dhol (a shrub-like lentil) looking green at this time of year, but soon to be reaped and stowed away; patches of potatoes, castor-oil plant, poppy in white flower, small guava trees, indigo, etc.; here and there a muddy pool or irrigation channel; a herd of slow, ungainly buffalo, or the more elegant humped cows, browsing miraculously on invisible herbage; a woman following them, barefoot and barehead, singing a sad-toned refrain, picking up the precious dung (for fuel) and storing it in a

* With an average density of population of 500 per square mile, or nearly double that of the United Kingdom!

basket; long expanses of mere sand with a few scrubby trees, brown crop-lands without a crop, straggling natural roads or tracks going to the horizon—not a hedge for hundreds of miles—strings of peasants passing from distant village to village, donkeys laden with produce, and now and then a great solid-wheeled cart laboring and creaking by over the unbroken land. The villages themselves are mostly mere collections of mud huts, looking when partially broken down very like ant-hills; and some villages are surrounded by rude mud walls dating from older and less settled times, and having a very primitive appearance. The people on the whole (after Southern India) look rather dirty in their unbleached cotton, but here and there one meets with bright colors and animated scenes.

Here are two peasants drawing water all day from the well to irrigate their field; one guides the bucket down to the water, the other runs out on the long lever arm of a horizontal pole—holding on to the branches of a neighboring tree as he does so—and so brings the bucket up again. And thus they continue from earliest dawn to latest dusk, with a few hours' rest at midday.

Here is one watering his fields by hand, carrying pots and emptying them over the thirsty plants—a fearful toil!

Here again is the classical picture—the two mild-eyed cows harnessed at the well mouth. The rope passes over a pulley and draws up a huge skin full of water as the cows recede from the well; then, as they remount the slight slope, the skin again falls to the water. To and fro go the cows; one man guides them, another empties the skins into the water channel; and so day-long the work continues.

But out on the great plain you may go for hundreds of miles, and mark but little change or variation. Flocks of green parrots, or of pigeons, fly by, or lesser birds; kites perpetually wheel and float overhead; occasionally you may see an antelope or two among the wilder scrub, or a peahen and her little family; the great cloudless blue (though not by any means always cloudless) arches over to the complete circle of the horizon, the whole land trembles in the heat, a light breeze shivers and whispers in the foliage, the sun burns down, and silence (except for the occasional chatter of the parrots or the plaintive song of the peasant) reigns over the vast demesne.

In many of these villages the face of a white man is seldom or never seen. Even such centres as Allahabad are mere specks in an ocean; the railway is a slender line of civilisation whose influence hardly extends beyond the sound of the locomotive whistle; over the northern borders of the plain the great snows of the Himálayas dawn into sight and fade away again mornings and evenings, and through its midst wind the slow, broad-bosomed waters of the sacred Ganges.

Over all this region, when night comes, floats a sense of unspeakable relief. The spirit—compressed during the day in painful self-defence against the burning sun above and the blinding glare below—expands in grateful joy. A faint odor is wafted from the reviving herbage. The flat earth—which was a mere horizon line in the midday light—now fades into nothingness; the immense and mystic sky, hanging over on every side like a veil, opens back into myriads and myriads of stars—and it requires but little imagination to think that this planet is only an atom in the vast dome of heaven. To the Hindu, Life is that blinding sun, that fever of desire and discomfort, and night is the blessed escape, the liberation of the spirit—its grateful passage into Nirwana and the universal.

One understands (or thinks one does) how these immense plains have contributed to the speculative character of the Hindu mind. Mountains and broken ground call out energy and invention, but here there is no call upon one to leave the place where one is, or to change one's habits of life, for the adjoining hundreds of miles present nothing new. Custom undisturbed consolidates itself; society crystallises into caste. The problem of external life once solved presents no more interest, and mechanical invention slumbers; the mind retires inward to meditate and to conquer. Hence two developments—in the best types that of the transcendental faculties, but in the worst mere outer sluggishness and lethargy. The great idea of Indifference belongs to these flat lands—in its highest form one of the most precious possessions of the human soul, in its lowest nothing better than apathy. The peasant, too, in these plains has for several months nothing to do. He sows his crop, waters it, and reaps it; works hard, and in a few months may painfully gain a year's subsistence; but he can do no more; the hot weather comes, and the green things are burnt up; agriculture ceases, and there remains nothing but to worship the gods. Hence from February to the end of May is the great time for religious festivals, marriages, and ceremonies and frolics of all kinds.

That the Ganges should be sacred, and even an object of worship, is easily intelligible—not only on account of its fertilising beneficence to the land, but there is something impressive in its very appearance: its absolute tranquillity and oceanic character as it flows, from half-a-mile to a mile wide, slowly, almost imperceptibly, onward through the vast hot plain. The water is greenish, not too clear, charged even in the lower portions of its course with the fine mud brought from the mountains; the banks are formed by sandy flats or low cliffs cut in the alluvial soil. As you stand by the water's edge you sometimes in the straighter reaches catch that effect—which belongs to such rivers in flat countries—of flowing broad and tranquil up to and *over* the very horizon—an effect which is much increased by the shimmer of heat over the surface.

In the Mahabhárata Siva is god of the Himálaya range—or rather he *is* the Himálayas—its icy crags his brow, its forests his hair. Ganga, the beautiful Ganga, could not descend to earth till Siva consented to receive her upon his head. So impetuously then did she rush down (in rain) that the god grew angry and locked up her floods amid his labyrinthine hair—till at last he let them escape and find their way to the plains. The worship of Siva is very old—was there perhaps when the ancestors of the Brahmins first found their way into these plains—though we do not hear of it till about 300 B.C.—one of those far-back Nature worships in which the phenomena of earth and sky are so strangely and poetically interwoven with the deepest intimations of the human soul.

On the banks of the Ganges, in the midst of the great plain, stands Benares, one of the most ancient cities of India, and the most sacred resort of Northern Hinduism. Hither come pilgrims by the hundred and the thousand all the year round, to bathe in the Ganges, to burn the bodies of their friends or cast their ashes into the stream, and to make their offerings at the 5000 shrines which are said to exist in the city. Outside the town, along the river-side and in open spots, may be seen the tents of pilgrims, and camels tethered. The city itself stands on the slightest rising ground—hardly to be called a hill—and the river-banks, here higher than usual, are broken and built into innumerable terraces, stairs, temples, and shrines. The scene is exceedingly picturesque, especially as seen from the river; and though taken in detail, the city contains little that is effective in the way of architecture—the shrines and temples being mostly quite small, the streets narrow, and the area of the place circumscribed considering its large population—yet it is the most characteristic and interesting town of India that I have hitherto seen.

The English make no show here—there are no residents, no hotels—the English quarter is four miles off, the names of the streets are not written in English characters, and you hardly see a shop sign in the same. And I must say the result of all this is very favorable. The sense of organic life that you immediately experience is very marked in contrast to a mongrel city like Calcutta. As you thread the narrow alleys, along which no vehicle can pass, with houses three or four storeys high forming a close lane above you, balconies and upper floors projecting in picturesque confusion, not unlike the old Italian towns, you feel that the vari-colored crowd through which you elbow your way is animated by its own distinct standards and ideals. A manifold ancient industry little disturbed by modern invention is going on in the tiny shops on either hand—workshops and saleshops in one. Here is a street full of brass-workers. The elegant brass pots which the whole population uses—for holding or carrying water or oil, for pouring water over the head in bathing, for offering libations in the temples, and so forth—and which form such a feature of Indian folk-life—are here being made, from miniature sizes up to huge vessels holding several gallons. Then there are little brass images, saucers to carry flowers in, and other fancy ware of the same kind.

Another street is full of sandal and leather workers; another of sweetmeat or sweet-cake confectioners; another is given to the sale of woollen and cotton wraps—which are mostly commercial products of the West; stone and marble effigies, and gems, form another branch of industry; and cookshops—innocent, fortunately, of the smell of meat—of course abound. There are many fine faces, both old and young, but especially old—grave, peaceful, penetrative faces—and among the better types of young men some composed, affectionate, and even spiritual faces—withal plenty of mere greed and greasy worldliness.

Niched among these alleys are the numerous shrines and temples already mentioned—some a mere image of Vishnu or Siva, with a lingam in front of it, some little enclosures with several shrines—the so-called Golden Temple itself only a small affair, with one or two roofs plated with gold. In many of the temples brahmin cows wander loose, quite tame, nosing against the worshipers, who often feed them; and the smell of litter and cow-dung mingles with that of frankincense and camphor. Vulture-eyed Brahmins are on the alert round the more frequented sanctuaries, and streams of pilgrims and devotees go to and fro.

The river-side is certainly a wonderful scene. A mere wilderness of steps, stairs, terraces, and jutting platforms, more or less in disorder and decay, stretching for a mile or more by the water. Flights of a hundred steps going up to small temples, or to handsome-fronted but decayed palaces, or to the Mosque of Aurungzebe, whose two tall red-sandstone minarets (notwithstanding the incongruity) are the most conspicuous objects in this sacred metropolis of Hinduism; the steps covered with motley groups going down to or coming up from the water—here an old man, a wanderer perhaps, from some distant region, sitting perched by himself, his knees drawn up to his chin, meditating; there another singing hymns; groups under awnings or great fixed straw umbrellas, chatting, or listening to stories and recitations; here a string of pilgrims with baskets containing their scanty bedding, etc., on their heads, just emerging from one of the narrow alleys; there on a balcony attached to a big building appear half-a-dozen young men, stripped, and with Indian clubs in their hands—their yellow and brown bodies shining in the early sun; they

The Ghauts at Benares

are students at some kind of native seminary and are going through their morning exercises; here are men selling flowers (marigolds) for the bathers to cast into the waters; here is a *yogi* squatted, surrounded by a little circle of admirers; there are boats and a quay and stacks of wood landed, for burning bodies; and there beyond, a burning ghaut.

One morning Panna Lall—who had come on with me from Calcutta—wanted to bathe at a particular ghaut (as each family or caste has its special sanctuaries), so we went off early to the river-side. He looked quite jaunty in his yellow silk coat with white nether garment and an embroidered cap on his head. As it happened, a spring festival was being celebrated, and everybody was in clean raiment and bright colors, yellow being preferred. As we approached the river the alleys began to get full of people coming up after their baths to the various temples—pretty to see the women in all shades of tawny gold, primrose, saffron, or salmon-pink, bearing their brass bowls and saucers full of flowers, and a supply of Ganges water.

The ghauts were thronged. Wandering along them we presently came upon a *yogi* sitting under the shade of a wall—a rather fine-looking man of thirty-five, or nearing forty, with a kindly, unselfconscious face—not at all thin or emaciated or ascetic-looking, but a wild man decidedly, with his hair long and matted into a few close ringlets, black, but turning brown towards his waist, a short, unkempt beard, and nothing whatever on but some beads round his neck and the merest apology for a loin-cloth. He sat cross-legged before a log or two, forming a small fire, which seemed grateful, as the morning was quite cold, and every now and then smeared his body with the wood-ashes, giving it a white and floury appearance. For the rest his furniture was even less than Thoreau's, and consisted apparently of only one or two logs of firewood kept in reserve, a pair of tongs, and a dry palm-leaf overhead to ward off the sun by day and the dews by night. I looked at him for some time, and he looked at me quietly in return—so I went and sat down near him, joining the circle of his admirers, of whom there were four or five. He seemed pleased at this little attention, and told me in reply to my questions that he had lived like this since he was a boy, and that he was very happy—which, indeed, he appeared to be. As to eating, he said he ate plenty "when it came to him" (*i.e.* when given to him), and when it didn't he could go without. I should imagine, however, from his appearance that he did pretty well in that matter—though I don't think the end of his remark was mere brag; for there was that look of *insouciance* in his face which one detects in the faces of the animals. His friends sat round, but without much communication—at anyrate while I was there—except to offer him a whiff out of their pipes every now and then, or drop a casual remark, to which he would respond with a quite natural and pleasant laugh. Of any conscious religion or philosophy I don't think there was a spark in him—simply wildness, and reversion to a life without one vestige of care; but I felt in looking at him that rare pleasure which one experiences in looking at a face without anxiety and without cunning.

A little farther on we came to one of the burning

ghauts—a sufficiently dismal sight—a blackened hollow running down to the water's edge, with room for three funereal pyres in it. The evening before we had seen two of these burning—though nearly burnt out—and this morning the ashes only remained, and a third fresh stack was already prepared. As we stood there a corpse was brought down—wrapped in an unbleached cloth (probably the same it wore in life) and slung beneath a pole which was carried on the shoulders of two men. Round about on the jutting verges of the hollow the male relatives (as we had seen them also the day before) sat perched upon their heels, with their cloths drawn over their heads—spectators of the whole operations. I could not help wondering what sort of thoughts were theirs. Here there is no disguise of death and dissolution. The body is placed upon the pyre, which generally in the case of the poor people who come here is not sufficiently large; a scanty supply of gums and fragrant oils is provided, the nearest male relative applies the torch himself—and then there remains nothing but to sit for hours and watch the dread process, and at the conclusion, if the burning is complete, to collect the ashes and scatter them on the water, and if not, to throw the charred remains themselves into the sacred river. The endurance of the Hindu is proverbial—but to endure such a sight in the case of a dear and near relative seems ultra-human. Every sense is violated and sickened; the burning-ground men themselves are the most abhorred of outcasts—and as they pass to and fro on their avocations the crowd shrinks back from the defilement of their touch.

We did not stay more than a few minutes here, but passed on and immediately found ourselves again amongst an animated and gay crowd of worshipers. This was the ghaut where Panna wished to bathe—a fine pyramidal flight of stairs jutting into the water and leading up to the Durga Temple some way above us. While he was making preparations—purchasing flowers, oil, etc.—I sat down in the most retired spot I could find, under an awning, where my presence was not likely to attract attention, and became a quiet spectator of the scene.

After all, there is nothing like custom. One might think that in order to induce people to bathe by thousands in muddy, half-stagnant water, thick with funeral ashes and drowned flowers, and here and there defiled by a corpse or a portion of one, there must be present an immense amount of religious or other fervor. But nothing of the kind. Except in a few, very few, cases there was no more of this than there is in the crowd going to or from a popular London church on Sunday evening. Mere blind habit was written on most faces. There were the country bumpkins, who gazed about them a bit, and the *habitués* of the place; there were plenty with an eye to business, and plenty as innocent as children; but that it was necessary for some reason or other to bathe in this water was a thing that it clearly did not enter into anyone's head to doubt. It simply had to be done.

The coldness of the morning air was forced on my attention by a group of women coming up, dripping and shivering, out of the river and taking their stand close to me. Their long cotton cloths clung to their limbs, and I wondered how they would dress themselves under these conditions. The steps even were reeking with wet and mud, and could not be used for sitting on. They managed, however, to unwind their wet things and at the same time to put on the dry ones so deftly that in a short time and without any exposure of their bodies they were habited in clean and bright attire. Children in their best clothes, stepping down one foot always first, with, silver toe-rings and bangles, were a pretty sight; and aged people of both sexes, bent and tottering, came past pretty frequently; around on the various levels were groups of gossipers, and parties squatting opposite each other, shaving and being shaved. Nearly opposite to me was one of the frequent stone lingams which abound here at corners of streets and in all sorts of nooks, and I was amused by the antics of a goat and a crow, which between them nibbled and nicked off the flowers, ears of barley, and other offerings, as fast as the pious deposited them thereon.

While I was taking note of these and other features of the scene, my attention was suddenly arrested by a figure standing just in front of me, and I found that I was looking at one of those self-mutilating fakirs of whom everyone has heard. He was a man of a little over thirty perhaps, clothed in a yellow garment—not very tall though of good figure; but his left arm was uplifted in lifelong penance. There was no doubt about it; the bare limb, to some extent dwindled, went straight up from the shoulder and ended in a little hand, which looked like the hand of a child—with fingers inbent and ending in long claw-like nails, while the thumb, which was comparatively large in proportion to the fingers, went straight up between the second and third. The man's face was smeared all over with a yellow pigment (saffron), and this together with his matted hair gave him a wild and demonish appearance.

One often reads of such things, yet somehow without quite realising them; certainly the sight of this deliberate and lifelong mutilation of the human body gave me a painful feeling—which was by no means removed by the expression of the face, with its stultified sadness, and brutishness not without deceit. His extended right hand demanded a coin, which I gladly gave him, and after invoking some kind of blessing he turned away through the crowd—his poor dwindled hand and half-closed fingers visible for some time over the heads of the people. Poor fellow! how little spiritual good his sufferings had done him. His heavy-browed face haunted me for some time. For the rest he was well-liking enough, and it must be said that these fellows for the most part make a fair living out of the pious charity of the people, though I would not be understood to say that all of them adopt this mode of life with that object.

When Panna came up out of the water and had dressed himself, and I had satisfied the curiosity of one or two bystanders who wanted to know whether I had come with him all the way on this pilgrimage out of friendship, we went up to the temple above—where a little band was playing strange and grisly music, and a few devotees were chanting before an image of Siva—and having made an offering returned to our hotel.

CHAPTER XV

THE ANGLO-INDIAN AND THE NATIVE

Allahabad.—It certainly is a very difficult thing to see the real India, the real life of the people. You arrive at a railway station, give the name of a hotel, and are driven there. When you wake up in the morning you find yourself in a region of straight shady avenues, villa residences, hotels and churches, lawn-tennis and whisky pegs. Except that the residences are houses of one storey instead of three, and that the sun is rather glaring for February, you might just as well be at Wandsworth or Kew. In some alarm you ask for the native city and find that it is four miles off! You cannot possibly walk there along the dusty roads, and there is nothing for it but to drive. If there is anything of the nature of a "sight" in the city you are of course beset by drivers; in any case you ultimately have to undergo the ignominy of being jogged through the town in a two-horse conveyance, stared at by the people, followed by guides, pestered for *bakshish*, and are glad to get back to the shelter of your hotel.

If you go and stay with your Anglo-Indian friend in his villa-bungalow, you are only a shade worse off instead of better. He is hospitality itself, and will introduce you cordially to all the other good folk, whom (and their ways) you have seen more than once before at Wandsworth and at Kew; but as to the people of the country, why, you are no nearer them physically, and morally you are farther off, because you are in the midst of a society where it is the correct thing to damn the "oyster" and all that is connected with him.

The more one sees of the world the more one is impressed, I think, by the profundity and the impassability of the gulf of race-difference. Two races may touch, may mingle, may occupy for a time the same land; they may recognise each other's excellencies, may admire and imitate each other; individuals may even cross the dividing line and be absorbed on either side; but ultimately the gulf reasserts itself, the deepset difference makes itself felt, and for reasons which neither party very clearly understands they cease to tolerate each other. They separate, like oil and water; or break into flame and fierce conflict; or the one perishes withering from the touch of the other. There are a few souls, born travelers and such like, for whom race-barriers do not exist, and who are everywhere at home, but they are rare. For the world at large the great race-divisions are very deep, very insuperable. Here is a vast problem. The social problem which to-day hangs over the Western lands is a great one; but this looms behind it, even vaster. Anyhow, in India the barrier is plain enough to be seen—more than physical, more than intellectual, more than moral—a deepset ineradicable incompatibility.

Take that difference in the conception of Duty, to which I have already alluded. The central core of the orthodox Englishman, or at anyrate of the public-school boy who ultimately becomes our most accepted type, is perhaps to be found in that word. It is that which makes him the dull, narrow-minded, noble, fearless, reliable man that he is. The moving forces of the Hindu are quite different; they are, first, Religion; and second, Affection; and it is these which make him so hopelessly unpractical, so abominably resigned, yet withal so tender and imaginative of heart. Abstract duty to the Hindu has but little meaning. He may perform his religious exercises and his caste injunctions carefully enough, but it is because he realises clearly the expediency of so doing. And what can the Englishman understand of this man who sits on his haunches at a railway station for a whole day meditating on the desirability of not being born again! They do not and they cannot understand each other.

Many of the I.C.S. are very able, disinterested, hard-working men, but one feels that they work from basic assumptions which are quite alien to the Hindu mind, and they can only see with sorrow that their work takes no hold upon the people and its affections. The materialistic and commercial spirit of Western rule can never blend with the profoundly religious character of the social organisation normal to India. We undertake the most obviously useful works, the administration of justice, the construction of tanks and railways, in a genuine spirit of material expediency and with a genuine anxiety to secure a 5 per cent. return; to the Hindu all this is as nothing—it does not touch him in the least. Unfortunately, since the substitution of mere open competition for the remains of *noblesse oblige*, which survived in the former patronage appointments to the I.C.S., and with the general growth of commercialism in England, the commercial character of our rule has only increased during the last thirty years. There is less belief in justice and honor, more in 5 per cent. and expediency—less anxiety to understand the people and to govern them well, more to make a good income and to retire to England with an affluence at an early date.

Curious that we have the same problem of race-difference still utterly unsolved in the United States. After all the ardor of the Abolitionists, the fury of civil war, the emancipation of the slaves, the granting of the ballot and political equality, and the prophecies of the enthusiasts of humanity—still remains the fact that in the parts where negroes exist in any numbers the white man will not even ride in the same car with his brother, or drink at the bar where he drinks. So long does it take to surpass and overcome these dividing lines. We all know that they have to be surpassed—we all know that the ultimate and common humanity must disentangle itself and rise superior to them in the end. The Gñáni knows it—it is almost the central fact of his religious philosophy and practice; the Western democrat knows it—it is also the central fact of *his* creed. But the way to its realisation is long and intricate and bewildering.

We must not therefore be too ready to find fault with the Anglo-Indian if he only (so to speak) touches the native with the tongs. He may think, doubtless, that he acts so because the "oyster" is a poor despicable creature, quite untrustworthy, incapable, etc.—all of which may be true enough, only we must not forget that the oyster has a corresponding list of charges against the Anglo—but the real truth on both sides is something deeper, something deeper perhaps than can easily be expressed—a rooted dislike and difference between the two peoples. Providence, for its own good reasons, seems to have put them together for a season in order that they may torment each other, and there is nothing more to be said.

And, putting race-difference aside, it is obvious that the circumstances of our presence in India make any fusion of the two parties very difficult. Certainly the spectacle of our domination of this vast region is a very remarkable one—something romantic, and almost incredible—the absorption and subjection of so many tribes and of such diverse elements under one political rule and standard, the mere handful of foreigners holding the country at such a vast distance from home and from their base of operations, the patience and pluck with which the problem has been worked out, the broad and liberal spirit of administration with less of rapine than perhaps ever known in such a case before, and even an allowance and tenderness for native customs and institutions which are especially remarkable considering the insular habits of the ruling race—all this makes one feel how wonderful an achievement the thing has been. But, so far as intercourse between the two peoples goes, the result has been inevitable. We came to India as foreigners, we remain there as a ruling caste. There is a gulf to begin with; how can it be bridged over?

A young man at the age of twenty-two or twenty-three comes out to join the official ranks. He finds two societies existing, quite sundered from each other. He cannot belong to both. He may have the most cosmopolitan ideas; he might even *prefer* to associate with the subject race, but that would be obviously impossible; he must join his own people —which means the use of the tongs when a native gentleman calls. As a mere lad, even though of strong character, it is impossible for him to withstand the tremendous pressure which the Anglos will bring to bear on him. When he is forty, he will have accommodated his views to his position. Thus the gulf remains as wide as ever.

Then the people themselves are the subject race, and *they* have learned their lesson only too well. Walking through an Indian city is as bad as walking through a Devonshire parish, where the parson and the squire have done their deadly work, and the school children curtsey to you and the farm-laborer pulls his forelock and calls you "Sir," if you only ask the way. I have walked alone through a crowded city in this part of India for two or three hours without seeing a single white face—one among scores of thousands—and the people officiously pushing each other out of the way to make room for me, the native police and soldiers saluting and shouldering arms as one went by, and if one chanced to look too straight at a man he covered his face with his hands and bowed low to the ground! This does not happen fortunately in the great centres like Bombay and Calcutta, but it does in some of the up-country cities; and it is a strange experience, impressing one no doubt with a sense of the power of the little mother-country ten thousand miles away, which throws its prestige around one—but impressing one also with a sinister sense of the gulf between man and man which that prestige has created. It may be imagined that a long course of this kind of thing soon convinces the average Anglo-Indian that he really does belong to a superior order of being—reacting on him just as the curtseys and forelock-pulling react on the class infatuation of squire and parson—and so the gulf gets wider instead of lessening.

At dinner last night I met a dozen or so of the chief officials here, and thought them a capable, intelligent, and good-hearted lot—steeped, of course, in their particular English class tradition, but of their class as good a sample as one could expect to meet. Talking with a Bengali gentleman who was present—one of the numerous Bannerji clan—he reiterated the usual complaint. "The official people," he said, "are very good as long as the governed submit and say nothing; but they will neither discuss matters with individual natives nor recognise the great social movement (National Congress, etc.) that is going on. Their methods, in fact, are those of a hundred years ago." "It is a great pity," he continued, "because in a few years the growing movement will insist on recognition, and then if that leads to altercation and division the future will be lost, both for the English and the native. The people of India are *most* friendly to the Government, and if the official classes would stretch out a hand, and give and take, so to speak, they would be loyal to death."

With these last expressions I am much inclined to agree, for having talked with natives of all classes on this subject—from the lowest to the highest—I have always found but one sentiment, that of satisfaction with the stability and security which our rule has brought to the country at large—not, of course, without serious criticisms of our policy, but with the general conviction, quite spontaneously expressed, that a change of government—as to that of Russia—or even a return to the divided rule of native princes, would be a decided change for the worse. While, however, thus gladly and unasked expressing their loyalty, my interlocutors have (I think in every case) qualified their remarks by expressing their dissatisfaction at the personal treatment they receive from the English. As one friend mildly expressed it, "The English official calls upon you, and you, of course, take care to return his call; but he takes care to confine the conversation to the weather and similar topics, and makes you feel that it is a relief when the visit is over, and so there is not much cordiality."

No doubt as rulers of the country and inheriting, as I have said, a tradition of aloofness and superiority over the ruled, it is difficult for our Anglo-Indian folk to act otherwise than they do. Some of them, I think, feel really grieved at the estrangement. One of the officials here said to me in quite a pathetic tone, "There is a gulf between us and the people which it is very difficult to bridge." The native gentleman, on the other hand, is, very naturally, extremely sensitive about his dignity, and not inclined—under such conditions—to make advances; or, if not sensitive, tends in some cases to be a toady for his own ends; in either case further estrangement results. If the English are to keep India together (supposing that really is a useful object) they must *rule* no doubt, and with a firm hand. At the same time the rapidly-growing public opinion beneath the surface *has* to be recognised, and will have to be recognised even more in the future. I myself am inclined to think that timidity has a good deal to do with the policy of the English to-day. Conscious that they are not touching the people's hearts, and cut off from them so as to be unable to fathom rightly what is going on in their minds, they magnify the perils of their own position, and entrenching themselves in further isolation and exclusiveness, by so doing create the very danger that they would avoid.

Aligurh.—This place affords a striking example of a *rapprochement* taking place between the rulers and the ruled. It is the only place in India which I have visited where I have noticed anything like a cordial feeling existing between the two sections; and this is due to the presence here of the Mohammedan Anglo-Oriental College, run by Englishmen whose instincts and convictions lie a little outside the Anglo-Indian groove. And the fact shows how much might be done by even a few such men scattered over India. Our friends, Theodore Beck and Harold Cox, both Cambridge men, and the latter a decided Socialist in opinion, being connected with the College at its first start a few years ago, naturally made a point of cultivating friendly relations not only with the boys but with their parents—especially those who might happen to be residing in the place. Being also, naturally, on friendly terms with the Anglo-Indians and officials of Aligurh, they (and the College) became a point of contact between the two sections of the community. At cricket-matches, prize-givings, supper-parties, etc., the good people of both sides met and established comparatively cordial relations with each other, which have given, as I say, a quite distinctive flavour to the social atmosphere here.

Last night (Feb. 17th) I came in for a dinner-party, given in the College reception-room by one of the Mohammedan *taluqdars*, or landlords, of the neighborhood—a little, grey, timid man with gold-braided cap and black coat—somewhat resembling the conductor of a German band. Very amusing. Gold caps on beaked and bearded faces, and gorgeous robes; speeches in Hindustani by Englishmen, and in English by Mohammedans; a few Hindus present, sitting apart so as not to eat at the table with us; healths enthusiastically drunk in tea, etc.! and to crown it all, when the health of the Mohammedans and Hindus present was proposed, and the English—including officials, collector, and all—stood up and sang, "For they are jolly good fellows"—the astonishment of the natives, hardly knowing what it all meant and unaccustomed to these forms of jollification, was quite touching.

But the influence of Sir Syed Ahmed here must of course not be overlooked. He is the originator and founder of the M.A.O. College, and one of the leading Mohammedans of India, as well as a confidant of the British and of the Government—a man of considerable weight, courage, and knowledge of the world, if a little ultra-Mohammedan in some of his views and in his contempt of the mild Hindu. He was a member of Lord Ripon's Council, and opposed Lord Ripon with all his might in the matter of the proposed system of popular election to Local Boards and Municipal Councils. The Mohammedan is poles asunder from the modern Radical, and Carlylean in his contempt of voting machinery. His fingers still itch, even in these degenerate days, to cut the Gordian knot of politics with the sword. He hates the acute and tricky Bengali, whom he cannot follow in his acuteness, and whom he disdains to follow in his tricks, and cannot away with his National Congress and representative reforms. But all this perhaps recommends him the more to Anglo-Indian sympathies. There is something in the Mohammedan, with his love of action and dogmatic sense of duty, which makes him more akin to the Englishman than is the philosophical and supple-minded Hindu. And one can easily understand how this race ruled India for centuries, and rejoiced in its rule.

Yet to-day it seems to be the fact that the Mohammedan population is falling into considerable poverty, which—according to some opinions—must end either in the extinction of their influence or their adoption of Western ideas and habits. With the advent of commercialism the stiff-necked son of Islam finds himself ousted in trade by the supple chetty or Brahmin. Hence the feud between the two races, which to a certain extent in the country parts was scarring over with mere lapse of time, seems likely now in the more advancing districts and commercial centres to break out afresh. "In Bundelkhand," says Beck, in his *Essays on Indian Topics*, "where society is very old-fashioned, the Rajas are quite Islamised in their customs and thoughts; while in Calcutta, where English influence has been longest, the anti-Mohammedan feeling reaches its greatest height." That is to say, that in Calcutta and such places the English have brought with them commercialism and a desire among the Hindus for political representation, both of which things have only served to enrage the two parties against each other—Hindu against Mohammedan, and Mohammedan against Hindu.

When a man of authority and weight could make such a jingo speech as that of Sir Syed Ahmed at Lucknow in 1887—who in the extremity of his contempt for the Hindu said, "*We* do not live on fish; nor are we afraid of using a knife and fork lest we should cut our fingers (cheers). Our nation is of the blood of those who made not only Arabia but Asia and Europe to tremble. It is our nation which conquered with its sword the whole of India, although its peoples were all of one religion"—one realises how deep-set is the antagonism still existing. Though forming a minority, fifty or sixty million descendants of a powerful race sharing such sentiments cannot be ignored; and it is obvious that the feud between the two races must for a long period yet form one of the great difficulties and problems of Indian politics.

A few years ago the Hindus tied a pig at nighttime in the midst of the Jumma Mosque at Delhi, where it was found in the morning by the infuriated Mahommedans. They in retaliation cut up a brahmin cow and threw it into a well used by Hindus. Street fights and assassinations followed and many people were killed—and the affair might have grown to a large scale but for the interference of British troops. Such little amenities are not infrequent, at any rate in certain districts.

There is a big horse-fair going on here just now. A hundred booths or more arranged in four little streets in form of a cross, with decorations. All round, bare sandy land with horses tied up for sale.

The Cabulees—great tall men with long hair and skin coats, fur inside, and ramshackle leggings and shoes—ride in with their strings of horses, 300 or 400 miles from the frontier—where they are obliged to pile their arms until they return, as they would play the deuce in the country if they were to bring their guns with them. They look tidy ruffians, and no doubt would overrun the country if not held back by the English or some military power.

Outside the fair is a wrestling arena, with earth-banks thrown up round it, on which a motley crowd of spectators was seated to-day. Saw several bouts of wrestling. The Aligurh champion's challenge was accepted by a big Punjaubee, a fellow from Meerut, over sixty years of age, but remarkably powerful—burly, with small nose, battered ears, and huge frontal prominences like some African chieftain or Western prize-fighter—good-humored too and even jolly till accused of unfair play, when he raged among the mob, and the meeting broke up in insane noise and blows of sticks—a small whirlwind of combatants eddying away for some distance over the plain. It was characteristic though, that when they had had enough of fighting, the two parties came back and appealed for fair play to Beck and me—the only two Englishmen present—though there did not seem the least reason why they should, and we were quite unable to afford them any proper satisfaction.

CHAPTER XVI

DELHI AND AGRA

THE train rushes over an iron girder bridge, crossing the Jumna, into Delhi. There are sandy flats and bits of garden by the river-side, and then the great red-sandstone walls of the fort, 30 or 40 feet high, surmounted by remnants of the old white marble palace of Shah Jehan, looking out eastward over the great plain. Here are the Pearl Mosque —a little pure white shrine—the Shah's private audience-hall, the zenana apartments, and the royal baths, still standing. The women's apartments are certainly lovely. White and polished marble floor and marble walls inlaid with most elegant floral and arabesque designs in mosaics of colored stones, and in gold; with marble screens of rich lace-like open work between the apartments and the outer world; and a similarly screened balcony jutting over the fort wall—through which the river and the great plains beyond are seen shimmering in the heat. The private audience-hall is of like work—a sort of open portico supported on some twenty marble columns, with marble floor and rich mosaic everywhere (see illustration), and the baths the same. Indeed the old Padishah with his fifty queens must have had some high old times in these baths—one for himself, one for the queens, and one for his children, all opening conveniently into each other.

Behind the fort used to be the densest part of the city; but after the Mutiny this was cleared away, and now an open space extends from the fort walls up to the Jumma Mosque and the present Delhi.

A large city of narrow alleys and courtyards—here and there a broad tree-planted avenue with

Dewan Khas, or Audience Hall, in Palace at Delhi

disheveled little two-storey houses on each hand, and occasional banks, hotels, and offices. Crowds of people. A finer-looking race than southwards—more of the Mohammedan element—and about the Hindus themselves more fling and romance and concreteness; some handsome faces, verging a little towards the Greek or Italian types—but looking fine with their dark skins. I suppose that in the Punjaub the men are finer and taller still, and look down a little on the folk at Delhi. Cows and brahmin bulls throng the streets, and come out of courtyards in the mid-city. Some of these bulls are public property, belong to no individual, and live on the highways and mingle with the herds of cows. When they want food they go into the market, and the Hindus feed them with their hands.

The Jumma Mosque is the first large mosque I have seen in India, but I am a little disappointed with it. These Indian mosques differ a little from the Turkish—being quite open to sun and sky. The idea seems to be, first a large open square, 100 feet across, or 100 yards, or more, paved with marble if possible, with a tank in the middle for worshipers to wash their feet in, and an arcade round three sides, very likely open-work of stone, with fine gateways in each side—and on the fourth side a sort of very handsome portico, with its floor raised above the general court, and surmounted by three domes. Right and left of the portico stand the two tall minarets. To be perfect the whole should be of white polished marble inlaid with arabesques and scriptures from the Koran. One of the main points is the absolute purity of the place. There is nothing whatever under the portico—no likeness of beast or bird—only three recesses in which one might fairly expect to see an altar or an image, a flight of three steps on which the reader stands to read the Koran, and that is all. Attendants continually dust the whole courtyard with cloths to keep it clean.

From a distance the effect of the domes, the minarets, the open-work of the arcade, the handsome gateways, and the little kiosks is very attractive; but within one misses something. It seems as if the portico ought to open back on a vast interior; but it doesn't. There is no mysterious gloom anywhere —not a cranny for a hobgoblin even. There is no nice Virgin Mary in the niches, or nasty gargoyle

The Jumma Mosque, Delhi

on the angles, no meditative Buddha or terrifying Kali with necklace of skulls, no suggestion of companionship human or divine, no appeal to sense. It doesn't give one a chance of even having a make-believe god. How different from Hinduism with its lingams and sexual symbols deified in the profound gloom of the temple's innermost recess!

What an extraordinary region is this to the south

and west of Delhi—a huge waste sprinkled with the ruins of six or seven previous Delhis! Emperors in those days had a cheerful way—when they thought they had found a securer or more convenient site—of calmly removing a whole city from its old location. Now you pass through an arid land, here and there green with crops, but running up into stony ridges and mounds, and dotted with ruins as far as the eye can see. Stumpy domes of decayed mosques in every direction looming against the sky, mere lumps of brickwork, now turned into barns and farmyards, or with herds of goats sheltering from the sun beneath their arches—the land in some parts fairly covered with loose stones, remnants of countless buildings. Here and there, among some foliage, you see a great mosque tomb in better preservation—kept up by the Government—that of Safdar Jung, for instance, who died 1753, Vizier of the Emperor Muhammad Shah, or of the Emperor Humayoun, or the marble shrine of the poet Khusro. Along the roads go bullock-carts of all kinds, some with curtains to them, concealing women-folk; and camels with loads of grass, and donkeys with huge panniers of cow-dung; and by the wayside are ash trees and peepul trees, and wells worked by brahmin cows drawing up water in huge skins.

Eleven miles south of Delhi stands the great Kutab Minar, a huge tower 240 feet high and 50 feet diameter at its base—tapering through five storeys to its summit, which unfortunately has lost its four-columned watch-turret and has only now a wretched iron rail—a kind of multiple column breaking out into a sort of scroll-work capital at each landing—not very beautiful, but impressive in its lonely vastness. The twin column or *minar*—hardly to be called minaret—was never finished; its base alone stands to a height of 40 or 50 feet. Between them lie the remains of a handsome mosque, and *within* the courtyard of the mosque the columned arcades of an ancient Hindu temple; while the whole group stands within the lines of the old Hindu fortress of Lalkab built about A.D. 1060. The mosque and minar were built by Kutab-ud-din about 1200 A.D.; but the Hindu temple is no doubt considerably older. Within the latter stands the celebrated iron pillar (22 feet high above ground—and said to be an equal depth below the surface—by 16 inches diameter at base)—whose construction at that early date is somewhat of a puzzle. It evidently is not a casting, but hammered. It is of pure iron, and was probably, I should say, welded to these huge dimensions piece by piece. A Sanskrit inscription on it recording a victory over the Bahilkas near the seven mouths of the Indus, fixes its date at A.D. 360-400.

This huge Kutab Minar is supposed to have been built as a kind of glorification of the triumph of Mohammedanism over Hinduism; but now from its top one looks out over a strange record of arid lands and deserted cities—both Mohammedan and Hindu—fortified places built one after another in succession and razed to the ground or deserted. The circles of their old walls are still, however, mostly traceable. One of these, which was called Toglakabad, and was destroyed by Tamerlane in 1398, lies to the south-east. Another, which the English call the old Fort, and which lies nearer Delhi, I visited on my way back to the city. Like most of the villages it stands on an eminence composed of the debris of former habitations. The walls, 40 feet high, of this little fortress, whose irregular sides are none of them probably much more than a quarter of a mile in length, are very rude but bold stonework, and command a dry ditch. Within there are now only a hundred or so mud huts, and a red-sandstone mosque of rather good appearance—from the terrace of which you look out over the Jumna and see the minarets of the present city only three or four miles off. Owing, however, to the dust flying in the air the views were by no means very clear.

Agra.—The fort here is quite on the same lines as that at Delhi, but of earlier date—built by Akbar in 1566 or so—and even finer in conception. There is indeed something very grand about this bold, stern, and practical Mohammedan structure, with its lofty seventy-foot walls and solid gateway of red sandstone, surmounted by the glitter of the marble and gilt-roofed domes and arcades and terraces which formed the royal palace within. All these buildings of the royal palace, like the Taj and other monuments, are now kept and repaired by the British Government, and with tender care; and are open for visitors to walk through at their own sweet will—subject to the trivial importunities of a few guides. One may wander for a whole day through the many courts of the palace at Agra and keep finding fresh beauties and interest. After one guide has been exhausted and paid off the others leave one respectfully alone, and one may sit down in the lovely arcade of the Dewan Khas, or in the canopied balcony called the Jessamine Tower, and enjoy the shade and coolness of the marble, or the sight of the brilliant landscape between the arches—the river-banks and the busy folk washing themselves and their linen—or study the beautiful floral mosaics upon walls and columns, at one's leisure.

In marble and mosaic it is impossible to imagine

Pertorated Marble Screen in Palace at Delhi

anything more elegant than the Mohammedan work of this period—as illustrated by numbers of buildings—the brilliant coloring and richness of inlaid stone in coral, agate, jade, bloodstone, turquoise, lapis-lazuli, or what not; the grace of running leaf and flower; the marble reliefs—whole plants—in panels, the lily or the tulip or the oleander conventionalised—one of the most beautiful in the Dewan Khas being a design of the tomato plant; and then the inimitable open-work screens (often out of one great slab of stone)—of intricately balanced yet transparently simple designs—some in the zenana apartments here almost as elaborate as lacework; and the care and finish with which they have all been wrought and fitted. It was from this fort and among these arcades and balconies that 500 English during the early days of the Mutiny watched the clouds of flame and smoke going up from their burning homes.

Here at Agra I find myself as usual at least an hour's walk from the native city, measuring by milestones—but how far I am from any possibility of converse with the people there, considering that I cannot speak their language, that they bow to the ground if I only look at them, and that my view of *noblesse oblige* as a Britisher should forbid my associating freely with them, is more than I can calculate. To go and see the Taj Mahal is easy enough; but to explore what lies behind some of these faces that I see on the road—beautiful as they are, something more wonderful than even the Taj itself—is indeed difficult. All this is very trying to people of democratic tendencies; but perhaps it will be said that such people ought not to visit India, at anyrate under its present conditions.

One must, I suppose, console oneself with the Taj. I saw it for a few brief minutes this evening under the magic conditions of deep twilight. I was standing in the middle of the garden which opens like a lovely park in front of the tomb. Cypresses and other trees hid its base; the moonlight was shining very tenderly and faintly on the right of the great white building; and on its left a touch of the blush of sunset still lingered on the high dome. The shadows and recesses and alcoves were folded as it were in the most delicate blue mist; the four minarets were (in the doubtful light) hardly visible;

The Taj, at Agra

and in the heart of the shrine, through the marble lacework of doors and screens, was seen the yellow glow of the lamps which perpetually burn there.

I think this is the best point of view. The garden foliage hides the square platform on which the Taj stands—which platform with its four commonplace minarets is an ugly feature, and looks too obtrusively like a table turned upside down. Indeed the near view of the building is not altogether pleasing to me. The absolute symmetry of the four sides, which are identical even down to the mosaic designs, and the abrupt right angles of the base give the thing a very artificial look. But the inlaid work of colored and precious stones—only to be seen on a near view—is, of course, perfect.

The Taj stands on a terrace which falls perpendicular into the Jumna river (behind the building in the above illustration). A mile and a half away to the west lies the sombre line of the fort walls crowned with the marble kiosks and minarets of the royal palace. A mile or two beyond that again lies the city of Agra, with one or two spires of English churches or colleges; while to the east the lovely tomb looks out over a wild ravine land, bare and scarred, which suggests a landscape in the moon as much as anything.

In the daytime the ornamental garden of which I have spoken, with its gay flowers, and water-tanks, and children at play, sets off the chaste beauty of the building; while the reflected lights from the marble platform, with their creamy tints, and blue in the shadows, give an added aërial charm. The thing certainly stands solid, as though it would last for centuries—and might have been built yesterday for any sign of decay about it. Indeed I was startled—as if my own thoughts had been echoed—when I heard a voice behind me say in good English, "This is rather a different style from your English jerry-building is it not?"—and looking round saw a somewhat jerry-built native youth, whose style showed that he came from one of the great commercial centres, saluting me in these mocking tones.

The small green parrots (the same that one commonly sees in cages in England) which are common all over India, and which haunt the Taj here and its garden, billing and chattering close by one, are quite a feature of the place; their flight, with the long tail straight behind, is something like a cuckoo's or a hawk's. Occasionally one may see a vulture perched upon some point of vantage looking down upon them with an envious eye. In Delhi, walking through a crowded street, I saw a kite swoop down and actually snatch something—some eatable I think—out of a child's hand a little in front of me. It then soared up into the air, leaving the little one terrified and sobbing on a doorstep.

This great river (the Jumna, and the Ganges the same) and the plain through which it slowly winds have a great fascination for me—the long reaches and sandy spurs, the arid steep banks and low cliffs catching just now the last red light of sunset—here and there a little domed building standing out on a promontory, with steps down to the water—or a brown grass-woven tent on the sands below; the great vultures slowly flapping hitherward through the fading light; a turtle splashing into the water; the full moon mounting into the sky, though yet with subdued glory, and already the twinkle of a light in a house here and there; and on my right this great mountain of marble catching the play of all the heavenly radiances.

She must have been very beautiful, that queen-wife, "the crown of the palace," to have inspired and become the soul of a scene like this; or very lovely in some sense or other—for I believe she was already the mother of eight children when she died. But, indeed, it does not matter much about external or conventional beauty; wherever there is true love there is felt to be something so lovely that all symbols, all earth's shows, are vain to give utterance to it. Certainly, if anything could stand for the living beauty of a loved creature, it might be this dome, pulsating with all the blushes and radiances of the sky, which makes a greater dome above it.

Across the river, just opposite, you dimly distinguish the outline of a vast platform—now mainly ploughed up and converted into fields—on which the good Shah intended to have built a similar or twin tomb for his own body; fortunately, however, he died long before this idea could be carried out, and now he lies more appropriately by the side of his loved one in the vocal gloom of that lofty interior.

"You say we Mohammedans do not respect our women, yet where in all Europe can you point out a monument to a woman equal to this?" said Syed Mahmoud triumphantly to me one day. And then one remembers that this precious monument (like so many others that the world is proud of) was made by the forced and famine labor of 20,000 workmen working for seventeen years—and one thinks, "What about them and *their* wives?"

Called on a coterie of professors connected with the university college at Agra—A. C. Bose, who is professor of mathematics; Gargaris, professor of physics; Nilmani Dhar, law lecturer; and A. C. Bannerji, judge of small cause court—an intelligent and interesting lot of fellows. I found Bose reading a book on Quaternions; when he learnt that I had known W. K. Clifford at Cambridge he was much interested, and wanted to hear all about him—has read his book on "The Common-Sense of the Exact Sciences," and was interested in the theory of "crumpled space" and the fourth dimension. They told me a good deal about family communism as it exists among the Bengalis, and spoke rather feelingly of its drawbacks—in respect of the incubus of poor relations, etc. They also asked some questions—rather touching—about sending their sons to study in England, and what treatment they might expect at the hands of the English at home—"if it were the same as we receive here, we would never consent to send our sons." Of course I assured them that their reception in England would be perfectly cordial and friendly. At the same time I said that they must not think ill of the English people generally because of the unfortunate gulf existing between the two races in India; because, after all, the officials and Anglo-Indians generally—though an honorable body—could not be taken to represent the whole people of England, but only a small section; and that, as a matter of fact, the masses of the people in England made much the same complaint against the moneyed and ruling sections there—namely, that they were wanting in good manners. Bannerji asked me if I saw the Lieut.-Governor (Sir A. Colvin) at Allahabad, and I said that I had had some conversation with him, and that I thought him a man of marked ability and culture, and probably having more liberality in his real opinions than his natural reserve and caution would allow him to give rein to.

Gargaris is a big-headed, logical-minded, slowish man who inquired much after the Positivists, and apparently thinks much of them—being indeed of that type himself. Nilmani Dhar seemed very enthusiastic about the Brahmo Somaj, which, I cannot say, I feel any interest in. He is, of course, a Theist, but most of the folk nowadays who go in for Western learning and ideas are Agnostics, and adopt the scientific materialism of Huxley and Tyndall.

The men in the streets here—and I noticed the same at Nagpore—are very handsome, many of them, with their large eyes and well-formed noses, neither snub nor hooked, and short upper lips. With great turbans (sometimes a foot high) on their heads, and fine moustaches, they look quite martial; but like mermaids they end badly, for when you look below you see two thinnest shins with little tight cotton leggings round them, and bare feet. How they get these leggings on and off is a question which I have not yet been able to solve. Anyhow, I have come to the conclusion about the Hindus generally that their legs are too thin for them ever to do much in the world.

The people sitting by the hundred at all the railway stations in this part of India, waiting for their trains, are quite a sight. They congregate in large sheds or areas—hardly to be called waiting-*rooms*—reserved for this purpose; and whether it be that their notion of time is so defective, or whether it be for the sake of society or of rest or shelter that they come there, certain it is that at any hour of day or night you may see these compacted crowds of thin-shanked, undemonstrative men, with wives and children, seated squatting on their hams, talking or meditating or resigning themselves to sleep, as if the arrival of their train was an event far remote, and of the very least importance. They must, however, really enjoy this method of traveling, for the third-class carriages are generally crowded with the poorer natives. They squat on the seats in all attitudes, and berth-like seats being let down overhead, they sometimes occupy these too—forming two storeys of cross-legged mortals. The women and children have a carriage to themselves—a fine exhibition generally of nose-rings and ear-rings. It is the third class that pays; first and second are only scantily used; the first by English alone, the second by mixed English and higher class natives. Though the distances to be covered by the traveling Englishman are generally large the conditions are not uncomfortable. Journeys are made largely by night, for coolness; first and second class are generally small saloons with couch-like seats; and these couches, with the berths available above, generally allow of one's having a good stretch and a sound sleep.

Traveling second class one meets (though not always) with some pleasant natives. As a specimen (and a favourable one) of the Young India that is growing up under modern influences I may mention a railway goods clerk who was my companion in the train between Nagpore and Bombay; a very bright face, with clear, well-balanced expression, and good general ability,—said he worked ten hours a day on the average, Rs. fifteen a month, but would be raised next year; was leaving Nagpore district because it was so out of the way—no papers, etc. "In Bombay you knew what was going on all over the world. Why, he had only heard of Mr Bradlaugh's death yesterday—two months after date." The English rule was very good. "Under the Mahrattas you were liable any day to have your goods stolen, but now there was general security, and peace between the different peoples instead of dissension, as there would be if the English were to go"—a real nice fellow, and I felt quite sorry when he left the train.

Later on the same evening, in the same train, a little incident occurred which may be worth recording. I and another Englishman were the sole occupants of the compartment; it was in fact near midnight, and we were stretched on our respective couches, when our slumbers were disturbed by the entrance of a family of four or five Parsees, among whom were a lady and a child and an old gentleman of somewhat feeble but refined appearance. Of course, though we were not disturbed, there was a little conversation and discussion while couches were being arranged and berths let down, etc.—till at last my fellow-countryman, losing his little store of patience, rolled over among his rugs with a growl: "I wish you would stop that chattering, *you Parsees.*" To which, when they had settled themselves a bit, one of them, looking over the edge of his berth, replied, "Please to sleep now, *Mr. Gentleman.*"

CHAPTER XVII

BOMBAY

THE native city of Bombay is really an incredible sight. I walked through some part of it I suppose every day for a week or more, trying to photograph its shows upon my brain, yet every day it seemed more brilliant and original than before—and I felt that description or even remembrance were nothing to compare with the actual thing. The intense light, the vivid colors, the extraordinarily picturesque life, the bustle and movement; the narrow, high, tumbled houses with projecting storeys, painted shutters, etc., and alleys simply *thronged* with people; the usual little shops with four or five men and boys squatted in each, and multifarious products and traffic—gold and silverwork of excellent quality, elegant boxes and cabinets, all being produced in full view of the public—embroidery and cap shops, fruit shops, sweetmeat shops, cloth merchants, money-changers; such a chattering, chaffering, and disputing, jokes shouted across the street from shop to shop; Hindu temples, mosques, opium dens, theatres, clubs; and at night, lights and open casements and balconies above with similar groups; handsome private houses too scattered about, but some of them now converted into warehouses or lodging-houses, and looking dirty enough.

Imagine a great house towering above the rest,

with projecting storeys and balconies and casements —the top tiers nothing but painted wood and glass, like the stern of a huge three-decker. The basement storey is open and fronted with great carved wooden columns. Here are a few plants standing,

Street in Bombay, Native Quarter

(Little shops on each side, a mosque on the left)

and among them—his gold-brown body thrown up against the gloom behind—stands a young boy of eight or nine, nearly naked, with silver wristlets and string of blue beads round his neck. The next houses are low, only two or three storeys, and their basements are let out in tiny shops only a few feet square each. Here, squatted among cushions, smoking his long pipe, sits an old money-lender with white cap and frock and gold-rimmed spectacles. Near him are boys and assistants, totting up accounts or writing letters on their knees. The man is worth thousands of pounds, but his place of business is not bigger than a dining-room table —and there are scores like him. The next few shops are all silversmiths—four or five in each shop, couches and cushions as before, and cabinets full of trinkets. Farther on they are hammering brass and copper—a score of shops at least consecutive. Now we come to an archway, through which behold a large reservoir, with people bathing. There is a Hindu temple here, and they do not like us to enter; but under the arch sits an old ascetic. He has sat cross-legged for so many years that he can take no other position; sometimes for extra penance he gets them to lift him up and seat him on a spiked board; but I fancy he is such a hardened old sinner that he does not feel even that much! He is a well-known character in the city.

A little farther on, in a balcony, is a group of girls, with henna-black eyes, somewhat daintily got up, and on the look-out for visitors. Now a covey of Parsee women and children comes by, brilliant in their large silk wraps (for even the poorer Parsee females make a point of wearing these)—pale-green or salmon color, or blue—drawn over their heads and depending even to their feet—their large dark eyes shining with fire and intelligence, not the timid glance of the general run of Indian women. Many of the Parsee fair ones, indeed—especially of the well-to-do classes—are exceedingly handsome. But the women generally in Bombay form quite a feature; for the Mahrattas, who constitute the bulk of the population, do not shut up their women, any more than the Parsees do, and numbers of these—mostly, of course, though not exclusively, of the

Parsee Woman

poorer classes—may be seen moving quite freely about the streets: the Mahratta fisher-women for instance, dressed not in the long depending cloak of the Parsees, but in the ordinary Indian *sari*, which they wind gracefully about the body, leaving their legs bare from the knees down. Of the

Parsees I understand that they are very helpful to each other as a community, and while leaving their women considerable freedom are at pains to prevent any of them falling through poverty into a life of prostitution.

If you take this general description of the native Bombay, and add to it a handsome modern city, with fine Banks, Post and Government offices, esplanades, parks, docks, markets, railway stations, etc.; and then again add to that a manufacturing quarter with scores of chimneys belching out smoke, ugly stretches of waste land, and all the dirt of a Sheffield or Birmingham (only with coco-palms instead of oak-trees shriveling in the blight); then distribute through it all a population, mainly colored, but of every nation in the world, from sheerly naked water-carriers and coolies to discreet long-raimented Parsees and English "gentlemen and ladies"—you will have an idea of Bombay—the most remarkable city certainly that I have visited in this part of the world.

The Parsee nose is much in evidence here. You meet it coming round the corner of the street long before its owner appears. It is not quite the same as the Jewish, but I find it difficult to define the difference; perhaps though larger it is a little suaver in outline—more *suaviter in modo,* though not less *fortiter in re.* It is followed by a pair of eyes well on the alert, which don't miss anything that the nose points out. At every turn you meet that same shrewd old gentleman with the beautifully white under-raiment falling to his feet, and a long China silk coat on, and black brimless hat—so collected and "all there"; age dims not the lustre of his eye to biz. Somehow he strangely reminds one of the neighborhood of the London Stock Exchange, only it is a face of more general ability than you often see in the City.

Parsee Merchants

And (what also is more than can be said for his City *confrère*) he is up early in the morning for his religious exercises. At sunrise you may see him on the esplanades, maidans, and other open places, saying his prayers with his face turned towards the east. He repeats or reads in an undertone long passages, and then bows three times towards the light; then sometimes turning round will seem to go through a similar ceremony with his back to it. The peculiarity of the physiognomy (not forgetting the nose of course) seems to lie in the depth of the eye. This together with the long backward line of the eyelid gives a remarkable look of intelligence and earnestness to the finer faces.

The younger Parsee is also very much to the fore —a smartish fellow, not without some Brummagem self-confidence — pushing in business and in his efforts to join in the social life of the English; who in revenge are liable to revile him as the 'Arry of the East. Anyhow they are a go-ahead people, these Cursetjees, Cowasjees, Pestonjees, and Jejeebhoys; and run most of the cotton mills here. Justice Telang spoke to me highly one day of them as a body—their helpful brotherly spirit and good capacity and versatility. He said, however, that they were not taking the lead in *business* quite so much as formerly, but turning rather more to poitical life.

Telang himself is of Mahratta extraction — a sturdy, well-fleshed man, of energy and gentleness combined—able, sound, and sensible, I should say, with good judgment and no humbug. He, of course, thinks the creation of a united India a long and difficult affair: but does not seem to despair of its possibility; acknowledges that the Mohammedan element is mostly indifferent or unfriendly to the idea, but the Parsees are favorable.

I was in Telang's court one day, and admired much the way he conducted the business. On the whole I thought the English barristers present showed up only feebly against the native judge and pleaders. I certainly am inclined to think the educated natives quite equal or if anything superior to the Englishman in matters of pure intellect (law, mathematics, etc.); where they are wanting—taking the matter quite in bulk, and with many individual exceptions—is in that quality which is expressed by the word *morale*; and it is that defect which prevents them being able to make the best use of their brain power, or to hold their own against us in the long run. So important is that quality. The Anglo-Saxons, with deficient brains, have it in a high degree, and are masters of the world.

I called another day on Tribhovan Das, who is head of the Bunyas here—a large and influential merchant caste. He occupies the house which belonged to his father, Sir Mungal Das, who was member of the Bombay Legislative Council and a great man in his time both in wealth and influence. The house is a large one standing in the native city. We went and sat in state in a big drawing-room, and then made a tour of the other reception-rooms and the library, and solemnly inspected and admired the works of art—oscillating models of ships in a storm, pictures with musical boxes concealed behind them, a huge automatic musical organ, wax-flowers and fruits in the library, fountains in the garden, etc.—all quite in the style of the reception-rooms of wealthy natives twenty years or so ago. Tribhovan showed me over it all with that mingled air of childlike pride and intense boredom which I have noticed before in Orientals under the same circumstances; then took me out for a drive in his swagger barouche, with white horses, and men in sky-blue livery—along the Malabar drive and up to the reservoir on the hill-top, a very charming seaside road, and thronged at that hour on Sunday evening with carriages and the motley aristocracy of the city. The view from the reservoir is famous. The Malabar hill is a promontory jutting southward into the sea, and occupied largely with villa residences. Westward from its summit you look over the open ocean, dotted with white sails; eastward, or south-eastward, across a narrow bay, is seen the long spit of flat land on which modern mercantile Bombay stands, with its handsome public buildings and long line of esplanade already at that hour beginning to twinkle with lamps. Beyond that spit again, and farther eastward, lies another much deeper and larger bay, the harbor proper, with masts of ships just discernible; and beyond that again are the hills of the mainland. At the base of the spit and a little inland lies the native portion of Bombay—largely hidden, from this point of view, by the masses of coco-nut trees which grow along its outskirts and amongst its gardens.

Tribhovan said he would much like to come to England, but that as head of the caste it was quite impossible. He told me that many people think the Bunyas took their dress (the cylindrical stiff hat like an English chimney-pot hat without a brim, and the long coat buttoned close round the neck) from the Parsees; but it was just the opposite—the Parsees when they came to India having adopted the dress of those Hindus amongst whom they first found themselves—namely, the Bunyas.

Whilst driving back through the city we came upon a marriage ceremony going on—a garden full of lights, and crowds of people conversing and taking refreshments. Two houses opened on the same garden, and one of these was occupied for the occasion by the bridegroom and his friends, and the other by the bride. This is the orthodox arrangement, enabling the bridegroom to descend into the garden and go through the ceremony of taking (capturing) his bride; and my host explained that houses thus arranged are often kept and let solely for this purpose—as few people have houses and gardens of their own large enough for the array of guests asked, or suitably built for the ceremony. In the thick of the city the bridegroom will sometimes manage to hire or get the loan of a house in the same street and opposite to that in which his bride dwells, and then the street is turned into a temporary garden with ornamental shrubs and branches, and lanterns are hung (for the ceremony is always in the evening) and chairs placed in rows, and a large part of the processions and festivities are as public as the gossips can desire. All this adds much to the charm of life in this most picturesque city.

The native theatres here are a great institution—crowded mostly by men and boys of the poorer sort—the performance a curious rambling business, beginning about 9 P.M. and lasting say till 2 or 3 in the morning! Murderous and sensational scenes carried out by faded girls and weak ambrosial youths, and protracted in long-drawn agonies of operatic caterwauling, with accompainment of wondrous chromatic runs on the *taus* and a bourdon bass on some wind instrument. Occasionally a few sentences spoken form a great relief. What makes the performance so long is the slowness of the action—worse even than our old-fashioned opera; if the youth is madly in love with the girl he goes on telling her so in the same "rag" for a quarter of an hour. Then she pretends to be indifferent, and spurns him in another "rag" for fifteen minutes more!

Another feature of Bombay nowadays, and indeed of most of the towns of India, including even quite small villages, is the presence and work of the Salvation Army. I must say I am Philistine enough to admire these people greatly. Here in this city I find "Captain" Smith and young Jackson (who were on board ship with me coming out) working away night and day in the "cause," and always cheerfully and with a smile on their faces—leading a life of extreme simplicity, penury almost, having no wages, but only bare board and lodging—with no chance even to return home if they get sick of the work, unless it were by the General's order. "I should have to work my way back on board ship if I wanted to go, but I shall not want to go, I shall be happy here," said Jackson to me. These two at anyrate I feel are animated by a genuine spirit. Whatever one may think of their judgment or their philosophy, I feel that they really care for the lowest and most despised people and are glad to be friends and brothers with them—and after all that is better philosophy than is written in the books. They adopt the dress of the people and wear turbans and no shoes; and most of them merge their home identity and adopt a native name. Of course, it is easy to say this is done out of mere religious conceit and bravado; but I am certain that in many cases it springs from something much deeper than that.

One day I joined a party of five of them on their way to the Caves of Elephanta—"Captain" and Mrs Smith, "Sikandra" (Alexander), and two others. Mrs Smith is a nice-looking and real good woman of about thirty years of age, and Sikandra is a boy of ability and feeling who has been out here about three years. They were all as nice and natural as could be (weren't pious at all), and we enjoyed our day much—a three hours' sail across the bay in a lateen-sailed boat with two natives—the harbor a splendid sight, with its innumerable shipping, native fish-boats, P. and O. and other liners, two or three ironclads, forts, lighthouses, etc.—and then on beyond all that to the retired side of the bay and the islands; picnic on Elephanta Island under the shade of a great tamarind-tree—visit to the caves, etc.; and return across the water at sundown.

Very *Indian* these islands—the hot smell of the ground covered with dead grass and leaves, the faint aromatic odor of sparse shrubs, with now and then a waft of delicious fragrance from the little white jessamine; the thorns and cactus, palms, and mighty tamarinds dropping their sweet-acid fruit. Then the sultry heat at midday, the sea lying calm and blue below in haze, through which the ridged and rocky mountains of the mainland indistinctly loom, and the far white sails of boats; nearer, a few humped cows and a collection of primitive huts, looking, from above, more like heaps of dead palm-leaves than human habitations.

The great cave impressed me very much. I have not seen any other of these Indian rock-sanctuaries, but this one gave me a greater sense of artistic power

The Great Cave at Elephanta

(Some of the rock-pillars being restored, sculptured figures visible in background)

and splendid purpose than anything in the way of religious architecture—be it mosque or Hindu temple—that I have seen in India. It is about half-way up the hillside from the water, and consists of a huge oblong hall, 50 yards square, cut sheerly into the face of the rock, with lesser halls opening into it on each side. Huge pillars of rock, boldly but symmetrically carved, are left in order to support the enormous weight above; and the inner roof is flat—except for imitations of architraves running from pillar to pillar. The daylight, entering in mass from the front, and partly also by ingenious arrangement from the sides, is broken by many great pillars, and subdues itself at last into a luminous gloom in the interior—where huge figures of the gods, 18 feet high, in strong relief or nearly detached, stand out from the walls all round. These figures are nobly conceived and executed, and even now in their mutilated condition produce an extraordinarily majestic effect, making the spectator fancy that he has come into the presence of beings vastly superior to himself.

On the back wall immediately opposite the entrance are three huge panels of sculpture—the most important objects in the temple. The midmost of these consists of three colossal heads—Brahma, Vishnu, and Siva—united in one; Brahma, of course, full faced, the others in profile. Each head with its surmounting tiara is some twelve feet high, and the portions of the busts represented add another six feet. The whole is cut deep into the rock so as to be almost detached; and the expression of the heads—which are slightly inclined forwards—is full of reserved power and dignity. It is Brahm, the unrealisable and infinite god, the substratum of all, just dawning into multiple existence—allowing himself to be seen in his first conceivable form.

In this trinity Vishnu, of course, represents the idea of Evolution—the process by which the inner spirit unfolds and generates the universe of sensible forms—as when a man wakes from sleep and lets his thoughts go out into light and definition; Siva represents the idea of Involution, by which thought and the sensible universe are indrawn again into quiescence; and Brahma represents the state which is neither Evolution nor Involution—and yet is both—existence itself, now first brought into the region of thought through relation to Vishnu and Siva.

Each figure, with a hand upturned and resting on the base of its neck, holds an emblem: Vishnu the lotus-flower of generation, Brahma the gourd of fruition, and Siva a cobra, the "good snake" whose bite is certain dissolution. Siva also has the third eye—the eye of the interior vision of the universe, which comes to the man who adopts the method of Involution. There is good reason to suppose, from marks on the rock, that the recess in which this manifestation of deity is carved, was closed by a veil or screen, only to be drawn aside at times of great solemnity. A hollow behind the triple head is pointed out, in which it is supposed that a concealed priest could simulate the awful tones of the god.

Of the three forms of the trinity Siva is the most popular in Hindu devotion, and he forms the centre figure of all the other panels here. The panel on the right of the principal one just described portrays the next devolution of godhead—namely, into the form of humanity—and represents Siva as a complete full length human being conjoining the two sexes in one person. This idea of the original junction of the sexes, though it may be philosophically tenable, and though it is no doubt supported by a variety of

Panel of Siva and his Consort Parvati, Elephanta

traditions—see the Bible, Plato, etc.—and by certain interior experiences which have been noticed (and which are probably the sources of tradition) is inartistic enough when graphically portrayed; and the main figure of this panel, with its left side projecting into a huge breast and hip, is only a monstrosity. As to the sexual parts themselves, they are unfortunately quite defaced. The cloud of moving figures, however, around and above, who seem to be witnessing this transformation, are very spirited.

The third panel—on the left of the principal one—in which the differentiation is complete, and Siva and his consort Sakti or Parvati are represented side by side as complete male and female figures in serene and graceful pose—he colossal and occupying nearly the centre of the panel, she smaller and a little to one side—is a great success. Round them in the space above their heads a multitude of striding clean-legged figures bear witness to the energy of creation now fully manifested in this glorious pair.

The rest of the panels, though still colossal, are on a slightly smaller scale, and seem to represent the human-divine life of Siva: his actual marriage, his abandonment of home, his contest with Rávana, his terrible triumph over and slaughter of his enemies, his retirement into solitude and meditation, and his ultimate reabsorption into Brahm, figured by his frenzied dance in the "hall of illimitable happiness"—that most favorite subject of the Hindu sculptors. This last panel—though the legs and arms are all broken—has extraordinary vigor and animation, and is one of the very best. The whole series, in fact, to those who can understand, is a marvelous panorama of the human soul. The work is full of allegorical touches and hints, yet hardly ever becomes grotesque or inartistic. It provides suggestions of the profoundest philosophy, yet the rudest peasant walking through these dim arcades could not but be affected by what he sees. In every direction there are signs of "go" and primitive power which point to its production as belonging to a time (probably about the tenth century A.D.) of early vigor and mastery and of grand conception.

I should not forget to mention that in a square chamber also hewn out of the rock, but accessible

Interior Shrine, Elephanta

by a door in each of the four sides, is a huge lingam—which was probably also kept concealed except on great occasions; and round the exterior walls of the chamber, looking down the various aisles of the temple, are eight enormous guardian figures, of fine and composed workmanship. (See illustration—in which a man is standing beneath the torso of the nearest figure.) Altogether the spirit of the whole thing is to my mind infinitely finer than that of the South Indian temples, which with their courts and catacomb-like interiors suggest no great ideas, but only a general sense of mystery and of Brahminical ascendancy.

March 6th.—A little after sunset yesterday "Sikandra" took me to see an opium den in the native quarter. It was rather early, as the customers were only just settling in, but the police close these places at nine. Much what I expected. A dark, dirty room, with raised wide bench round the sides, on which folk could lie, with little smoky lamps for them to burn their opium. For three pice you get a little thimbleful of laudanum, and by continually taking a drop on the end of a steel prong and frizzling it in the flame, you at last raise a viscid lump hardly as big as a pea, which you put in a pipe, and then holding the mouth of the pipe in the flame, draw breath. Two or three whiffs of thick smoke are thus obtained—and then more stuff has to be prepared; but the poison soon begins to work, and before long the smoker lies motionless, with his eyes open and his pipe dropping out of his hand. I spoke to a man who was just preparing his dose, and who looked very thin and miserable, asking him if he did not find it damage his health; but he said that he could not get along without it—if he gave it up for a day or two he could not do his work, and felt nervous and ill.

The effect of these drugs, opium, haschisch (hemp or ganja),* as well as of laughing gas, sulphuric

* As a curiosity of derivation it appears that these two words *hemp* and *ganja* are from the same root: Sanskrit *goni*, *ganjika*;

ether, etc., is no doubt to produce a suspension of the specially bodily and local faculties for the time, and with it an inner illumination and consciousness, very beatific, and simulating the real "ecstasy." Laughing gas (nitrous oxide) produces a species of illumination and intuition into the secrets of the universe at times—as in the case of Sir Humphry Davy, who first used it on himself and who woke up exclaiming, "Nothing exists but thoughts! the universe is composed of impressions, ideas, pleasures, and pains." The feelings induced by opium and haschisch have often been described in somewhat similar terms; and it has to be remembered that many much-abused practices—indulgence in various drugs and strong drinks, mesmeric trance-states, frantic dancing and singing, as well as violent asceticisms, self-tortures, etc.—owe their hold upon humanity to the same fact—namely, that they induce in however remote and imperfect a degree, or by however unhealthy a method, some momentary realisation of that state of cosmic consciousness of which we have spoken, and of the happiness attending it—the intensity of which happiness may perhaps be measured by the strength of these very abuses occurring in the search for it, and may perhaps be compared, for its actual force as a motive of human conduct, with the intensity of the sexual orgasm.

One evening two or three friends that I had made among the native "proletariat"—post-office and railway clerks—insisted on giving me a little

Persian, Greek and Latin, *cannabis*; French *chanvre*; German *Hanf*; Dutch *hennep*. *Canvas* also is the same word.

entertainment. I was driven down to the native city, and landed in a garden-like court with little cottages all round. To one of these we were invited. Found quite a collection of people; numbers increasing on my arrival till there must have been about fifty. Just a little front room nine feet square, with no furniture except one folding chair which had been brought from heaven knows where in my honor. A nice rug had been placed on the ground, and pillows round the walls; and the company soon settled down, either inside the room (having left their shoes at the door), or in the verandah. A musician had been provided, in the shape of an old man who had a variety of instruments and handled them skilfully as far as I could judge. But the performance was rather wearisome and lasted an unconscionably long time.

It was very curious to me, as a contrast to English ways, to see all these youngish fellows sitting round listening to this rather stupid old man playing by the hour—so quiescent and *resigned* if one might use the word. They are so fond of simply doing nothing; their legs crossed and heads meditatively bent forward; clerks, small foremen, and book-keepers, and some probably manual workers—looking very nice and clean withal in their red turbans and white or black shawls or coats.

There is a certain tastefulness and grace always observable in India. Here I could not but notice, not only the Mahratta dress, but all the interior scene; plain color-washed walls edged with a running pattern, the forms of the various instruments, a few common bowls brought in to serve as musical glasses, the brass pot from which water was poured into them—all *artistic* in design and color, though the house was of tiniest proportions—only apparently two or three rooms, of the same size as that one.

After the music a little general conversation ensued, with coffee and cigarettes, talk, of course, turning on the inevitable Congress question and the relations of England and India—a subject evidently exciting the deepest interest in those present; but not much, I think, was added to former conversations. One of the company (a post-office clerk) says that all the educated and thoughtful people in India are with the Congress, to which I reply that it is much the same with the Socialist movement in the West. He thinks—and they all seem to agree with him—that the condition of the agricultural people is decidedly worse than it used to be; but when I ask for evidence there is not much forthcoming, except references to Digby. I guess the statement is on the whole true, but the obvious difficulty of corroborating these things is very great; the absence of records of the past, the vastness of India, the various conditions in different parts, etc. etc., make it very difficult to come to any general and sweeping conclusion. The same friend pointed out (from Digby) that mere statistics of the increasing wealth of India were quite illusive, "as they only indicated the increase of profits to merchants and foreigners, and had nothing to do with the general prosperity"; and to this I quite agreed, telling him that we had had plenty of statistics of the same kind in England; but that this was only what might be expected, as the ruling classes in both countries being infected with commercialism would naturally measure political success by trade-profits, and frame their laws too chiefly in view of a success of that kind.

Several of those present maintained that it was quite a mistake to say the Mohammedans are against the Congress; a certain section of them is, but only a section, and education is every day tending to destroy these differences and race-jealousies. I put the question seriously to them whether they really thought that within 50 or 100 years all these old race-differences, between Mohammedan and Hindu, Hindu and Eurasian, or between all the sections of Hindus, would be lost in a sense of national unity. Their reply was, "Yes, undoubtedly." Education, they thought, would abolish the ill-feeling that existed, and indeed was doing so rapidly; there would soon be one common language, the English; and one common object—namely, the realisation of Western institutions. Whether right or not in their speculations, it is interesting to find that such is the ideal of hundreds of thousands of the bulk-people of India nowadays. Everywhere indeed one meets with these views. The Britisher in India may and does scoff at these ideals, and probably in a sense he is right. It may be (indeed it seems to me quite likely to be) impossible for a very long time yet to realise anything of the kind. At the same time who would not be touched by the uprising of a whole people towards such a dream of new and united life? And indeed the dream itself—like all other dreams—is a long step, perhaps the most important step, towards its own realisation.

Thus we chatted away till about midnight, when with mutual compliments, and the usual presents of flowers to the parting guest, we separated. These fellows evidently prize a little English society very much; for though they learn our language in the schools and use it in the business of every-day life, it rarely, very rarely, happens that they actually get into any friendly conversation with an Englishman;

Side Cave, Elephanta

and I found that I was able to give them useful information—as, for instance, about methods of getting books out from England—and to answer a variety of other questions, which were really touching in the latent suggestion they contained of the utter absence of any such help under ordinary circumstances. It struck me, indeed, how much a few unpretending and friendly Englishmen might do to endear our country to this people.

It is quite a sight at night walking home—however late one may be—to see on the maidans and open spaces bright lamps placed on the dusty turf, and groups of Parsees and others sitting round them on mats—playing cards, and enjoying themselves very composedly. Round the neighborhood of the Bunder quay and the club-houses and hotels the scene is rather more gay and frivolous. How pleasant and cool the night air, and yet not too cool! The darkies sleep out night-long by hundreds in these places and on the pavements under the trees. They take their cloths, wrap them under their feet, bring them over their heads, and tuck them in at the sides; and lie stretched straight out, with or without a mat under them, looking for all the world like laid-out corpses.

Indian Ocean.—On the way to Aden. The harbor of Bombay looked very beautiful as we glided out in the ss. *Siam*—with its variegated shore and islands and shipping. I went down into my berth to have a sleep, and when I awoke we were out of sight of India or any land. Most lovely weather; impossible to believe that England is shivering under a March sky, with north-east winds and gloom. The sea oily-calm; by day suffused with sunlight up to the farthest horizon—only broken, and that but seldom, by the back-fin of a porpoise, or the glance of flying-fish; by night gleaming faintly with the reflection of the stars and its own phosphorescence. Last night the sea was like a vast mirror, so smooth—every brighter star actually given again in wavering beauty in the world below—the horizon softly veiled so that it was impossible to tell where the two heavens (between which one seemed suspended) might meet. All so tender and calm and magnificent. Canopus and the Southern Cross and the Milky Way forming a great radiance in the south; far ahead to the west Orion lying on his side, and Sirius, and the ruddy Aldebaran setting. Standing in the bows there was nothing between one and this immense world, nothing even to show that the ship was moving, except the rush of water from the bows—which indeed seemed an uncaused and unaccountable phenomenon. The whole thing was like a magic and beautiful poem. The phosphorescent stars (tiny jelly creatures) floating on the surface kept gliding swiftly over those other stars that lay so deep below; sometimes the black ocean-meadows seemed to be sown thick with them like daisies. The foam round the bows lay like a luminous necklace to the ship, and fell continually over in a cascade of brilliant points, while now and then some bigger jelly tossed in the surge threw a glare up even in our faces.

One might stand for hours thus, catching the wind of one's own speed—so soft, so mild, so warm—the delicate aroma of the sea, the faint, far suggestion of the transparent air and water, wafting, encircling one round. And indeed all my journey has been like this—so smooth, so unruffled, as if one had not really been moving. I have several times thought, and am inclined to think even now, that perhaps one has not left home at all, but that it has been a fair panorama that has been gliding past one all these months.

THE OLD ORDER

AND

THE NEW INFLUENCES

CHAPTER XVIII

THE OLD ORDER: CASTE AND COMMUNISM

THERE is certainly a most remarkable movement taking place in India to-day, towards modern commercialism and Western education and ideas, and away from the old caste and communal system of the past—a movement which while it is in some ways the reverse of our Western Socialist movement answers curiously to it in the rapidity and intensity of its development and in the enthusiasm which it inspires. The movement is, of course, at present confined to the towns, and even in these to sections and coteries—the 90 per cent. agricultural population being as yet practically unaffected by it—but here again it is the old story of the bulk of the population being stirred and set in motion by the energetic few, or at anyrate following at some distance on their lead; and we may yet expect to see this take place in the present case.

Knowing as we do at home the evils which attend our commercial and competitive order of society it is difficult to understand the interest which it arouses in India, until we realise the decay and degradation into which caste and the ancient communism have fallen. On these latter institutions commercialism is destined to act as a solvent, and though it is not likely that it will obliterate them—considering how deeply they are rooted in the genius of the Indian people, and considering how utterly dissimilar that genius is to the genius of the West—still it may fairly be hoped that it will clean away a great deal of rubbish that has accumulated round them, and free them to be of some use again in the future, when the present movement will probably have had its fling and passed away. On all sides in India one meets with little points and details which remind one of the Feudal system in our own lands; and as this passed in its due time into the commercial system so will it be in India—only there is a good deal to indicate that the disease, or whatever it is, will not be taken so severely in India as in the West, and will run its course and pass over in a shorter time.

The complexity into which the caste system has grown since the days when society was divided into four castes only—Brahmins, Kshattriyas, Vaisyas, and Sudras—is something most extraordinary. Race, occupation, and geographical position have all had their influence in the growth of this phenomenon. When one hears that the Brahmins alone are divided into 1886 separate classes or tribes, one begins to realise what a complicated affair it is. "The Brahmins," says Hunter, in his *Indian Empire*, "so far from being a compact unit are made up of several hundred castes who cannot intermarry nor eat food cooked by each other." Of course, locality has a good deal to do with this subdivision; and it is said that a Brahmin of the North-West is the most select, and can prepare food for all classes of Brahmins (it being a rule of all high caste that one must not touch food cooked by an inferior caste); but family and genealogical descent also no doubt have a good deal to do with it; and as to employment, even among the Brahmins, though manual labor is a degradation in their eyes, plentiful individuals may be found who follow such trades as shepherds, fishermen, porters, potters, etc. Dr. Wilson of Bombay wrote two large volumes of his projected great work on Caste, and then died; but had not finished his first subject, the Brahmins!

In the present day the Brahmins are, I believe, pretty equally distributed all over India, forming their own castes among the other races and castes, but, of course, not intermarrying with them, doing as a rule little or no manual work, but clustering in thousands round temples and holy places, full of greed and ever on the look-out for money. Though ignorant mostly, still they have good opportunities in their colleges for learning, and some are very learned. They alone can perform the temple services and priestly acts generally; and oftentimes they do not disguise their contempt for the inferior castes, withdrawing their skirts pharisaically as they pass, or compelling an old and infirm person to descend into the muddy road while they occupy the narrow vantage of the footway.

This pharisaism of caste marks not only the Brahmins, but other sections; a thousand vexatious rules and regulations hedge in the life of every "twice-born" man; and the first glance at the streets of an Indian town makes one conscious of something antagonistic to *humanity*, in the broad sense by which it affords a common ground to the meeting of any two individuals. There are difficulties in the way of mere human converse. Not only do people not eat together (except they belong to the same section); but they don't *touch* each other very freely; don't shake hands, obviously; even the terms of greeting are scanty. A sort of chill strikes one: a *noli-me-tangere* sentiment, which drives one (as usual) to find some of the most grateful company among the outcast. Yet the people are disposed to be friendly, and in fact are sensitive and clinging by nature; but this is the form of society into which they have grown.

The defence of the system from the native religious point of view is that Caste defines a man's position and duties at once, limits him to a certain area of life, with its temptations and possibilities and responsibilities (caste for instance puts a check on traveling; to go to sea is to break all bounds), and saves him therefore from unbridled licence and the insane scramble of the West; restricts his outward world and so develops the inward; narrows his life and so causes it to reach higher—as trees thickly planted spire upward to the sky. Caste, it is said, holds society in a definite form, without which vague turmoil would for ever ensue, distracting men to worldly cares and projects and rendering them incapable of the highest life. When, however, this last, the truly highest, is developed within an individual, then—for him—the sanction of caste ceases, and he acknowledges it no more. As to the criticism—so obvious from the Western point of view—of the unfairness that a man should be confined all his life to that class or stratum in which he is born, to the Indian religioner this is nothing; since he believes that each man *is* born in those surroundings of life which belong to his stage of progress, and must get the experience which belongs to that stage before moving farther.

However this may be, the rigidity of caste as it yet exists gives a strange shock to one's democratic notions. "Once a *dhobi* always a *dhobi*," says the proverb. The washerman (dhobi) is one of the poorest and most despised of men; the word is in fact a common term of reproach; but once a washerman, a washerman (save in the rarest cases) you will remain. And once a pariah always a pariah—a thing that no caste man will touch. Yet—and here comes in the extraordinary transcendental democracy (if one may call it so) of the Hindu religion—Brahm himself, the unnameable God, is sometimes called the *dhobi*, and some of the greatest religious teachers, including Tiruvalluvar, the author of the Kurral, have been drawn from the ranks of the Pariahs.

The English themselves in India hardly realise how strong are the caste feelings and habits among all but the few natives who have fairly broken with the system. At a levee some few years back a Lieut.-Governor, to show his cordial feeling towards a native Rajah, put his hand on the prince's shoulder, while speaking to him; but the latter, as soon as he could decently disengage himself, hurried home and took a bath, to purify himself from the touch! Nor to this day can the mass of the people of India get over the disgust and disapprobation they felt towards the English when they found that they insisted on eating *beef*—a thing that only the very lowest classes will touch; indeed this habit has not only done a good deal to alienate the sympathies of the people, but it is one of the chief reasons why the English find it so hard or next to impossible to get servants of good caste.

An acquaintance of mine in Ceylon who belongs to the Vellála caste told me that on one occasion he paid a visit to a friend of his in India who belonged to the same caste but a different section of it. They had a Brahmin cook, who prepared the food for both of them, but who being of a higher caste could not eat *after* them; while *they* could not eat together because they did not belong to the same section. The Brahmin cook therefore ate his dinner first, and then served up the remainder separately to the two friends, who sat at different tables with a curtain hanging between them!

I myself knew of a case in which an elderly native gentleman was quite put to it, and had to engage an extra servant, because, though he had a man already who could cook and draw water for him to drink, this man was not of the right caste to fill his bath! Can one wonder, when caste regulations have fallen into such pettiness, that the more advanced spirits hail with acclaim any new movement which promises deliverance from the bondage?

Another curious element in the corruption of caste is the growth of the tyranny of respectability. Among certain sections—mainly, I imagine, the merchant and trading castes—some of the members becoming rich form themselves into little coteries which take to themselves the government of the caste, and while not altogether denying their communal fellowship with, do not also altogether conceal their contempt for, the poorer members, and the divergence of their own interests and standards from those of the masses. Of course, with this high-flying respectability goes very often (as with us) a pharisaical observance of religious ordinances, and a good deal of so-called philanthropy.

I have before me a little book called "The Story of a Widow Remarriage," written by a member of the Bunya caste, and printed (for private circulation) at Bombay in 1890. The author of this book some years ago married—in defiance of all the proprieties of high-caste Hinduism—a lady who was already a widow; and he tells the story of this simple act and the consequent caste-persecution which he had to endure in a style so genuine and at once naïve and shrewd that the book is really most interesting. The poor girl whom he married had lost her husband some years before: he in fact was a mere boy and she a child at the time of his death. Now she was an "unlucky woman," a widow—one of those destined to spend all her life under a ban, to wear black, to keep away from any festivity lest she should mar it by her presence. "What happiness in the world have I," said she, when the author at their first meeting condoled with her on her fate; "nothing but death can relieve me of all my woes. I have abjured food for the last twelve months; I live only on a pice-worth of curd from day to day. I starve myself, in order that any how my end may come as soon as possible. I have often thought," she continued, "of committing suicide by drowning myself in the sea or in the neighboring tank of Walkeshwar, or by taking opium. But there are many considerations which hold me back. According to our Brahmins the Shastras say that those who commit suicide are doomed to die a similar death seven times over in their future existence.

Moreover, I myself believe that taking one's own life is as sinful as taking the life of any other person. This gives me pause, and I do not do what I would do. I have, however, forsaken all food, in order that the happy deliverance may come to me in a short time. I have nothing in this life to live for. If I had a child of my own, I would have had some cause for hope."

Moved by the sufferings of the unhappy Dhunkore, as well as by her youth and beauty, Madhowdas fell genuinely in love with her; and she, in return, with him; and ere long they determined—notwithstanding the relentless persecution of the more influential members of the caste, which they knew would follow—to get married. Madhowdas was in business, and there was the utmost danger that he would be boycotted and ruined. To Dhunkore her chief trouble was the thought of the grief this step would occasion to her mother (with whom she lived). She might be intimate with Madhowdas "under the rose"—that would be venial; she might if there were any serious consequences go a "pilgrimage," as so many widows do, to some quiet place where a delivery would not attract attention; but to be publicly married—that could never be forgiven. Not only her wealthy relations, but even her mother, would never see her again. So inexcusable would be the act, so dire its consequences.

Nevertheless the pair decided to go through with it. With the utmost secrecy they made their preparations, knowing well that if any rumors got abroad the arrangements would likely be interfered with by mercenary violence; the young woman might even be kidnapped—as had happened in a similar case before. Only sympathisers and a few witnesses were invited to the actual ceremony, which, however, was safely performed—partly owing to the presence of an European officer and a body of police! The next morning the *Times of India*, the *Gazette*, and other Bombay papers were out with an account of the widow remarriage, and the native city was convulsed with excitement—the community being immediately divided (though very unequally) into two hostile camps over their views of it.

The mother's alarm at the mysterious disappearance of Dhunkore was only partly allayed when she found among her daughter's trinkets a little note: "Be it known to my dear mother that not being able to bear the cruel pangs of widowhood, I forsook all kinds of food, and ate only a piece of curd every day. The consequence was that I became very weak, but did not die, as I hoped. . . . My dear mother, it is not at all likely that we shall meet again hereafter. You may therefore take me for dead. But I shall be very happy if I ever hear from the lips of anyone that you are all doing well. I have not done this thing at the instigation of anyone, but have resolved upon it of my own free will; so you will not blame anybody for it. I have taken away nothing from your house, and you will kindly see for yourself that your property is quite safe. . . ." And the alarm was changed into dismay when the news came of what had really happened. A meeting of wealthy relations and influential members of the caste was called; everything was done to damage the credit and ruin the business of Madhowdas; and finally he and his wife were solemnly excommunicated!

The pair, however, struggled on, contending against many difficulties and trials, and supported by a few friends, both among their own caste and the resident English, for some years. Though crippled, their worldly prospects were not ruined. Gradually Madhowdas established himself and his business, drew round him a small circle of the more advanced spirits, settled in a roomy house at Girgaon, and snapped his fingers at his enemies. Indeed his house became a centre of propaganda on the subject of widows' wrongs, and an asylum for other couples situated as he and his wife had been; meetings, of both English and native speakers, were held there; quite a number of marriages were celebrated there; and it appears that the house, to confirm its mission, now goes by the name of "Widow Remarriage Hall"!

But what I set out to note in telling this story was the curious way in which wealth asserts itself even in the caste system of India to form a tyranny of so-called respectability and of orthodoxy—dividing the caste, in some cases at anyrate, into distinct parties not unlike those which exist in our society at home. "The real opponents of widow remarriage," says Madhowdas in his book, "are not generally the simple and poor members of a caste, but its Shetthias. They pose before the public as the most enlightened members of their caste. In their conversation with European or Parsi acquaintances they declare themselves to be ardent advocates of social reform, and they pretend to deplore the folly, the stupidity, and the ignorance of their caste-fellows. But, as a matter of fact, it is these same Shetthias, these leading citizens, these enlightened members of society, who are really the bitterest and most uncompromising enemies of social progress. . Can the reformer turn to the educated classes fo help? I am grieved to say, yet the truth must be told, that their moral fibre is capable of a great deal of strengthening; and as to their active faculties, they still lie perfectly dormant. They have indeed the intelligence to perceive social evils. But their moral indignation on the tyranny and barbarism of custom evaporates in words. . . . A race of idle babblers these. They will speak brave words from the political platform about their country's wrongs and their countrymen's rights. But talk to them of something to be done, some little sacrifice to be made, they will shrink away, each one making his own excuse for his backsliding. . . . The world generally believes them; and if they occasionally give a few thousand rupees towards some charity, their reputation for liberality and large-mindedness is confirmed still more, and their fame is trumpeted forth by newspapers as men of munificence and enlightenment."

It must not be thought, however, because the caste-system is in many ways corrupt and effete, that it is without its better and more enduring features—even in the present day. Within the caste there is a certain communal feeling, which draws or tends to draw all the members together, as forming a corporate body for common ends and fellowship, and giving every member a claim on the rest in cases of distress or disability. Moreover, a great many of the castes, being founded on hereditary occupation, form trade societies, having their own committees of management, and rules and regulations, fines, feasts, and mutual benefit arrangements, almost quite similar to our old trade-guilds and modern unions. Thus there are the goldsmiths (a powerful caste which in South India, says Hunter, for centuries resisted the rule of the Brahmins, and claimed to be the religious teachers, and wore the sacred thread), the brass-workers, the weavers, the fishers, and scores of others—each divided into numerous subsections. The caste-guild in these cases regulates wages, checks competition, and punishes delinquents; the decisions of the guild being enforced by fines, by causing the offender to entertain all his fellows at a feast, and by other sanctions. The guild itself derives its funds not only from fines, but also from entrance-fees paid by those beginning to practise the craft, and from other sources. In any case, whether trade-guild or not, the caste—while it assures its members against starvation—exercises a continual surveillance over them, as we have seen in the case of Madhowdas—extending to excommunication and even expulsion. Excommunication being of three kinds: (1) from *eating* with other members of the caste, (2) from *marriage* with them, and (3) from use of the local barber, washerman, and priest. Expulsion is rare; and it is said that it seldom takes place unless the offender is a real bad lot.

As an instance of trade-unionism in caste, Hunter mentions the case of the bricklayers at Ahmedabad in 1873. Some of the bricklayers were working overtime, and thus were getting a few pence a day extra, while at the same time others of them were unemployed. The guild therefore held a meeting, and decided to forbid the overtime — the result of which was that employment was found for all.

When I was at Kurunégala in Ceylon, an amusing dispute took place between the barber caste and the Brahmins of the locality. The barbers—though a very necessary element of Hindu society, as shaving is looked upon as a very important, almost religious, function, and is practised in a vast variety of forms by the different sections—are still somewhat despised as a low caste; and it appeared that the Brahmins of the place had given offence to them by refusing to enter the barbers' houses in order to perform certain religious ceremonies and purifications—the Brahmins no doubt being afraid of contaminating themselves thereby. Thereupon the barbers held a caste meeting, and decided to boycott the Brahmins by refusing to shave them. This was a blow to the latter, as without being properly scraped they could not perform their ceremonies, and to have to shave themselves would be an unheard-of indignity. *They* therefore held a meeting, the result of which was that they managed to get a barber from a distant place—a kind of blackleg—who probably belonged to some other section of the barber community—to come over and do their scraping for them. Things went on merrily thus for a while, and the blackleg no doubt had good times, when—in consequence of another barbers' meeting—he was one day spirited away, and disappeared for good, being seen no more. The barbers also, in defiance of the Brahmins, appointed a priest from among their own body to do their own religious choring for them—and the Brahmins were routed all along the line. What steps were taken after this I do not know, as about that time I left the place.

When at Bombay I had another instance of how the caste-guild acts as a trade-union, and to check competition among its members. I was wanting to buy some specimens of brasswork, and, walking down a street where I knew there were a number of brass-workers' shops, was surprised to find them all closed. I then proposed to my companion, who was a Hindu, that we should go to another street where there were also brass-workers' shops; but he said it would be no good, as he believed this was a half-holiday of the brass-workers' caste. "But," I said, "if it is a half-holiday, there may yet be some who will keep their shops open in order to get the custom." "Oh no," he replied, with a smile at my ignorance; "they would not do that; it would be against all caste rules."

Thus we see that the caste-system contains valuable social elements, and, ancient as it is, may even teach us a lesson or two in regard to the organisation of trades.

When we come to the other great feature of Indian social life, Communism, we find it existing under three great forms—agricultural, caste, and family communism. Of the first of these—agricultural communism—I know personally but little, having had no opportunity of really studying the agricultural life. The conditions of village tenure vary largely all over India, but apparently in every part there may be traced more or less distinctly the custom of holding lands in common, as in the primitive village life of Germany and England. In most Indian villages there are still extensive outlying lands which are looked upon as the property of the community; and of the inlying and more settled lands, their cultivation, inheritance, etc., are largely ruled by common custom and authority. Maine, however, points out in his *Village Communities* that the sense of individual property, derived from contact with the West, is even now rapidly obliterating these ancient customs of joint tenure.

Of the second, the caste communism, I have already spoken. It no doubt is less strongly marked than it was; but still exists, not certainly as an absolute community of goods, but as a community of feeling and interest, and some degree of mutual assistance among the members of the caste. The third is the family communism; and this is still pretty strongly marked, though the first beginnings of its disintegration are now appearing.

In speaking of the Family it must be understood that a much larger unit is meant than we should denote by the term—comparatively distant relations being included; and there seems to be a tacit understanding that the members of this larger Family or Clan have a claim on each other, so that anyone in need can fairly expect support and assistance from the others, and without feeling humiliated by receiving it. This has its good side—in the extended family life and large-heartedness that it produces, as well as in its tendency to keep wealth distributed and to prevent people playing too much for their own hands; but it has its drawbacks, chiefly in the opportunity it affords to idle "ne'er-do-weels" to sponge upon their friends.

I have mentioned the case (p. 87) of a young

man who came to read English with me in Ceylon, and who, though married and having children, turned out to be living with and dependent on his parents. I must not speak of this as a case of a ne'er-do-weel, as the fellow was genuinely interested in literature, and was in the habit of giving lectures on philosophy in his native place—and if one began calling such people names, one might not know where to stop; but to our Western notions it was a curious arrangement. Certainly a Bengali gentleman whom I met one day complained to me very bitterly of the system. He said that he was in an official position and receiving a moderate salary, and the consequence was that his relatives all considered him a fair prey. He not only had his own wife and children, and his father and mother, to support—of which he would not make a grievance; but he had two or three younger brothers, who, though of age, had not yet found anything to do, and were calmly living on at his cost; and besides these there were two aunts of his, who had both married one man. The husband of the aunts had died leaving one of them with children, and now he, the complainant, was expected to provide for both aunts and children, besides the rest of his family already mentioned! To a man once bitten with the idea of "getting on" in the Western sense of the word, one can imagine how galling it must be to have indefinite strings of relations clinging around one's neck; and one can guess how forcibly the competitive idea is already beginning to act towards the disruption of family communism.

In Calcutta and other places I noticed considerable numbers of grown youths loafing about with nothing to do, and apparently with no particular intention of doing anything as long as their friends would support them. And this, no doubt, is a great evil, but I think it would be hardly fair to lay it all at the door of the family communal habits. It is rather to the contact of the old communal life, with the new order of things, and to the dislocation of the former which ensues, that we must attribute the evil. For under the old order, a youth growing up, would, no doubt, by the obligations of his caste, religion, etc., have his duties and calling so distinctly set out for him, that the danger of his giving himself up to idleness and infringing on the hospitality of his family would seldom arise; but now the commercial and competitive *régime*, while loosening his old caste and religious sanctions, often leaves him quite unprovided with any opening in life—indeed forbids him an opening except at the cost of a struggle with his fellows—and so tempts him to relapse into a state of dependence.

The closeness of the family tie still subsisting is, when all is said, a beautiful thing. The utmost respect is accorded to parents; and to strike a father or mother is (as I think I have already remarked) an almost unheard-of crime. I was much impressed in talking to Justice Telang at Bombay by the way in which he spoke of his parents. I had asked him whether he intended coming over to England for the National Congress—to be held in London in 1893—and his reply was that he should like to, but his parents "would not let him" (no doubt on account of the loss of caste in crossing the sea). This from a man of forty, and one of the leading Mahrattas, indeed one of the most influential politicians in Bombay, was sufficiently striking; but it was said with a tenderness that made one feel that he would forego almost anything rather than wound those of whom he spoke.

In the social progress of the West, the sword descending divides, with often painful estrangement, brother from sister, and child from parent; so is it also in the East. Only in the East, the closeness of the parental tie makes the estrangement more odious and more painful, and adds proportionately to the obstacles which lie in the path of progress.

CHAPTER XIX

THE NEW INFLUENCES: WESTERN SCIENCE AND COMMERCIALISM

THE first objects that I saw in India—indeed I saw them while still well out at sea—were a lighthouse and a factory chimney! This was at Tuticorin, a little place in the extreme south; but afterwards I found that these objects represented remarkably well the vast spread of Western influences all over the country, in their two great main forms, science and commercialism.

I had no idea, until I landed, how Western ideas and education have of late years overrun the cities and towns, even down to the small towns, of India; but I was destined to be speedily enlightened on this subject. Having a few hours to spare at Tuticorin, I was walking up and down by the sad sea waves when I noticed a youth of about seventeen reading a book. Glancing over his shoulder, to my surprise I saw it was our old friend "Todhunter's Euclid." The youth looked like any other son of the people, undistinguished for wealth or rank —for in this country there is no great distinction in dress between rich and poor—simply clad in his cotton or muslin wrap, with bare head and bare feet; and naturally I remonstrated with him on his conduct. "O yes," he said in English; "I am reading Euclid—I belong to Bishop Caldwell's College."—

"Bishop Caldwell's College?"—"Yes," he said; "it is a large college here, with 200 boys, from ages of 13 or 14 up to 23 or 24."—"Indeed! And what do you read?"—"Oh, we read Algebra and Euclid," he replied enthusiastically, "and English History and Natural Science and Mill's 'Political Economy,' and" (but here his voice fell a semitone) "we learn two chapters of the Bible by heart every day." By this time other boys had come up, and I soon found myself the centre of a small crowd, and conversing to them about England, and its well-known scholars and politicians, and a variety of things about which they asked eager questions. "Come and see the college," at last they said, seeing I was interested; and so we adjourned—a troop of about fifty—into a courtyard containing various school buildings. There did not seem to be any masters about, and after showing me some of the class-rooms, which were fitted up much like English class-rooms, they took me to the dormitory. The dormitory was a spacious room or hall, large enough, I daresay, to accommodate most of the scholars, but to my surprise it contained not a single bit of furniture—not a bed or a chair or a table, far less a washstand; only round the wall and the floor were the boys' boxes—mostly small enough—and grass mats which, unrolled at night, they used for sleeping on. This (combined with J. S. Mill) was plain living and high thinking indeed. Seeing my look of mingled amusement and surprise, they said with a chuckle, "Come and see the dining-hall"—and lo! another room of about the same size—this time with *nothing* in it, except plates distributed at equal distances about the floor! The meal hour was just approaching, and the boys squatting down with crossed feet took each a plate upon his lap, while serving-men going round with huge bowls of curry and rice supplied them with food, which they ate with their fingers.

It certainly impressed me a good deal to find a high level of Western education going on, and among boys, many of them evidently from their conversation intelligent enough, under such extremely simple conditions, and in so unimportant a place as Tuticorin might appear. But I soon found that similar institutions—not all fortunately involving two chapters of the Bible every day, and not all quite so simple in their interior instalments—existed all over the land. Not only are there universities at Madras, Calcutta, and Bombay, granting degrees on a broad foundation of Western learning, and affiliated to Oxford and Cambridge in such a way that the student, having taken his B.A. at either of the Indian universities, can now take a further degree at either of the English ones after two years' residence only; but there are important colleges and high schools in all the principal towns; and a graduated network of instruction down to the native village schools all over the land. Besides these there are medical colleges, such as the Grant Medical College at Bombay; women's colleges, like the Bethune College at Calcutta, which has fifty or sixty women students, and which passed six women graduates in the Calcutta university examinations in 1890; and other institutions. In most cases the principals of these higher institutions are English, but the staff is largely native.

And as a part of Western education I suppose

one may include our games and sports, which are rapidly coming into use and supplanting, in populous centres, the native exercises. It is a curious and unexpected sight to see troops of dark-skinned and barefooted lads and men playing cricket—but it is a sight one may meet with in any of the towns nowadays in the cooler weather. At Bombay the *maidans* are simply crowded at times with cricketers —Parsee clubs, Hindu clubs, Eurasians, English—I reckoned I could count a score of pitches one day from the place where I was sitting. The same at Calcutta. The same at Nagpore, with golf going on as well. Yet one cannot help noticing the separation of the different sections of the population, even in their games—the English cricket-ground, the "second-class" English ground, the Eurasian ground, the Hindu and Mohammedan—all distinct!

The effect of this rush of Western ideas and education is, of course, what one might expect—and what I have already alluded to once or twice—namely, to discredit the old religion and the old caste-practices. As my friend the schoolmaster said at Calcutta, "No one believes in all this now"; by no one meaning no one who belongs to the new movement and has gone through the Western curriculum—the "young India."

The question may be asked then, What does the young India believe in? It has practically abandoned the religion of its fathers, largely scoffs at it, does it accept Christianity in any form in its place? I believe we may reply No. Christianity in its missions and its Salvation Armies, though it may move a little among the masses, does not to any extent touch the advanced and educated sections. No;

the latter read Mill, Spencer, and Huxley, and they have quite naturally and in good faith adopted the philosophy of their teachers—the scientific materialism which had its full vogue in England some twenty years ago, but which is now perhaps somewhat on the wane. As one of these enthusiasts said to me one day, "We are all Agnostics now." With that extraordinary quickness and receptivity which is one of the great features of the Hindu mind, though beginning the study so much later in the day, they have absorbed the teachings of modern science and leapt to its conclusions almost as soon as we have in the West. That the movement will remain at this point seems to me in the highest degree unlikely. There may be a reaction back to the old standpoint, or, what is more hopeful, a forward effort to rehabilitate the profound teachings of their forefathers into forms more suited to the times in which we live, and freed from the many absurdities which have gathered round the old tradition.*

* The Theosophical Society, chiefly under the direction of Annie Besant and Col. Olcott, has already (1903) done a great work in this direction. It has brought back the ancient teachings of their Sages, with a certain admixture of Western thought and science, to scores and hundreds of thousands of Hindus who were weary of religious formalism; and has given them a fresh interest in their own traditions. And in Europe and America it has also been invaluable in familiarising the Western mind with those Oriental religious conceptions which it so greatly needs—the conceptions of *karma* and reincarnation, and the redeeming power of involution. If it has erred in the tendency to fall into a certain cant and jargon, and to elaborate "systems" and doctrines more as an intellectual exercise than as an expression of facts really experienced, this is only after all what happens in case of almost every new religious movement; and when these little accretions

The second great factor in modern India is the growth of Commercialism. This is very remarkable, and is likely to be more so. Not only at Tuticorin, but at a multitude of places are factory chimneys growing up. At Nagpore I saw a cotton-mill employing hundreds of hands. At Bombay there are between thirty and forty large cotton-mills, there is a manufacturing quarter, and a small forest of chimneys belching forth their filth into the otherwise cloudless blue.

I visited one of the largest of these mills (that of the United Spinning and Weaving Co.) with a friend who at one time had worked there. It was the counterpart of a Lancashire cotton-mill. There was the same great oblong building in three or four storeys, the same spinning-jenny and other machinery (all, of course, brought out from England, and including a splendid high-pressure condensing engine of 2000 h.-p.), the same wicked roar and scream of wheels, and the same sickening hurry and scramble. But how strange to see the poor thin "oysters" working under the old familiar conditions of dirt and unhealth—their dark skins looking darker with grease and dust, their passive faces more passive than ever—to see scores of Hindu girls with huge ear-rings and nose-rings threading their way among the machinery, looking so small, compared with our women, and so abstracted and dreamy that it hardly seemed safe. And here a little naked boy about 10 years of age, minding a spinning-jenny and taking up the broken threads,

fall away again, it will be found, I think, that the Theosophical movement has left a solid contribution behind, to the growth of humanity. (*Note Second Edition.*)

as clever and as deft as can be. Fortunately the Hindu mind takes things easier than the English, and refuses to be pressed; for the hours are shamefully long and there is but little respite from toil.

There is no doubt that great fortunes have been and are being made in this cotton business. It can hardly be otherwise, for as long as Manchester is in the market the goods of Bombay are in a line as to prices with the products of English manufacture; but they are produced at very much less cost. I suppose the average wage for adults in one of these mills is not more than 8d. a day (if so much), and the difference between this and 2s. 8d. a day say, as in England, gives 2s. per diem saved on each employee. In the mill that I visited there are 1100 hands—say 1000 adults; that gives a saving of 1000 × 2 shillings, or £100, a day; or £30,000 a year. Against this must be set the increased price of coal, which they get all the way from England (the coal of the country being inferior) at Rs.15 to 17 per ton—say 25 tons a day at 20s. added cost to what it would be in England—*i.e.* £25 a day, or £7500 a year. Then it is clear that despite this and some other drawbacks, the balance in favor of production in India is very great; and the dividends of the cotton-mills at Bombay certainly show it, for they run at 20, 25, 50, and even 80 per cent., with very few below 20.

It is clear that such profits as these are likely to draw capital out to India in rapidly increasing degree, and we may expect a vast development of manufacturing industry there during the next decade or two. The country—or at anyrate the town-centres—will be largely commercialised. And as far as the people themselves are concerned, though the life in mills is wretched enough, still it offers a spacious change from the dull round of peasant labor, and something like a secure wage (if only a pittance) to a man who in his native village would hardly see the glint of coin from one year's end to another; the bustle and stir of the town, too, is an attraction; and so some of the same causes which have already in England brought about the depletion of the land in favor of the congestion of the cities, are beginning to work in India.

Then besides the manual employment which our commercial institutions provide there are innumerable trading posts and clerkships, connected with merchants' houses, banks, railways, post-offices, and all manner of public works, all of which practically are filled by natives; and some of which, with the moderate salaries attached, are eagerly sought after. One hardly realises till one sees it, how completely these great organisations are carried on—except for perhaps one or two Englishmen at the head—by native labor; but when one does see this one realises also how important a part of the whole population this section—which is thus ministering to and extending the bounds of modern life—is becoming. And this section again is supplemented by at least an equally numerous section which, if not already employed in the same way, is desirous of becoming so. And, of course, among both these sections Western ideals and standards flourish; competition is gradually coming to be looked on as a natural law of society; and Caste and the old Family system are more or less rapidly disintegrating.

Such changes as these are naturally important, and indeed in an old and conservative country like India strike one as very remarkable—but they are made even more important by the political complexion they have of late years assumed. In the National Indian Congress we see that not only the outer forms of life and thought, but the political and social ideas which belong to the same stage of historical development, have migrated from West to East. The people—or at least those sections of it of which we are speaking—are infected not only with Darwin and Huxley, but with a belief in the ballot, in parliaments and town-councils, and in constitutionalism and representative government generally. The N.I.C. brings together from 1000 to 1500 delegates annually from all parts of India, representing a variety of different races and sections, and elected in many of the larger towns with the utmost enthusiasm; and this by itself is a striking fact—a fact quite comparable in its way with the meetings of the Labor Congresses in late years in the capitals of Europe. Its conferences have been mostly devoted to such political questions as the application of the elective principle to municipal and imperial councils, and to such social questions as that of child-marriage; and these subjects and the speeches concerning them are again reviewed and reported by a great number of newspapers printed both in English and the vernacular tongues, and having a large circulation. Certainly it is probable that the Congresses will not *immediately* lead to any very striking results—indeed it is hard to see how they *could* do so; but the fact of the existence of the N.I.C. movement alone is a pregnant one, and backed as it is by economical changes, it is not likely—though it may change its form—to evaporate into mere nothingness.

In fact—despite the efforts of certain parties to minimise it—it seems to me evident that we are face to face with an important social movement in India. What the upshot of it may be no one probably can tell—it may subside again in time, or it may gather volume and force towards some definite issue; but it certainly cannot be ignored. The Pagetts, M.P., may be ponderously superficial about it, but the Kiplings merry are at least equally far from the truth. Of course in actual numerical strength as compared with the whole population the party may be small; but then, as in other such movements, since it is just the most active and energetic folk who join them, their import cannot be measured by mere numbers. It is useless again to say that because the movement is not acknowledged by the peasants, or by the religious folk, or because it is regarded with a jealous eye by certain sections, that therefore it is of no account; because similar things are always said and always have been said of every new social effort—in its inception—however popular or influential it may afterwards become.

The question which is most interesting at this juncture to anyone who recognises that there really is something like a change of attitude taking place in the Indian peoples, is: How do the Anglo-Indians regard this change? and my answer to this—though given with diffidence—since it is a large generalisation and there may be, certainly are, many exceptions to it—is: I believe that taken as a whole the Anglos look upon it with a mingled sentiment of Fear and Dislike. I think they look upon the movement with a certain amount of Fear—perhaps not unnaturally. The remembrance of the Mutiny of '57 is before them; they feel themselves to be a mere handful among millions. And I am sure they look upon it with Dislike, for as said above there is no real touch, no real sympathy, between them and the native races. However it may be for the liberalising Englishman at home to indulge in a sentimental sympathy with the aspiring native, the Britisher in India feels that the relation is only tolerable as long as there is a fixed and impassable distinction between the ruler and the ruled. Take that away, let the two races come into actual contact on an equality, and . . . but the thought is not to be endured.

And this feeling of race-dislike is, I think—as I have hinted in an earlier chapter—enhanced by the fact that the Britisher in India is a "class" man in his social feeling. I have several times had occasion to think that the bulk-people of the two countries—though by no means agreeing with each other—would, if intercourse were at all possible, get on better together than the actual parties do at present. The evils of a commercial class-government which we are beginning to realise so acutely at home—the want of touch between the rulers and the ruled, the testing of all politics by the touchstone of commercial profits and dividends, the consequent enrichment of the few at the expense of the many, the growth of slum and factory life, and the impoverishment of the peasant and the farmer, are curiously paralleled by what is taking place in India;

and in many respects it is becoming necessary to realise that some of our difficulties in India are not merely such as belong to the country itself, but are part and parcel of the same problem which is beginning to vex us at home—the social problem, namely. The same narrowness of social creed, the entire decadence of the old standards of gentle birth without their replacement by any new ideal, worthy to be so called, the same trumpery earmarks of society-connection, etc., distinguish the ruling classes in one country as in the other; and in both are the signals of coming change.

At the same time it would be absurd to assume that the native of India is free from serious defects which make the problem, to the Anglo-Indian, ever so much more difficult of solution. And of these probably the tendency to evasion, deceit, and underhand dealing is the most serious. The Hindu especially with his subtle mind and passive character is thus unreliable; it is difficult to find a man who will stick with absolute fidelity to his word, or of whom you can be certain that his ostensible object is his real one; and naturally this sort of thing creates estrangement.

To my mind this social gulf existing between the rulers and the ruled is the most pregnant fact of our presence in India—the one that calls most for attention, and that looms biggest with consequences for the future. Misunderstandings of all kinds flow from it. "When this want of intercourse," says Beck, in his *Essays on Indian Topics*, "between the communities or a reasonable number of people of each, is fixed on my attention, I often feel with a sinking of the heart that the end of the British Indian Empire is not far distant."

I have already pointed out (p. 271) how clear it is by the example of Aligurh that friendly intercourse is *possible* between the two sections—though we have allowed that it is difficult to bring about. Mr Beck corroborates this in his *Essays* by strong expressions. He says (p. 89), "An Englishman would probably be dubbed a lunatic if he confessed that the only thing which made life tolerable in his Indian exile was the culture, the interest, and the affection he found in native society. Such an Englishman will therefore at most hint at his condition"; and again—"As one whose circumstances have compelled him to see more of the people of India than the average Englishman, I can only say that the effort repays itself, and that, incredible though it may appear, all degrees of friendship are possible between the Anglo-Indian and his Eastern fellow-subject." And, further on, after urging the importance, the vast importance, of cultivating this intercourse, and so attempting to bridge the fatal gulf, he says:—"To know the people, and to be so trusted by them that they will open out to us the inmost recesses of their hearts; to see them daily; to come to love them as those who have in their nature but an average share of affection cannot help loving them when they know them well—this is our ideal for the Indian civilian. Some Englishmen act up to this ideal: in the early days of our rule several did. If it become the normal thing the Indian Empire will be built upon a rock so that nothing can shake it. Agitation and sedition will vanish as ugly shadows. Had it existed in 1857 the crash would not have come."

The writer of the above paragraphs thinks

nothing of the N.I.C. movement, or rather I should say thinks unfavorably of it; but of the importance of bridging the social gulf he cannot say enough—and in this latter point, as far as I feel competent to form an opinion at all, I entirely agree with him. But will it ever be bridged? Unfortunately the few who share such sentiments as those I have quoted are very few and far between—and of those the greater number must, as I have already explained, be tied and bound in the chains of officialdom. "The Anglo-Indian world up to the hour when the great tragedy of '57 burst upon them was busily amusing itself as best it can in this country with social nothings"—and how is it amusing itself now? The most damning fact that I know against the average English attitude towards the natives, is the fact that one of the very few places besides Aligurh, where there is any cordial feeling between the two parties, is Hyderabad—a place in which, on account of its being under the Nizam, *the officials are natives,* and their position therefore prevents their being trampled on!

If the Congress movement is destined to become a great political movement, it must, it seems to me, eventuate in one of two ways—either in violence and civil war, owing to determined hostility on the part of our Government and the continual widening of the breach between the two peoples; or—which is more likely—if our Government grants more and more representative power to the people—in the immense growth of political and constitutional life among them, and the gradual *drowning out* of British rule thereby. There is a third possibility—

namely, the withdrawal of our Government, owing to troubles and changes at home. Either of these alternatives would only be the beginning of other long vistas of change, which we need not attempt to discuss. They all involve the decadence of our political power in India, and certainly, situated as we are—unable to really *inhabit* the country and adapt ourselves to the climate, and with growing social forces around us—I can neither see nor imagine any other conclusion.

The Congress movement being founded on the economical causes—the growth of commercialism, etc.—it is hard to believe that it will not go on and spread. Certainly it may alter its name and programme; but granted that commercialism is going to establish itself, it is surely impossible to imagine it will do so, among so acute and subtle a people as the Hindus, without bringing with it the particular forms of political life which go with it, and really belong to it.

One of the most far-reaching and penetrating ways in which this Western movement is influencing India is in its action on the sense of *property*. The conception of property, as I have already pointed out once or twice, is gradually veering from the communistic to the highly individualistic. In all departments, whether in the family or the township or the caste, the idea of joint possession or joint regulation of goods or land for common purposes is dying out in favor of separate and distinct holding for purely individual ends. It is well-known what an immense revolution in the structure of society has taken place, in the history of various races and peoples, when this change of conception has set in. Nor is it likely that India will prove altogether an exception to the rule. For the change is going on not only—as might fairly be expected—in the great cities, where Western influence is directly felt, but even in the agricultural regions, where, ever since the British occupation, it has been slowly spreading, partly through the indirect action of British laws and land settlements, and partly through the gradual infiltration, in a variety of ways, of commercial and competitive modes of thought.

Now no estimate of Indian affairs and movements can be said to be of value, which does not take account of the weight—one might say the dead weight—of its agricultural life: the 80 or 90 per cent. of the population who live secluded in small villages, in the most primitive fashion, with their village goddess and their Hindu temple—hardly knowing what government they live under, and are apparently untouched from age to age by invention and what we call progress. Nor can the conservative force so represented be well exaggerated. But if even this agricultural mass is beginning to slide, we have indeed evidence that great forces are at work. If the village communities are going to break up, and the old bonds of rural society to dissolve, we may be destined to witness, as Henry Maine suggests, the recurrence of "that terrible problem of pauperism which began to press on English statesmen as soon as the old English cultivating groups began distinctly to fall to pieces." "In India, however," he says, "the solution will be far more difficult than it has proved here."*

* See Appendix.

All this assumes the continued spread and growth of the commercial ideal in India—which is a large question, and wide in its bearings. Considering all the forces which tend nowadays in that direction, and the apparent inevitableness of the thing as a phase of modern life at home, its growth in India for some years to come seems hardly doubtful. But it is a curious phenomenon. Anything more antagonistic to the genius of ancient India—the Wisdom-land—than this cheap-and-nasty, puffing profit-mongering, enterprising, energetic, individualistic, "business," can hardly be imagined; and the queer broil witnessed to-day in cities like Bombay and Calcutta only illustrates the incongruity. To Hindus of the old school, with their far-back spiritual ideal, a civilisation like ours, whose highest conception of life and religion is the General Post Office, is simply *Anathema.* I will quote a portion of a letter received from an Indian friend on the subject, which gives an idea of this point of view. Referring to the poverty of the people—

"All this terrible destitution and suffering throughout one-seventh of the world's population has been brought about without any benefit to the English people themselves. It has only benefited the English capitalists and professional classes. The vaunted administrative capacity of the English is a fiction. They make good policemen and keep order, when the people acquiesce—that is all. If this acquiescence ceases, as it must, when the people rightly or wrongly believe their religion and family life in danger from the government, the English must pack up and go, and woe to the English capitalist and professional man! I feel more and more strongly every day that the English with their commercial ideals and standards and institutions have done far more to ruin the country than if it had been overrun periodically by hordes of savage Tatars."

That Commercialism is bringing and will bring great evils in its train, in India as elsewhere—the sapping of the more manly and martial virtues, the accentuation of greed and sophistry, the dominance of the money-lender—I do not doubt; though I do not quite agree with the above denunciation. I think if the English have infested and plagued poor India, it is greatly the fault of the Indians themselves, who, in their passiveness and lethargy have allowed it to be so. And I think—taking perhaps on my side a too optimistic view—that this growing industrialism and mechanical civilisation may (for a time) do much good, in the way of rousing up the people, giving *definition*, so much needed, to their minds and work, and instilling among them the Western idea of progress, which in some ways fallacious has still its value and use.

Only for a time, however. We in England, now already witnessing the beginning of the end of the commercial *régime*, are becoming accustomed to the idea that it is only a temporary phase; and in India where, as I have said, the whole genius of the land and its traditions is so adverse to such a system, and the weight of ancient custom so enormous, we can hardly expect that it will take such hold as here, or run through quite so protracted a course of years. Commercialism will no doubt greatly modify and simplify the caste system—but to the caste system in some purified form I am inclined to think the people will return; it will do something also to free the women—give them back at least as much freedom as they had in early times and before the Mohammedan conquests, if not more; and finally Western science will strongly and usefully criticise the prevalent religious systems and practices, and give that definition and *materialism* to the popular thought which is so sadly wanting in the India of to-day; but the old underlying truths of Indian philosophy and tradition it will not touch. This extraordinary possession—containing the very germ of modern democracy—which has come all down the ages as the special heritage and mission of the Indian peoples, will remain as heretofore indestructible and unchanged, and will still form, we must think, the rallying point of Indian life; but it is probable and indeed to be hoped that the criticism of Western thought, by clearing away a lot of rubbish, will help to make its outline and true nature clearer to the world. However, there we must leave the matter.

APPENDIX

SINCE the foregoing was written, in 1892, a terrible succession of famines in India—probably the worst ever known there, and followed, apparently, by a condition of chronic destitution and agricultural paralysis over an immense area—is giving rise to the most gloomy forebodings in the heart of every lover of that great country. Have agricultural depression, and the loss of the peasant's working stock gone so far there, that recovery, even with good seasons, is dubious? Are the conditions of agricultural life under the British rule—the conditions of land-tenure, taxes, rents, markets, mortgages, etc.—such that a downward drift is in the long run inevitable? Will our Government and people ever make a sincere and deep-reaching effort to rehabilitate the prosperity of the Indian masses, even (as it must be) at some considerable cost to themselves? Such are some of the questions which force themselves upon us.

A cry for Empire, hollow-sounding and sinister, has gone up in Britain during the last few years. Were that cry whole-hearted and genuine, backed by a real belief in our mission to other peoples, and a real effort to fulfil such mission, there would be little to be said against it. But what do we see? While the sound and fury are great, the signification is practically nothing. Having added some country to our Imperial demesne, we practically cease to take any interest in it. The people at home, as a body, with the exception of a few privately interested individuals, forget all about it. The official class administers it as a matter of the most otiose routine. Indifference and neglect rule; and it is these which make the cry of Empire so utterly hollow.

Who, for instance, cares for India? What body of people at home makes it its business to consider its welfare, or even to plant there the high ideals of British civilisation, of which we hear so much. Why is it that, year after year, and year after year, when the Indian budget comes on, the destinies of these 250 millions of people are dealt with and despatched in the House of Commons before empty benches? Why is it that even all the sufferings of that immense population during the last few years have failed to arouse any effective interest? Let us confess it: we do not administer India, we simply let her drift.

The people at home do not, and cannot, attend to other people's business (and that is the sufficient and conclusive retort to all great schemes of domination). They have, or ought to have, their own affairs to attend to. If our people had taken the trouble to know what was really going on in the Transvaal in 1899 there would have been no war there. But they didn't. Now that the Transvaal is under British domination, there is not one man in a thousand who knows how it is being administered—or who cares. And what shall we say of Ireland, to whose plaint (be it just or unjust) the Houses of Parliament, and the people of England, have so long refused to listen?

But if the cry of Empire is hollow, it is also something worse—it is sinister. It is full of evil foreboding, even for those who utter it, for it is put into their mouths for a false purpose, and for ill designs. When the people know and care nothing about a matter, how shall the Government represent them rightly in it? And when Government is an otiose official routine, how shall it not fall a prey to ambitious schemers either within or outside of its ranks? It is the powerful monetary and commercial interest which, for its own private ends, puts the cry of Empire in the people's mouths. That this was so in the case of Johannesburg in 1899 was obvious to anyone at that time who looked into the matter, and is now, of course, known and acknowledged by everybody. It is the same interest which is continually pushing the nation forward, at immense expense of blood and treasure, in the prosecution of small wars over the globe, for the purpose of opening up foreign markets. And it is the same interest, alas! which rules our policy towards India, and prevents us from ever taking a fair and impartial look at the problem there before us, or making any real effort for the rescue of its suffering millions. There are too many private hands in India's pocket.

Here, in the case of India, the monetary influence has not been so deliberate and designed as in many more modern cases. But there it is, as it has slowly grown up in the course of history, and the fact lies patent before us that India is now being slowly bled to death. The following passages are reprinted from an article of mine in the *Humane Review* for October 1900, entitled "Empire in India and Elsewhere":—

"The main explanation of the sad plight and worse prospects of our great dependency lies in the fact that we are steadily and systematically draining away her resources; we have our hands perpetually in her pocket. Refer to the current number (1899) of the *Statistical Abstract relating to British India*, which brings the accounts down to 1897-98; turn to pp. 112-113, and you will almost wonder that our Government has the hardihood to print the figures! This table gives the annual charges made by our Home Government upon India,—claims of various kinds, some of them presumably for expenses incurred on behalf of India. There is first of all (of course) the interest on Indian State loans, and the interest and annuities on State railways and guaranteed lines, which all have to be paid through the Banks of England and Ireland, practically to British holders. These altogether amount to £8,770,000 for 1897-98. Then there are the charges made by our Government for military establishments in England supposed to be connected with India, but largely availed of for South African and other uses, also for pensions for retired officers, etc.; these together total up to £3,717,000. Then similar charges for civil establishments in England and pensions for retired civilians, etc. which come to £2,289,000. There are a few other charges, on account of Post Office, Telegraphs, Political and other departments, amounting to over £1,000,000; and thus the whole charge made by England totals up to £16,198,000.

"This, remember, is not Indian Revenue to be spent in India, but it is Indian Revenue paid over to England to be spent here. Which of its items really benefit India, and to what extent they do so, I must leave the reader to judge. What we cannot get over is that the yearly tribute exacted from this poverty-stricken population is stated by our own Blue-books to be this enormous sum; and that, be it remembered, in gold. Collected as it is in silver, the exchange alone is a huge item; and the total (in tens of rupees) figures out at Rx. 25,320,000.

"Yet this only represents *Government* charges. To estimate the total drain we must include the enormous *private* remittances home made by civilian and military officials, and the interest on private loans and commercial undertakings, similarly sent home. With regard to the first item, Mr Hyndman,* in his 'Approaching Catastrophe in India,' puts the total salaries of the English

* Mr Hyndman is one of the few Englishmen who have gone thoroughly into this great question of India's bankruptcy; and his work is ignored with almost ludicrous care by all the official people.

officials in India at £15,000,000 a year. The salaries are mostly on a handsome scale, and possibly one half of them is saved and sent home for use in England; but if we put down £5,000,000 we shall certainly not be in danger of exaggeration. With regard to the profits on commercial undertakings and what portion of these is yearly remitted to England, it is difficult to arrive at any certainty, but from the figures available one may conclude that a similar sum of £5,000,000 is not too high. Thus we have some £10,000,000 to add * to the £16,000,000 Government charges—giving an approximate estimate (probably under the mark) of £26,000,000 a year for the total drain from India to England—or in tens of rupees, say Rx. 40,000,000.

"Now, if for a moment we put all other causes aside, it is not difficult to see that a drain of this kind steadily going on must bring ruin behind it. Think what a drain of twenty-six millions annually on the wealth of England would mean! But on poverty-stricken India it is crushing. In only twenty-five years it amounts to £650,000,000. The mass of the peasants of India are so poor, even in average years, that they have to go on one meal a day, and even then vast numbers of them cannot afford rice, but content themselves with some coarser grain! The *average* income of the Indian native is placed by Mr Digby at less than 1d. per diem. To see their poor, thin bodies is to wonder how they have strength to work. Broken down, with boils and blains from insufficient food, many of them tramp long distances to the nearest hospital, recover under the better conditions there, and are soon discharged—only to return

* Mr J. M. Maclean, M.P., in his evidence on East Indian Finance before the House of Commons, 1873, placed "the amount of the annual earnings of Englishmen connected with India which are transmitted home,' at not less than £20,000,000.

again when the same causes bring on the same results. Destitution may be said to be the normal condition of the Indian peasant of late years (*see* pp. 42 and 234, *supra*).

"Yet he has to pay (calculated in tens of rupees) Rx. 25,000,000 in Land Revenue to the Indian Exchequer annually. And the Government is ever pressing for more. At its wits' end to find cash for its railways, forts, frontier expeditions, military establishments, and home charges, it neglects measures and expenditure which might be really serviceable for the prosperity of the peasant, and is only occupied in considering how to extract more out of him. It is simply killing the goose for the sake of its eggs.

"For instance, it may be noticed that the Land Revenue has gone up from Rx. 23,016,000 in 1888-89 to Rx. 25,683,000 in 1897-98, or over 2½ millions in ten years. Over a large portion of Bengal the land tax is permanently settled; but outside that region reassessments are periodically made, and generally at a higher figure —with the result that, while the retail prices of food grains (see *Stat. Abstr.*, table 198) and the general condition of the cultivator have steadily gone down, the levy has been increased by the amount indicated.* The reserve stock of the peasant is constantly falling, and this makes the danger of bad seasons so much greater than it was. At the same time the land is being exhausted. Fallowing is discouraged by our system, on which lands without crops are taxed the same as lands with crops (while in some Native States they are only taxed one-eighth); and thus overcropping results. Manure is burnt for fuel. In a little time things will have come to such a pass that even a diminution of taxation will

* *See* Notes by my late brother, C. W. Carpenter, B.C.S., in the Report of the Deccan Riots Commission, 1870.

be of little use. Says Sir James Caird in his Report on the Condition of India (dated 31st October 1879):

"'An exhausting agriculture and an increasing population must come to a deadlock. No reduction of the assessment can be more than a postponement of the inevitable catastrophe.'*

"But nothing shows the desperation of our efforts to obtain money more than the salt tax. To tax a necessary of life of this kind — and at the rate of some ten or twenty times its value — is an absolute outrage; and indeed a thing no Government in its senses would do, if it could possibly invent any other way of obtaining money. But I suppose it is well understood that the limits of taxation have been reached in this unfortunate country. We obtain a little over Rx. 8,000,000 annually from salt, and as we have no intention of diminishing our *expenditure*, the tax is maintained in face of the discontent which it engenders.†

"But when the revenue thus ground out of the Indian people has been collected, there are two grave questions which arise with regard to its expenditure. One is that which has been touched on already, the drain of a large portion of it out of the country. The revenue from a people may not be very wisely spent by its Government; but if it is spent *in* the country it returns to the people in some form. The money circulates back among those it was taken from. This is one reason, doubtless, why the Native States of India are more prosperous, and, on the whole, far less famine-stricken than those directly under our rule. Though taxation in these provinces is, in many cases, considerably heavier than

* In this year of Famine, 1900 A.D., I have a letter from a small proprietor in South India, saying that his lands have not produced enough this year even to meet the Government taxes, which he has consequently to pay out of his reserve.

† This tax is now reduced by 25 per cent. (1903).

in British territory, yet practically *all* is spent in the province from which it is drawn; but in the case of British India there is a dead loss to the people every year.* What this means with regard to the recurrence of famine is obvious enough. Every country suffers from fluctuations of harvest, and, in a country like India, a failure of crops (except in very well irrigated regions) must every now and then be expected. But then in every country the peasant depends for these occasions on his storage power, his banks, his reserves, his actual stacks and stores of grain. In every village in India you see those enormous earthenware jars standing by the side of his cabin in which the peasant stores his grain. But now, if the country is drained every year, there is so much loss of storage power. If, taking the above figures, there is a drain say of £250,000,000 in ten years, this enables us to realise the loss of storage power to the peasant. But if his grain jars are empty, if he has already mortgaged his crops and sold the heavy silver bangles off his wife's ankles to pay his taxes, what can he do but die when the year of famine comes; and how can it other than happen that the famine years get more frequent?

"In the native provinces it would seem that the revenues (with the exception of what goes to the rajahs and their courts) are spent with considerable regard for the general prosperity of the people. And this brings us to the second question, namely, whether the same can be said of our territory, whether that part of the revenue which

* "Lord Curzon has issued a strongly-worded circular with regard to the growing practice of native chiefs to neglect their States and visit Europe. These repeated absences, says the circular, are regarded as a dereliction of duty, and in the future leave for travelling will only be given where it will result in personal and public advantage." In view of the above remarks, and of our own absentee landlordism on an enormous scale both in India and Ireland, this circular of Lord Curzon's may be regarded in the light of a pleasant little repartee!

is spent in the country, and not drained away, is wisely spent? And to this I fear we must answer No.

"There is no necessity to launch accusations of deliberate mismanagement or neglect against the *personnel* of the administration. Everyone must feel that on the whole their intentions have been sincere, but their standard, of course, is that of the country in which they have been born and bred.

"When we consider how little of our vast revenue at *home* is spent for the welfare and prosperity of the mass of the people; when we consider that of the £103,000,000 sterling expenditure of the United Kingdom for 1899 (before the Transvaal War), close on 70 millions went in naval and military service and interest on public debts; when we consider that our home policy (like that of the other Western nations) is a merely *commercial* policy—that is, to stimulate trade, especially foreign trade, to protect our trade by our fleet, and to embark in small wars for the purpose of opening up markets and compelling payment of interest on British loans—that it is a policy directed to benefit the trader, the merchant, the British capitalist, and the landlord, and that in favoring these it neglects agriculture and the cultivator of the soil and does not really consider the artisan—then I say it seems unlikely that our policy will be any better in India. As a matter of fact, it is quite the same. Our statesmen (pardon the term!) have no grander idea of policy in this our vast dependency than to open up the country with railways (working at a loss) in order to encourage trade with England and the investment of British industrial capital; to embark in frontier wars and to incur a vast civil and military expenditure for the supposed purpose of safe-guarding our interests, but really very largely for the purpose of finding 'places' for the sons of the well-to-do middle classes at home; and to squeeze the people to the last drop in order to pay these dues and maintain this system.

"It is the policy of infidelity. Our 'statesmen' seem to forget that the agricultural population of India numbers some 150,000,000, and that no policy which does not first consider the interests of this vast multitude is itself worth considering. They do not seem to see that to make this ocean of people prosperous and contented would—as a mere matter of policy—be worth all the forts we have built to dominate and guard them; that it would be the one way to really retain our hold over them; and to ensure the elasticity of that revenue for which (if it must be so) we so greatly hanker. And they do not see (for alas! how should they?) that to adopt this policy would be not only to gladden the hearts of these millions and knit them to us in bonds of affection and gratitude, but that it would be to gladden the heart of the whole world, witnessing for once the spectacle of a strong nation helping a weak one, and even cast a little ray of light back on England herself, where beneath her fogs and amid her sad and squalid cities she sits and clutches at her gold-bags.

"It is not railways that are wanted for the prosperity of India, but irrigation. Irrigation is the prime need, the absolute necessity, of such a land; and with a thorough system of irrigation India might be one of the richest and most productive of countries—as indeed it once was. Railways may be useful, but they do not increase the *productiveness* of a country. We, in the West, are liable to forget that. They are part of our system of division of labour. The hides, grown in Texas, are sent 1000 miles to Chicago to be cured and tanned, then 500 miles farther to Massachusetts, to be made into boots, and then perhaps return to Texas to be worn; but in the East, where the peasant in his village fulfils all trades himself, this ponderous circumlocomotion (which after all is mainly for the benefit of the trader and the shareholder) is not needed. Railways are useful for the trader and the commercial man; they are convenient for the dispatch of troops; they afford an excellent investment (if properly guaranteed by the State) for single ladies; and, in India, they might even open up a market for British goods (that great purpose of civilisation) *if* the peasant of India had a surplus of products to send in return. But as, under our rule, and of late years, the surplus is rapidly diminishing, that object does not appear to be fulfilled. As a matter of fact (*Stat. Abstr.*, p. 209), the export of rice from India to the United Kingdom has fallen from value Rx. 1,462,000 in 1890-91 to Rx. 1,100,000 in 1897-98; of wheat in the same period from Rx. 3,437,000 to Rx. 930,000; and of raw cotton * from Rx. 4,324,000 to Rx. 424,000, or to about one-tenth! And even the total exports of these articles to all parts of the world have fallen in much the same ratios. Practically, by crushing taxation and neglect of his interests, we have destroyed the small cultivator's trading power.

"Irrigation, I say, is a prime need of Indian prosperity. But it does not follow from that, that in order to carry out great irrigation works, we should borrow large sums from Western capitalists and then tax the cultivator up to the hilt in order to pay the interest on these loans, for this would only be to undo with one hand what we were doing with the other. No, we should have encouraged the village communities themselves, with wise help and direction from the State, to carry out these works.

"But here we come to the root-evil of our policy in India —our treatment of the land question. We have practically destroyed the village community. It no longer exists,

* While the import of manufactured cotton (from Manchester, etc.) has similarly fallen from Rx. 27,242,000 to Rx. 22,902,000.

and we cannot make use of it. To go into the whole question of land-settlement in India would take us far beyond our limits. Sufficient to say that from centuries back the land has been held by the village communities under the State. The village commune, represented by the head-man, has paid its yearly rent or tax to the State; the individual ryot or peasant has been responsible to the commune. From our first appearance in India, and largely from the sheer ignorance necessarily arising out of one country meddling in the affairs of another, we have disintegrated this system. Our early officials, finding a head-man in each village, concluded that he *must* be either a landlord or a tax-gatherer. It did not enter into their heads that he could be anything else! They treated him accordingly; and thus it has come about that we have alienated the State's right over the land, have displaced the head-man, and have destroyed the corporate life of the village. We have introduced (in accordance with our Western notions) private property in land, with the sequent rights of sale and mortgage; we have thrown the people into the hands of the professional tax-gatherers, the landlord, and the money-lender; and we have brought on them that financial ruin which now is not only completing itself in India, but threatens also all the Western governments with their insane policy of commercial and military expansion, accompanied by utter neglect of the actual peasant and cultivator.

"What might we not have done in India is, indeed, a touching question. Among a people so gratefully affectionate—as a thousand stories of personal devotion testify —so dependent as the Indians are by nature, and inclined to lean upon others for guidance, a frank and friendly amalgamation of interests would, I believe, have been amply repaid. But the British public, while friendly in their general attitude towards the Indians, and perfectly ready to treat them in a generous manner when they visit our shores, are in darkest ignorance as to the real state of affairs in the country itself."

What *will* be done for India is another question which one hardly ventures to consider. If there is any truth in the indictment outlined in the few preceding pages—an indictment, indeed, which has been presented by so many critics much more capable than myself—nothing can save India from ruin and bankruptcy except a complete change of British policy towards her; a change which shall terminate, once for all, that terrible drain which is going on, and which shall be directed, before all else, to the rehabilitation in prosperity of the peasant and cultivator. Of such a change of policy, it is scarcely necessary to say, there is no sign. The people of England do not care, the official classes are content just to get through their daily work, keeping to the barest routine. Individual advantage and interest is all in favor of keeping things as they are. The outlook is dark, and the hours hurry only towards disaster.

THE END